An Invitation to The Great Awakening

An Invitation to The Great Awakening

by WWG1WGA

©2019, all rights reserved
ISBN 978-1-942790-13-6

The chapters in this book were written by Anons (anonymous authors) and are published or re-published with their permission. We gratefully acknowledge and thank the many Anons who have worked to share truth with friends, family, co-workers and followers. Many of the author/contributors who are featured in this book have websites, sub-Reddits, YouTube channels, Twitter followings, etc. and we encourage you to subscribe and support their ongoing work. We hope that sharing this book with others will help awaken the people you care about. Thank you for your prayers and sharing. Reviews are extremely helpful, and deeply appreciated. We are all in this together. WWG1WGA

The 2016 inauguration photo was by official White House photographer Greg E. Mathieson Sr. The meme on page 26 was created by Qurious @FuriousQurious (Twitter). If you were the creator of any of the memes used in this book, and you would like to be acknowledged, please let us know. We are always happy to make corrections, updates, include missing sources, or remove images used inadvertently without permission if requested. You may contact us at:

Published by Relentlessly Creative Books
http://relentlesslycreativebooks.com/
books@relentlesslycreative.com

Dallas, Texas, USA

Contributing Editors

Captain Roy D
Dustin Nemos

Author/Contributors

Chrystal/Scorpio Patriot
Joe M
Liberty Lioness
Linda Paris
Lori Colley
Pamphlet
Radix
RedPill78
Sarah Westall
SerialBrain2
SpaceShot76
ZackoDaFracko

Where We Go One We Go All
(WWG1WGA)

Contents

An Introduction

This is the beginning.

There is so much to tell you, so much has happened, and so much has been hidden. But we have to start somewhere, so this is it.

A book is typically a big project. But we are from the era of DMs and PMs and online comments. So, we are going to do this one together like we always do.

There's this old saying from back in the last century: Many hands make light work. We know all about that working together idea. We call it "Where We Go One We Go All." So, that's who we are as a team: WWG1WGA. The reality that we share the same future encourages us to work together.

Yes, we are real people with real jobs, real families and real futures. But many of us prefer to remain anonymous. We don't think we should have to put the things we value the most at risk to make a contribution to our world when our names aren't important. What we have to say could be. We'll let you be the judge.

Mostly, we'd like to share about what has happened in the recent past that has changed so many things for us, both together and as individuals. One of the things we have in common is that we all discovered QAnon, an online poster (or a group that speaks as one) with a different voice and an insider's perspective.

The messages QAnon has offered have been cryptic, but at the same time insightful and full of foresight. We work together to understand the messages and share them with the larger world.

While we know that our interest in QAnon has been vilified by the mainstream media, following QAnon's posts has given us insights and flashes of the future, taught us history, shown us fresh possibilities, and challenged us to think on our own and to dig for information. QAnon has also inspired us to work together, probably the primary reason for the suppression we're experiencing.

At last, it seems, we've been befriended by someone who has our best interests at heart. As decades of deceit and lies are revealed, so is the plan for dealing with them. As thinking, caring people, we know that there is a great deal at stake. We trust that the plan is well underway and that the plan is working. The intensity of the media's ridicule and social media censorship tells us that we are "over the target."

Our job is to generate a future that reclaims the reins of power from the forces that would abuse our children and enslave us. Our intention is to take them back and restore power to "We the People." We are committed to achieving that for all of us, you included.

So, welcome to our book about our experiences with QAnon. We hope you find it both revealing and empowering.

This is your invitation to The Great Awakening.

Please read this book with an open mind and an open heart. There are real consequences for all of us from what you'll be learning here. And when you're done with the book, please share it with someone you care about.

Thank you.

The Plan to Save the World communicates a fundamental understanding of what is going on in our world and why we have Q. It is a 40,000-foot overview that explains so many things. You may initially appreciate it as a story, a fantasy. Or you may see it cynically as politically-motivated lies. But for many of us who have followed Q for over a year, this is the frame that the pieces fit into. It is the first "big picture" view that makes sense of what we are discovering, and the last story you will hear about on the mainstream news. When you understand The Plan to Save the World, you will have a better understanding of why Donald Trump was elected president and what exactly is meant when he talks about "draining the swamp."

The Plan to Save the World

by Joe M

Have you ever wondered why we go to war or why you never seem to be able to get out of debt?

Why there is poverty, division and crime?

What if I told you, there was a reason for it all?

What if I told you it was done on purpose?

What if I told you, that those corrupting the world, poisoning our food and igniting conflict were themselves about to be permanently eradicated from the earth?

You might think that is an idealistic fantasy.

Well let me tell you a story.

We acknowledge there are criminals, of course.

They rob your house, they steal your phone, they can murder you too if they think they can get away with it.

We have all experienced criminals in one way or another.

Criminals, as we know, are those who choose personal gain over the rights of others with no regard for laws.

But here's where you need to expand your thinking.

Criminals can also succeed in business and politics, and can be elected as our leaders.

If a criminal became the president, imagine what they could achieve!

They could use the full weight of their executive power to commit much larger crimes, and ensure they and their friends were enriched to the fullest extent possible.

A criminal president could create alliances with other criminal presidents, and then collaborate on more global criminal activities.

Anything goes, drug-running, human trafficking, whatever makes the big bucks.

The 20th Century was turbulent with war, economic disaster, famines and displacement.

We have always accepted these as just human nature and simply the way the world works—something inevitable and due to the weaknesses of human nature that lead us to these actions.

This is where we were all tragically wrong.

You are not a criminal. I am not a criminal.

So how can we just assume it is human nature that is driving all this pain and misery?

What if it wasn't human nature at all, and as a result of something more deliberate?

We were taught Capitalism was the cause of a massive rich/poor divide, and the reason for poverty—which in turn is the reason for war, crime and starvation.

Others were taught that Communism, the system of equal wealth across all people, was really to blame for the mess.

But you see folks, it is none of these things. It is not our nature to fight and be racist, it is not in our nature to rob from others.

You must learn is that it was the CRIMINALS all along!

Yes. They got power. More power than a criminal should ever have.

They rose to the top of media companies that control our news and entertainment.

They ascended to the top of the banking system.

Also to the Oval Office.

To Brussels.

To the Vatican

To the Crown.

They crept in quietly.

They became leaders of agricultural companies who have control over food supply.

Also big pharmaceutical companies; the ones we trust to help us when we are sick.

Nobody stopped them and they just recruited more criminals to help them.

First they accumulated the world's wealth.

They invented a system of money called Central Banking which lends money to governments with interest, placing countries into eternal debt.

People's wealth got less, their wealth got more. Much more.

When a criminal is already as rich as they can get, then protecting their ill-gotten gains becomes the priority.

Angry citizens tired of being poor are a major obstacle and can revolt if they suffer enough.

The criminals needed to prevent this.

So they diverted attention to their last remaining competitor—the people of the world: You and me.

We are not happy being ruled by criminals and having to work 3 jobs just to survive.

They know we won't accept it.

So they used their control of the media to set black against white,

woman against man,

young against old,

Muslim against Christian.

They convinced us WE were the problem so that we would fight and destroy ourselves.

To get it done faster, they attacked all aspects of humanity that make us strong.

Like family.

Using their influence over culture, they popularized lifestyle choices that led to a surge in broken homes, lost youth and substance abuse.

I could talk all day about how else they deliberately weakened us, and it would turn your stomach.

We were just trying to get on with living.

So where are all the good guys?

Good people just want to get married, have kids, make a living and enjoy their liberty.

Well, there WERE good guys. Many.

One became the president of the United States in January 1961.

He knew about these criminals and wanted them gone.

He knew their intentions for us all and he wanted to fight them.

Sadly, he had no idea how powerful they had become.

Reagan also had good intentions for the American people.

He knew this criminal mafia controlled almost everything by this stage, including the powerful rogue intelligence agencies.

His economic policies were promising, but the criminals needed a weak America to hold onto their power.

Reagan was shown with a bullet that a growing US economy and prosperous citizens were not what the criminals wanted.

It was looking pretty grim for good people.

Every time someone wanted to stand up and do the right thing, they get stopped.

Were we ever to be freed?

The criminals are also known as the Deep State, or cabal, because of how they control things behind the scenes.

Every president after Reagan was one of these Deep State criminals, and their empire grew even stronger.

With each bad president came new depths America and the world would sink.

The world collapsed into darkness.

Do you need me to tell you how?

Destroyed factories, declining job numbers, sicker people, opioids, destruction of Iraq, Syria and Yemen with pointless war, displacement of people into Europe, Isis, terrorism, collapsed governments, poverty and genocide.

TOTAL MISERY.

Do you think that was inevitable?

Hell no!

Well, here is where things start to take a new turn.

When the full picture comes to be known, it will forever be regarded as the greatest story ever told.

Well, here is the top line:

Some good people still held positions of power.

They valued humanity and the rule of law.

While the criminals discussed their game plan at the annual Bilderberg meetings, the good guys were making plans of their own.

The Information age was coming to change history forever.

As the Internet flooded into every home, and appliances became smarter, and when people started carrying tracking devices, an opportunity to put an end to criminal control over the world was emerging.

We became connected, trackable and surveilled,
but SO DID THEY.

They became dependent—just like we did—on email, SMS and instant communication.

It made crime much easier, but it also put them on a grid that, if accessed by the right people, would expose their crimes to the public and end their iron grip on us once and for all.

In this new age of information, it was thought that the military should also have its own intelligence agency to focus on cyber crime and espionage.

They called this the NSA, the National Security Agency.

The relevance of the NSA in the story cannot be understated.

Here we had every phone call, email and text from every device, stored and archived.

Whether it be someone making a doctor's appointment or the Deep State setting up a massive heroin purchase from the Taliban.

In the right hands it would be enough information to expose the entire sinister criminal plot to rob us blind and wipe us out.

Hold that thought, now I need to explain the PLAN.

The good guys were devising a PLAN to reclaim the world from the cabal and return it to the people.

It would involve alliances with multiple countries, since the criminals had global rat lines, trade and other infrastructure in place that would need their cooperation.

It came down to two choices for America.

Launch a military coup to seize the government from whichever cabal puppet was in the White House.

Or win legitimately, take control of the NSA, expose the criminals for what they are and arrest them all.

Obviously, the first option would be very troubling for the public.

With people still preoccupied with cabal-engineered social issues, they would likely revolt and hurt themselves and others.

No, it would have to be the latter.

So they needed a candidate who could win and who could win big.

Many states like California had been so heavily inundated by criminals that even the voting machines were electronically set up to swing votes any which way.

It would need to be a very decisive victory.

Good patriots in the US military, and their global partners asked Trump to run for president so that they could take back control of America legitimately without alarming the public.

Trump was a good choice, obviously, because he overcame the voter fraud and won.

But he was a patriot and he was loved and admired by the public.

He was not interested in joining the cabal, mainly because they hated America and he did not agree with them on that point.

As soon as he showed interest in taking power, they activated their media assets to viciously turn on him.

That's when we saw the sudden hatred emerge.

Even when he won, the cabal still had no idea what he was part of, and the sophisticated plan that was about to unfold against them.

Shocked at their loss, they mobilized their full arsenal of intelligence, media, money and technology to try and take back power.

Their people at the top of the DOJ and FBI then put together a plan to frame Trump and have him impeached.

This is where we come back to the NSA again.

All messages were stored and could be used to expose this plot and prevent Trump's overthrow.

An entire book will be written about the first two years of Trump's presidency, false flag terror attacks, downed planes, missile alerts, assassination attempts.

Here is the point.

The world is currently experiencing a dramatic covert war of biblical proportions, literally the fight for earth, between the forces of good and evil.

I can't put it in simpler terms but I can say it appears the good guys are winning.

The cabal had complete control over North Korea.

They hijacked the Kim Dynasty, took them hostage and worked to build up a nuclear arsenal to threaten the world.

Kim Jong-Un suddenly embracing peace was simply because the Deep State were beaten and driven out.

ISIS was also destroyed in the year after Trump's win.

We are all starting to see the pattern now that enough time has passed; that our biggest global concerns are starting to recede, and peace is returning.

It is all evidence that the good guys are winning the war.

But we are still in the middle.

While a lot is improving, it still puzzles many that most of these known criminals are still free.

Especially higher ups like the Hillary Clinton, the Bushes and Obama.

That is coming in the next chapter of the story.

That's why we have Q.

The good guys, with control over the NSA, began the Q intelligence dissemination program to invoke an online grassroots movement called "The Great Awakening."

It started on underground Internet channels and then moved to the mainstream.

Q has been a fun distraction for those who follow world events and desire truth, but it is about to begin a much more important and necessary phase—keeping the public informed when the Deep State war breaks out onto the surface.

By this, I mean high-profile arrests.

Yes folks. The criminals I am referring to are famous politicians, actors, singers, CEOs and celebrities.

People who have earned our trust, respect and admiration.

They have done very bad things that are all fully known and documented, and they will be severely punished.

Those of us who have followed Q since the beginning will be here to help you make sense of upcoming events.

We are among the first to realize that our petty partisan divisions are just trivial distractions, and we are all enslaved by a hidden enemy.

We realize that the problem was never Capitalism or Socialism, Democrat or Republican, black or white, Muslim or Christian.

We know it was just very powerful criminals who had too much power.

Fellow slaves. It's time to buckle your seatbelt, recognize your true enemy, and embrace a new future that we all owe to the brave patriots who risked their lives to achieve victory against the greatest force of evil the world has ever known.

May God bless America.

About the Author

Joe M

Joe M agreed to contribute to this publication but elected NOT to participate in any royalty or payment, now or in the future. Joe M has made the personal choice not to monetize his platform until the war is over, the Fed is dead, gold backs our dollar and our Republic is 100% debt free.

https://www.youtube.com/watch?v=3vw9N96E-aQ
https://www.youtube.com/watch?v=NGuyUyRBsA4
https://www.youtube.com/watch?v=MRtEgdgj_XQ
https://www.youtube.com/watch?v=80s5xuvzCtg

General Michael Flynn
Describing the Digital Army

"We have an army... We have an army of digital soldiers. That's what we call them, what I call them, because this was an insurgency folks, this was run like an insurgency. This was irregular warfare at its finest in politics and that story will will continue to be told. But we have what we call citizen journalists because the journalists that we have in our media did a disservice to themselves actually—more than they did to this country. They did a disservice to themselves because they displayed an arrogance that is unprecedented. And so the American people decided to take over the idea of information. They took over the idea of information and they did it through social media."[1]

While these words were spoken some time before the first QAnon posts, Flynn was aware of the countless patriots, in every conceivable digital channel, who were standing by ready to fight the MSM and support their president. This was the same digital army who instantly saw the validity of Q when the first crumbs started to be dropped in the chans.

---

[1] https://youtu.be/W0CThXL37Jk

Who is Q? That is the first question we usually get asked. At the very simplest, Q is an anonymous and somewhat mysterious person who leaves cryptic posts on 8Chan using the handle Q. There is the strong suggestion that Q is Military Intelligence with a close connection to the White House. Although he posts on 8Chan, you may prefer reading his or her posts (Q could be a woman or even a team) via a more direct and civilized route, for example at qmap.pub or qanon.pub. (8Chan is kind of a zoo and hard for newbies to navigate.) The 2nd question is typically something like: How do you know that Q is "real?" That's what his chapter is all about. You might say that it is mathematically impossible for him not to be who he says he is. But don't take our word for it. Do the math.

When Will It Become Mathematically Impossible?

by SpaceShot76 & RedPill78

What is a Proof?

In its simplest form, a proof is an argument for the validity of a fact. Claims require evidence to back them up, that necessary cogency of evidence which can prove beyond a shadow of a doubt, mathematically or philosophically, the establishment of those statements as fact. In the scope of research, in order to establish what is true, validation is everything. On this subject in particular, the weight of these posts and the power they hold, literally pertain to our very freedom. The claims we make and the implications therein require bodies of evidence which support those claims as legitimate.

In the world of Q, proofs are as good as gold. We are going to run you through some of the best Q proofs, that in our opinion, lend credibility to the fact that Q is a person or group of people who are very close to President Donald Trump.

In the beginning, when we first learned about this Anon posting on the boards, a great number of us were very excited because we had been researching this type of content for many years. This line of research brings with it the ire of the establishment and Q was no exception. However, early on there was very little pushback, as the media wanted to steer as clear as possible and Q's messages were not as popular, nor as widespread as today. Now, with Q gaining a larger foothold in the conscious awareness of more people, proofs are more necessary than ever.

As long as Q has been posting, Anons on the boards have been taking those posts, combining them with tweets by POTUS along with news and and real world events, in order to create proofs. Proofs are our evidence, our argument of fact that establishes the validity of these posts. The number of proofs you can create from the variety of posts, tweets, future news and world events is staggering. Although Q's first post has yet to be proven true, many more crumbs have been dropped in its wake that have been. These crumbs, taken by other Anons and arranged into pictographic memes have given us the body of evidence required to establish, with statistical certainty, the legitimacy of the anonymous Q.

Try Explaining This to Your Mom

The validity of Q can be difficult to explain to the average person in brief terms. Try telling your average normie that a faceless, unnamed poster on an Internet research board, (known primarily among the public for trash talk and politically incorrect language), is dropping crumbs for us Anons to decipher, what is essentially, direct communication from the President. Then tell them that the end goal of these communications is to free ourselves from the Deep State. Unless you were lucky enough to have been watching from the beginning, this claim would be easy to dismiss.

However, after more than a year of such posts, replete with messages that do indeed seem to come directly from the President himself, coupled with seemingly precognitive statements predicting world events, the fact has been established: Q is real, and we can prove it. This is why proofs are so important.

For myself, the first proof took place on Oct. 5, 2017, before the Q posts even began. The President and First Lady were hosting a dinner at the White house for Military leaders and their wives. During the photo op with the press prior to the dinner, President Trump asked cryptically, "Do you guys know what this represents? Maybe it's the calm before the storm. Could be. The calm, the calm before the storm..."

The press, stymied as they usually were, asked repeatedly what he meant. Was he referring to Iran, to ISIS, what storm was he hinting at?

When asked directly, "What storm Mr. President?" President Trump answered flatly, "You'll find out." No one could have known at that exact moment, except for The President and the great Military minds in that room, exactly what he meant, but many of us had an instinct that something big was coming.

Trump: Could be the calm before the storm.

On Nov. 2, 2017, Q posted a message that for the first time echoed the exact same phrase by ending the post with, "The calm before the storm." For those fortunate enough to have heard the President on that day and then see the post that followed, the fact that something truly great was happening was evident. Since that time, "The Calm Before The Storm" is a phrase that has gone on to be spoken many times, has been the name of numerous boards, graced many a meme and become burned into the fabric of this movement.

As soon as this anonymous poster, (who had yet to become known as Q), started writing, one of the biggest questions on most people's minds was, who was this person? Was Q a larp (live action role play), a government official, perhaps another Edward Snowden or Julian Assange, etc.?

Well, that question may have been answered on Nov. 1, 2017, at least in part. At 10:56 am on Nov. 1, 2017 post 34 began with the heading, Q Clearance Patriot and included a message to "My fellow Americans," an introduction often used by Presidents when addressing the nation. This was the first reference we received to "Q" and the meaning of the title. Q clearance refers to a high-level security clearance designation, a level above "Top Secret," the same level as the President and other high-level officials in his stable of Military leaders.

Moments later, in post 35, another message regarding the course of operations yet to come was dropped, that was signed off with 4 10 20. It didn't take long for many on the boards to realize that using the A1Z26 cipher, a simple letter/number code, the corresponding letters to those numbers in that signatory are DJT, the initials of The President. This had the potential to mean that Donald J Trump himself was addressing us as Q. Many people from the beginning had hoped this was the case, but many others dismissed it just as easily.

In February 2018, Q began to sign off on some posts using Q+, the first being post 791. Post 791 was a verse from the Bible, Jeremiah 29:11: "For I know the plans I have for you," declares the Lord, "plans to prosper you and not to harm you, plans to give you hope and a future." The next lines were the same, repeated twice, followed by

Q+:
:Protect 6/14-46
:Protect 6/14-46

The verse from Jeremiah, although a message from God to to the Exiles, in this context was a message directly from the President, telling those on the boards as well as those listening outside, that plans were in place, patriots were firmly in control. He had plans and they were being carried out, we had nothing to worry about. If successful, we would take back our lives and our future from the evil cabal that had taken over not only our country but our entire world. The numbers after Protect, were equal to the birthdate of our President, June 14, 1946. Donald Trump was hinting to us that he himself was most certainly part of team Q. While later posts would continue to be signed Q, only a relatively few were signed Q+.

As time went on, it became obvious that there was a synchronicity between Q's posts and President Trump's tweets. For example, on February 21, 2018, President Trump visited Marjory Stoneman Douglas High School in Broward County Florida, to visit with some of the surviving students of the tragic shooting that took place earlier that month on the 14th.

Just prior to the beginning of the meeting, President Trump was photographed holding a piece of White House stationary, with some notes written on the back. Two fingers on his right hand and three on his left gripped the notes, obscuring most of the writing. The odd way he held the paper garnered much attention in the media, with the picture circulating widely. The stationary held a numbered list, with the fifth and final line reading, "I hear you." After the meeting, Q posted a picture of the President holding the list and later that evening in post 435, Q posted a list of stringers that ended with, [SIG_5:5_READ], followed by brackets filled with 58 spaces. With the five on the paper combined with five of the President's fingers showing (5:5), it was speculated that perhaps the message was not intended for the students, but rather, for those of us following Q.

On Feb. 22 the connection was confirmed when the President sent out a tweet that contained 58 empty spaces, similar to Q's post from the day before. Was it possible that The President had allowed his notes to photographed accidentally? Perhaps, however it is highly unlikely that both Q and the President would both post messages containing 58 unnecessary spaces within 24 hours of each other. The President was listening and we received the message, loud and clear. 5:5 Mr. President. We hear you too.

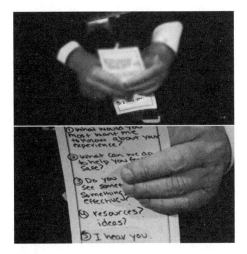

In another example, on June 17th, 2018, Father's Day, Q posted Happy Father's Day at 12:48 p.m. Exactly 7 minutes later at 12:55 p.m. President Donald Trump retweeted The White House's Happy Fathers

Day tweet. Since then, Q and The President have shared the same message within short time spans a number of times. These instances are Q's little way of letting us know that he is working hand-in-hand with Donald Trump.

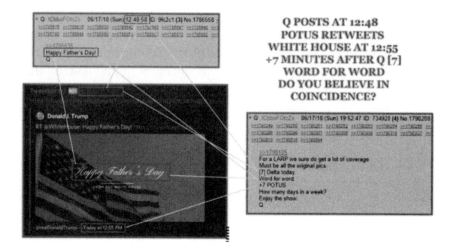

Q POSTS AT 12:48
POTUS RETWEETS
WHITE HOUSE AT 12:55
+7 MINUTES AFTER Q [7]
WORD FOR WORD
DO YOU BELIEVE IN
COINCIDENCE?

Not Lord Voldemort, But Close

As far back as November of 2017, Q had posted regarding Arizona Senator John McCain who eventually came to be known primarily as NO NAME because, "we don't like to say his name," as revealed in Q post 357. Senator NO NAME first appeared in post 436 on December 22, 2017 in a post that laid out the plan to take down the President through the "insurance policy" discovered in the Strzok-Page text messages. The "insurance policy" was hinted as having begun with Hillary Clinton and the DNC's financing of the Steele Dossier, as well as pointing to NO NAME in disseminating it to *Buzzfeed* and other media outlets.

The post is an example of "future proves past," a phrase used often by Q, because we came to learn that HRC and the DNC did in fact pay for the dossier and it was in fact a long-time associate of NO NAME who first gave the dossier to the press. This was also the first time an "insurance policy" was mentioned in the posts and months before it would be revealed in the media. From that point forward, the name McCain was rarely spoken, either by Q or the President. McCain all but disappeared from the public eye in Dec. 2017, almost immediately after Q began posting.

In a February 11, 2018 post, 732, Q posted a photo of NO NAME with ISIS rebels in Syria, along with, "We don't say his name returning to Primetime wonder if his so-called illness or condition will flare up," in reference to McCain taking a leave of absence and ultimately passing away, as the mainstream story would go. Again, Q knew before the media or anyone else did. Numerous times throughout the year, Q published regarding the nameless Senator, including post 1706 that said, "no name returning to headlines," and days later, the media was awash in news covering his failing condition. Q was right every time.

On August 13, 2018 the *New York Times* had posted regarding a speech President Trump made, introducing the John S. McCain National Defense authorization act for fiscal year 2019. In an article in the New York Times on August 13th 2018 it was reported that President Trump made a speech in front of soldiers and Senior Military leaders at Fort Drum in New York. The President spoke for 28 minutes without once mentioning McCain's name, calling it the most significant investment in our military and our warfighters in modern history. President Trump never made any reference to John McCain's military service, nor to his decades-long career in the Senate. Some may say it's coincidence, but going out of your way to not say a person's name, the name that adorns the bill you're hailing, is a little unusual.

How Much Proof Do We Need?

A question Q poses quite often is, "How many coincidences before mathematically impossible?" Over the past year or more of posts, there have been so many coincidences that it is beyond mathematical probability that Q is not with President Trump, or in his administration at the very least.

Another impossible coincidence was from post 521 on January 13th, 2018 in which Q posted, "Do you TRUST the chain of command?" Two days later, on January 15th, the US Department of Defense (@DeptofDefense), tweeted a post regarding a program airing that night on The National Geographic Channel, using the hashtag #chainofcommand. When the program aired, there was a scene with a coffee mug with a big letter Q emblazoned on it! Again, some may suggest that this is merely a coincidence, but we say again, what are the chances, really?

One of our favorite proofs was posted on May 10th, 2018. On that day Q posted on his private board posts numbered 72 through 76. Some may recall President Trump had made a deal with North Korea at that time to secure the release of three American prisoners being held there.

The day of the release, President Trump posted on his Twitter a video of the three hostages returning home, and in that video there were two fire trucks with their booms extended, holding a huge American flag between them. That same day, Q posted a picture of an American flag, post 74 on Patriots Fight, with the words, "Castle Lock," below. In another astounding coincidence, the fire truck holding up the flag on the right when the hostages came home, had a large Q74 on the side of it. That my friends, is too coincidental for our taste!

There have been many times over the past year where people in the growing audience have lashed out against Q, throwing doubt on his legitimacy. But what are the odds on a day Q is publishing posts 72 through 76, that there would be a video released by President Trump that has Q 74 in it?

Due to all of the push back we have received since this movement began, we did due diligence every single time Q's validity was in question, with the Q74 being no exception. In order to verify the probability that a fire truck would be labeled as Q74, hours were spent poring over images of fire trucks and yet we were unable to find any fire trucks at all that had one letter and two digits. Most fire trucks found had three or four letters in their identifier, so the fact that that fire truck had Q74 on it is odd enough. Add to the fact that Q74 was the middle post that day and the chances are nearly impossible.

On April 24th, 2018, post 1254, Q posted:

> **Iran is next**
> **[MARKER]**
> **Re_read.**
> **POTUS today.**
> **"Mark it down."**
> **"Bigger problems than ever before."**
> **Sig to Iran?**
> **Q**

Well coincidentally, approximately two-weeks later on May 8, 2018, President Trump gave remarks on the joint comprehensive plan of action regarding Iran and in that speech he says quote, "It will have bigger problems than it has ever had before." Once again we have a post where Q gave us foreknowledge of a statement that President Trump was going to make ahead of time.

Another one of our favorites came on Easter. We admit this one is a little bit ridiculous, but if anything, it increases the likelihood of its validity. An anon on 8chan asked, "maybe Q can work the phrase, 'Tip Top' into the SOTU (State of The Union speech)," as the State of the Union Address was scheduled for January 30th, 2018 at 9 p.m. EST. However, this request came only the night before on January 29th at 6:56 p.m. A tall order in any event, but fitting a phrase like "Tip Top" into the State of the Union when given less than a day's notice would have been pretty difficult regardless of the time. In our opinion, the State of the Union Address was most likely already well completed at that point.

Fast forward to April 2nd, 2018 when Q was responding to an anon on the board who said, "Tip top tippy-top shape," and Q answered, "It was requested, did you listen today? Q." Q was referring to President Trump's addressing the nation on Easter Sunday, on the White House balcony with First Lady Melania Trump and an Easter Bunny. Perhaps more specifically, the Easter Bunny was an aide in a rabbit suit with freaky looking glasses. Follow the white rabbit has come to mean much more to us since then, more than just a phrase from *Alice in Wonderland* or the film *The Matrix*. President Trump used the requested phrase while thanking Melania for getting the White House into great shape saying, "We keep it in tip-top shape, we sometimes call it tippy-top shape."

The use of this phrase was so strange, and the repetition was seen by anons as being done to match the requested phrase. What are the odds that a President of the United States would ever use the words, tip-top tippy-top, in a sentence naturally? How many times in your life have you heard anyone use that phrase? Even for those of who were on the fence about Q saw that one as a clear sign that President Trump was talking directly to us.

Credit: Huffington Post online 4/2/2018

Q Followers Learn Weeks Before World Events

On November 14th, 2017, Q posted the full text of the Lord's Prayer, which stood out at the time as there was no context or relevance given for the post. On December 8th, 2017, news broke that Pope Francis had proposed a slight change to the words of The Lord's Prayer.

The next day, December 9th, 2017 in post 306, Q posted, "Which version? Why is this relevant? What just came out re: The Lord's Prayer?" As you can see, Q hinted at something regarding The Lord's Prayer less than a month before anyone knew. It's yet another proof of foreknowledge that Q has on world events. In yet another proof regarding world events, specifically with regard to the Pope, was a post on April 3rd, 2018. In post 997 Q stated, "[Pope] will be having a terrible May."

Q !xowAT4Z3VQ ID: 463ae0 No.884799
Apr 3 2018 19:45:50 (EST)

>>884748
[Pope] will be having a terrible May.
Those who backed him will be pushed into the LIGHT>
Dark to LIGHT.
TRUTH.
Q

A little more than a month later on May 18th, stories began to circulate around the Internet under the headline, "Every Bishop in Chile Submits Resignation to Pope Francis," due to the many sexual abuse allegations facing priests in Chile, allegations which purportedly transpired and were subsequently covered up by top leadership in the Vatican, presumably up to and including, the Pope.

Every bishop in Chile just resigned over the child sex abuse scandal

The move comes days after Pope Francis met with bishops to discuss the crisis.

By Tara Isabella Burton | @NotoriousTIB | tara.burton@vox.com | May 18, 2018, 3:00pm EDT

Considering Q's propensity for telling us about happenings ahead of time, such as the Pope's terrible May that was followed by the resignations of Chile's Bishops, what else has Q told us about ahead of time? On January 19, 2018 in post 559, Q posted, "HUSSEIN CABINET / STAFF Who used private email addresses?" Q went on to list many sets of initials that stood for: Loretta Lynch, Hillary Clinton, James Comey, James Clapper, Chuck Schumer, Andrew McCabe, John McCain, Rod Rosenstein, Susan Rice, John Brennan, Huma Abedin and Valerie Jarrett, after which asking, "Did Hussein use a private email address?" These Obama administration officials, listed by Q, were all part of Crossfire Hurricane, the operation to keep President Trump, then candidate Trump, from gaining post-election access to the White House. With the end result being the removal of President Trump from office should he attain it.

From the Inspector General's report dated June 14, 2018, it was revealed that, "FBI analysts and prosecutors told us that former president Barack Obama was one of the 13 individuals with whom Clinton had direct contact using her Clintonemail.com account." Obama, like the other high-level government officials, used a pseudonym for his username on his Clintonemail.com account.

Coincidentally, all of the people noted in this post are either removed from office, under investigation, or about to be under investigation if they are not already under a sealed grand jury. As early as November of 2017 we were seeing quotes like this by Q, far prior to any removal or criminal disclosures. Those who have been listening to Q, have been a step ahead of the public revelations.

Obama Admin Emailgate   559

Q !UW.yye1fxo 19 Jan 2018 - 2:45:44 AM

HUSSEIN CABINET / STAFF
Who used private email addresses?
What was the purpose?
LL.
HRC.
JC.
JC.
CS.
AM.
We don't say his name.
RR.
SR.
JB.
HA.
VJ.
Did Hussein use a private email address?

As you can see, the number of coincidences continued to mount. As the evident "coincidences" grew in number, so too did the pushback against Q and his validity. On July 24th, 2018, in post 1682, the first line of Q's post read, "Sea to shining sea." That night, President Trump was entering the stage as he usually does, while the song, "God Bless the U.S.A." by Lee Greenwood played. As most people know, there is a line in the lyric that says, "From sea to shining sea." Once again, coincidentally, right before the song let out the words "sea to shining sea," President Trump put his finger to his ear as if to say, listen up! He then pointed up with both hands as the words rang through the arena.

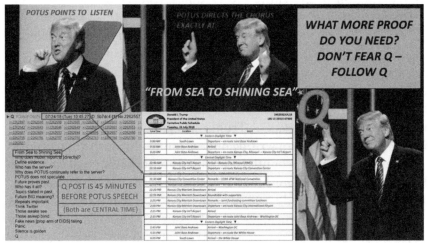

Credit for meme creation: Qurious @FuriousQurious (Twitter)

More or Less Exactly 17 Times

On the topic of President Trump and his incredible rallies, there was one hosted July 31, 2018 in Tampa, Florida and as all Q followers know—and using the A1Z26 cypher—the letter Q is the 17th letter of the alphabet and therefore equals 17. Here is a direct quote from President Trump's speech that day in Tampa, "You know, I told the story the other day, I was probably in Washington in my entire life 17 times. True, 17 times. I don't think I ever stayed overnight. You know what I'm getting at, right?" The president continued on to say, "But I've made some choices that I wouldn't have made. But I'm riding down Pennsylvania Avenue. Again I've only been here about 17 times. And probably seven of those times were to check out the hotel I'm building on Pennsylvania Avenue and then I hop on the plane and I go back. So I've been there 17 times, never stayed there at night."

First off, what are the odds that somebody is going to say "I've been there about 17 times," and as many times as he said it? As the reader, think about times in your life when you've generalized, you probably have used numbers like we've used, in multiples of 5 or 10. "Oh I've been there about 15 or 20 times 20 or 25 times," but to use the number 17 and then to use that number four times within the space of a few moments, is very specific, he was very clearly talking to us. Add to the fact that he kept saying it and asking if we understood, "I was probably in Washington in my entire life 17 times, true 17 times. *You know what I'm getting at, right?*"

Yes Mr. President, anons know exactly what you're getting at sir.

At another rally on June 20, 2018 President Trump walked down to the stage and right up to a person in the crowd who had a big Q on their t-shirt and pointed directly at him. Later, Q posted the picture that the Anon took of President Trump pointing directly at him. On multiple occasions President Trump has gone on stage and literally made the hand gesture of writing out a Q, quite obviously for us anons.

There have been countless mainstream articles, well into the hundreds, that have gone out of their way to try to discredit Q. However not one pundit will actually ask President Trump the one question we all want them to ask, "President Trump, do you know anything about this person or entity that is Q Anon?" There has been so much media buzz, (most of it negative) about Q, one would think at least one reporter would try to discredit Trump and Q by asking the question.

As stated previously, every single time there was a question of Q's validity, we went out of the way to ensure nothing was reported to viewers that was fake or fraudulent. Early on as a means of validation, Q began to use an identifier known on 8chan as a "trip code," as a means to ensure that we know we are reading posts from the same poster each time. As 8chan is generally an anonymous board, the trip code was essential in knowing who to trust, as only Q (or the group of people posting as Q) could use it. This trip code system is not a simple cipher, for example if you typed in an A 3 times, the first one might be A equals X, but the second time might be A equals a question mark, and so on. So the trip code is not overly simple, but not totally unbreakable.

The Deep State that President Trump and Q are fighting have very good resources and access to excellent computing power with powerful decryption and hacking tools, so given time it is possible to crack. Operatives made it their mission to try to exploit Q and his or her trip code, as gaining access to the account would mean potential control of the movement. On one occasion Q's trip code was exposed, and over time it became necessary to change it on several additional occasions. Along the way however, Q kept providing proofs, even going so far as to hold some proofs back for months at a time.

After the trip code was exposed, there was much discussion regarding the continued veracity of the information Q was providing. Was this still really Q? Many people went out of their way to show the trip codes were not secure, inferring anybody could post under it if they figured out the code. Back in November of 2017, Q was using the trip code "!lTPb.qbhqo" and while using this trip code on November 9, 2017, Q posted two pictures showing the Korean Peninsula through the window of Air Force One. This trip code "!lTPb.qbhqo" has never been cracked and apparently the bad actors were focusing their attention on cracking the current codes in April and May 2018.

Q !lTPb.qbhqo 9 Nov 2017 - 11:31:45 PM

To once again prove his validity, Q posted a picture that was taken between the first two pictures posted on November 9. These pictures were all three taken in succession, however Q posted only the first and third in the series in November, with the second posted under the new trip code on May 22, 2018. To which Q stated, "Why not post an original picture plus or minus 1 2 3 seconds to establish credibility, prepared, predictable, this is not a game these people are stupid." Identity proven once again.

On Nov 8, 2017 while aboard Air Force One President Trump tweeted:

Congratulations to all of the "DEPLORABLES" and the millions of people who gave us a MASSIVE (304-227) Electoral College landslide victory!

Accompanying this tweet was an image of President Trump and some senior advisors, all giving the thumbs up in victory. When the image was down-loaded, it discovered that the name of the file was DOITQJ8UIAAowsQ.jpg. Coincidence? When uploading an image to Twitter, the name of the file is randomly assigned, generally characters of random numbers and letters, you cannot choose the name of the file. If you go now and download any image from Twitter you will see that the Code assigned is random. Additionally, if you trace around the hands of the people in the image it creates a Q!

On July 3rd, 2018, Q posted photos that were pictures taken off of the back of a reflective iPhone. These pictures showed the inside of The President's office aboard Air Force One, a highly secured area that only The President or those in his inner circle would have access to. After anons did some digging, they quickly realized that to obtain the image shown by Q, the photo would have to have been taken by somebody sitting in the chair of the president on Air Force One. Now who could that have been? Furthermore, the photo displayed a crucial element added by President Trump that was not present during the Obama Administration: a cup holder.

Air Force One has taken many flights, but recently, in December 2018 and early January 2019, on some of those flights, the Air Force One call sign has been changed to Q 0 (Q zero). Anyone with a cell phone knows if you needed to make a plus sign like this "+", it would be under the zero. Now begs the question, who has the power to change the call sign of Air Force One? You guessed it; none other than POTUS 45 meaning that is was highly likely that the President changed the call sign of Air Force One, to Q+.

Any one of these instances taken on their own could be written off as a coincidence, but taken together, it is statistically impossible that all of these individual coincidences are coincidences at all. That leads us to several conclusions: A) that Q is real, B) that Q is a team working with President Trump and C) that Q+ is President Trump. WWG1WGA

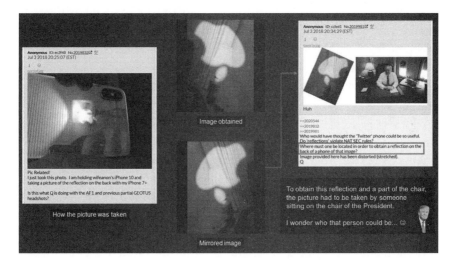

About the Authors

SpaceShot76
(*World Patriot News*)
@SpaceShot76 on Twitter and www.youtube.com/c/SpaceShot76

As far back as I can remember, I've always felt something was off or odd about the world we live in. I am 42 years old, married with an eight-year-old son. I grew up in Rhode Island, living life as normally as can be expected. About three weeks after 9/11 things changed for me. News reports kept repeating Osama Bin Laden was responsible, that he planned the attack, which will be proven to be false after a very recent Grand jury has been empanelled to look into that fateful day. Three weeks later, "WE'RE GOING TO IRAQ"! This puzzled me and reignited my inquisitive side. As they say, the rest was history. I consumed all types of "useless" info for nearly 20 years, I was so shocked at the things I discovered and wondered why more people did not know, why weren't more people outraged? I used to say, "Please God, there must be a way to awaken the masses." After even forgetting about those prayers I heard about Q. The Q team and President Trump have been an answer to prayer. As well as helping expose vast corruption, Q introduced me to many great World Patriots and new friendships along the way. Peace!!!

RedPill78
(*Red Pill News*)
@RedPill78 on Twitter and www.youtube.com/c/RedPill78

RedPill78 is a lifelong seeker of truth, who began his journey to uncover the real story when he learned about the assassination of JFK at a very young age. Throughout his life, each tragic world event, every "official story," every explanation from the powers that be, made less and less sense. Watching the world slip further into darkness, he almost gave up hope. When Donald Trump was elected, he knew that something had changed, that this was the moment we as a nation needed to finally break free from the shackles of slavery. When Q emerged, it was 100% confirmation that the time had come. More people awake every moment and with a critical eye and a fair amount of humor, he reports world events and more through his daily program, Red Pill News on Youtube and Twitter.

Trust does not come easily. Nor should it. Trust must be earned, not given away—not to the talking heads on television, even the ones full of confidence who speak with such authority and not to the grinning politicians in the expensive suits who convey such sincerity and conviction. He or she is probably not our friend. In fact, many of us have indeed trusted people who were not worthy of the faith we placed in them. If we required of them the same level of proof of their sincerity and authenticity that Q has given us, we'd know that they were at least worth listening to. And over time, as we've discovered that the things Q told us days, weeks or even months earlier have come to pass, not only do we listen (and then still verify), we know this is someone who is genuinely on our side. Q implores us to do our own research, to think logically, to question everything. We do, starting with questions about whether or not Q was who he said he was.

The Day I Knew Q Wasn't a Hoax

by Lori Colley

(NOTE: THESE ARE MY PERSONAL OPINIONS ONLY, AND SHOULD NOT BE CONSTRUED AS FACT ABOUT ANY PERSON, EVENT, OR ENTITY. PLEASE DO YOUR OWN RESEARCH.)

My Moment of Truth

Everyone who follows Q had one: a day when you knew, that you knew, that you knew, that Q wasn't a hoax. When you were sure that Q wasn't a hoax, or a LARP (live-action role play), or a too-good-to-be-true conspiracy theory. My day came when Trump used the words, "tip-top, tippy top" in April, 2018—but the set-up started on January 29, a few months after I began following Q.

That day, an anonymous person posted a request on the 8Chan board, a website where Q writes messages. He or she wanted Q to ask President Trump to work the phrase "tip top" into the State of the Union Address.

It didn't happen during that speech. Instead, the validation came in a much cleverer way. The President spoke those very words from the South Lawn of the White House at the traditional Easter Egg Roll. He was standing next to a giant, white "Alice in Wonderland" rabbit.

You'll see the connection in a minute.

Trump began by thanking the First Lady and acknowledging the White House Historical Association for their work on the event. Then he said those magic words that rocked my world:

*"We keep [the White House] in tip-top shape.
We call it sometimes tippy-top shape."*

Q posted later that night:

*Tip Top Tippy Top Shape.
It was requested. Did you listen today?*

That did it for me. That's the day I knew Q wasn't a hoax.

The ride with Q has had its ups and downs. We've waited for the arrests and, to our knowledge, they haven't yet materialized. But because of Trump's tweets and his speeches that coordinate with Q's posts, we know without a shadow of a doubt that Q and Donald John Trump are a team. And Q followers are part of it: spreading the word, helping people wake up, and remaining p-a-t-i-e-n-t.

Following Q is like working a 50,000-piece puzzle. It's slow, but intriguing and fun—as we wait for clues and put the pieces together. I've also loved watching Trump poke the other side. People in the Fake News media were flummoxed by Trump's words "tippy top." Some said the President "struggled to describe the White House." One debunking website said, "A Q made him do it."

BuzzFeed News, the epitome of Fake News, called QAnon an "evidence-free mega-conspiracy." The irony is staggering, since *BuzzFeed* gave credence to the phony "dossier" that accused Trump of working with Russia.

Yet, the more they ridicule the "conspiracy," the more they prove the point. Why make a ruckus about something that isn't real? If the Q movement (as it has now become) is a hoax, it will die on its own. Fourteen months later and counting, we're still here and our ranks are growing.

These People Are Pure Evil

The elite cabal fills the DC swamp. They are wicked, sick, and stupid people who never thought Hillary would lose. They've made too many critical mistakes, and very soon the hammer will drop. There will be nowhere for them to hide.

The ascendancy of evil is not just a US problem, it's worldwide. The Q slogan, "Where we go one, we go all," is being echoed by people in England, Germany, Sweden, Italy, Korea, and Australia, just to name a few. The whole world is watching to see if the clean-up of America will spread.

The elite cabal, which includes compromised people in the Fake News media, Hollywood, politics, academia, and business, have a vested interest in debunking Q. You can tell from their panicked tweets that they know their days are numbered.

Those who have the most to lose scream the loudest, like Obama's former CIA Director John Brennan. He was a top player in the attempted coup to oust Trump, and continues to viciously attack the President on Twitter.

> *"Whenever you send out such inane tweets, I take great solace in knowing that you realize how much trouble you are in & how impossible it will be for you to escape American justice. Mostly, I am relieved that you will never have the opportunity to run for public office again." —John Brennan*

The way to properly interpret Brennan's tweet is to think of it as a mirror. Whatever he accuses Trump of, Brennan himself is doing. Whatever he says is in store for Trump, that's what is waiting for him. This tactic is called *psychological projection*, and the elite use it to get ahead of (and attempt to control) a story in order to frame the narrative. According to Q, for Brennan there is "No Escape and will get No Deals"—just an open-ended ticket to the military detention center in Guantanamo Bay.

How I Got Here

Like many in our community, I stumbled upon Q by accident. I was on YouTube doing research for my *Praying Citizen* newsletter, which I started in 2015. I felt compelled to reach Christians who were not planning to vote in 2016. So, I began writing about the issues of the day, telling both sides of the story, explaining why voting matters, and how one might pray about it.

It was easy in the beginning, but the Fake News media doubled-down on their attacks after Trump's victory. Every day, finding and reporting truth became more challenging and the list of trusted sources grew shorter. The first casualty was trust in the government. From the JFK assassination, to 9/11, to government mind control programs like Project MK-Ultra, I have become a bona-fide conspiracy believer. If you haven't taken the time to look into these and other crisis events, like the Pulse Night Club, Las Vegas, Parkland High School, and Sutherland Springs Baptist Church shootings, you really should. Nothing about the official stories about them adds up.

Like Q says, we have been lied to by the people we trust the most.

While I was trying to get to the truth on the Las Vegas shooting, I stopped to watch a Q video. My interest was piqued by crumbs of information such as:

> They never thought she would lose...
> This was [an attempted] hostile takeover from an evil corrupt network of players.
> Many in our government worship Satan...
> Good people were forced into bed with this evil under personal and family threats.

Right from the beginning Q said we can trust Trump and the US military. Those were the only two entities I was prepared to trust! Q also said, "Patriots are in control. Sit back and enjoy the show." As time went on, Q added names to the trustworthy list: Attorney General Jeff Sessions, FBI Director Christopher Wray, and US Attorney John Huber. Most of all, Q said to trust "The Plan"—an effort by Trump and the good guys to take control away from the evil globalist elite and return power to We, the People.

Q has given me hope by saying things like:

> Rest assured POTUS is backed by the absolute finest people alive who are all dedicated to the eradication of evil and corruption from the US/World.

My relationship with Q evolved as I began putting the information into my newsletter. I felt impressed to create YouTube videos for those who would rather watch than read. As time went on the posts got to be so huge, deep, and challenging, that I began devoting videos just to Q. My approach now is to report the Q post, present the research, add my thoughts, and finish with prayer. Many of the questions Q raises haven't been fully answered yet. But like with any great story, when we get to the end we'll understand it all.

Why Some Struggle to Believe Q

Those in the truth movement were hoping against hope that Q was real, but the first post promising Hillary's arrest on October 30, 2017, was curious. No arrest was made public. Subsequent posts that day said her extradition was already in motion; she was detained but not yet arrested. After that, the most fascinating drops of clues and facts began to follow.

It wasn't always easy to keep the faith. Some of the most frustrating aspects have been Q's promises that, "This week is going to be huge," or "2018 is going to be glorious." Q had us all believing, several times, that THIS WOULD BE THE WEEK we would see Hillary in custody and the Fake News media eating crow.

Because "The Plan" is earth-shattering, the way had to be prepared: The Department of Justice cleaned out—which it was with an unprecedented numbers of resignations, terminations, and retirements. The Senate had to be solidly Republican—which was delivered as a 53-47 majority after the midterms. And finally, the Supreme Court needed another conservative justice, which we got with Brett Kavanaugh.

It has been a long road, and the hype and lack of visible action took its toll. During the first year, some Q followers fell by the wayside. But those who have kept the faith, following, praying, and spreading the word, have been richly rewarded. Hints from Q have led us down more rabbit holes than we can keep up with! Our patience has paid off, and we are probably the most informed people around.

The Calm Before the Storm

The President himself announced the start of this awakening on October 6, 2017, several weeks before the first Q post. Flanked by military commanders and their spouses in the State Dining Room, Trump asked the press corps, "Do you know what this represents? Maybe it's the calm before the storm."

A reporter asked, "What's the storm?"

Trump responded, "Could be the calm before the storm," and then he gave a sly smile.

Reporters scrambled to figure out what he meant and the resulting conjectures were wild and irrational. Sara Huckabee Sanders straightened them out, saying the President was sending a message. She said: "I think we have some serious world issues here. I think that North Korea, Iran both continue to be bad actors, and the president is somebody who's going to always look for ways to protect Americans, and he's not going to dictate what those actions may look like."

Later, Trump was asked again what he meant. He responded, "You'll find out."

We have since learned that Trump and his team are pursuing enemies both foreign and domestic, and we've passed from the calm into The Storm. The other side has fought back with the lie that Trump is a Russian agent; but also with several false flags. These are acts perpetrated by one entity, but blamed on another. The name comes from the days when pirates on the high seas would capture a ship and sail under a "false flag."

Many times during The Storm, Q has warned us to stay alert, be vigilant, and above all, pray. Some of the false flags were averted, like a bombing in New York's subway. Others took the lives of innocent Americans in places like Parkland, Florida, where the shooting may have been orchestrated by people within our government in order to elicit support for a gun-grab. There are still many never-Trumpers in all levels of our government who are doing whatever they deem necessary to carry out the globalists' agenda to reduce population and take worldwide control. If you have any doubt, research the UN's Agenda 21 (now called Agenda 2030). It is chilling.

The purest of pure evil—beyond theft, corruption, murder, and blackmail—is the kidnapping, torture, raping, and sacrificing of children. The perpetrators are Luciferians and Satan-worshippers. They run pedophile networks across continents, through the Vatican, and underneath the cover of charities and child protective services. In short, they target and infiltrate any organization that puts them closest to their victims.

It All Ties to the White Rabbit

Q's post on October 29, 2018, refers to a 2010 email that was exposed by Judicial Watch. The email exchange itself is uninteresting. What matters are the references to *Alice in Wonderland*. Hillary is "Madam Alice," and her correspondent is Clinton buddy Marty Torrey, the "Mad Hatter."

The earliest communications by Q refer to Alice and "bloody wonderland," and Q's December 20, 2018, post circled back:

ALICE & MAD HATTER

Remember, Trump stood on the South Lawn flanked by a gigantic white rabbit when he affirmed Q by using the words, "Tip-top, tippy top." As we've discovered, there are no coincidences.

Bloody Wonderland

The kingdom of Saudi Arabia (SA) is known for strict adherence to Islamic law and bloodlust—the beating and beheading of offenders. But Q suggests it goes deeper, that SA is a hub for human trafficking—or rather it *was* a hub. Everything changed after Trump visited the kingdom on his first official trip.

Shortly thereafter, the SA was rocked by a palace coup. Prince Alwaleed bin Talal was captured and imprisoned (he eventually bought his way out of jail) and was replaced by his nephew Mohammad bin Salman—the 32-year-old son of the King.

Q told us there was an order to the cleanup, with SA being first and the US right behind it. Other nations in the "queue" were NK, Iran, Europe, and Israel—which is being saved for last.

Trump famously referred to Alwaleed bin Talal as the "Dopey Prince." As usual, the President nailed it. This is the same guy who:

- Led in the funding drive to pay for Barack Obama's education at Harvard (how did he pay off that debt?)
- Gave multiple millions to the Clinton Foundation
- Gave multiple millions to John McCain's Foundation
- Gave multiple millions to Nancy Pelosi's Foundation

Further posts suggested that these foundations were created in order to facilitate trafficking and launder money.

August 31, 2018 Q wrote:

> **HRC = Alice**
> **SA = Wonderland**
> **WHO ARE THE WHITE RABBITS?**

Before we answer that question, let's explore the identities of the other characters in Q's posts: Godfather III, Snow White, and Wizards & Warlocks. So far, we've been told that the Wizards and Warlocks are in the intelligence agencies, and Snow White may refer to the computer system they use—or it may be something else entirely.

What about Godfather III? In the movie, an aging mafia don named Michael Corleone tries to assuage his guilty conscience by donating huge sums of money to various charities. He asks his children to come to a ceremony where he will be honored by the Pope. Corleone tells them, "The only wealth in this world is children; more than all the money, power on earth, you are my treasure."

Is Q saying that kids are the cash cow?

Another post says this:

> **"Who is the broker for underage sex?**
> **Think SA with FB, Instagram playing a role in capturing kids.**
> **Think movie Taken."**

In *Taken*, Liam Neeson's daughter is kidnapped and sold as a sex slave to a Saudi prince.

According to this post, Facebook and Instagram are being used by human traffickers in SA. Was the Dopey Prince the ringleader?

Now let's take a look at two creepy Clinton associates and their sick proclivities.

John Podesta was a top aide for both Hillary and Bill. His brother Tony ran the very powerful Washington DC lobbying organization called the Podesta Group, which closed its doors in December 2016. No surprise there, as they lost access to power when Hillary lost the election. The Podesta brothers love and follow the dark side. First of all, they're fans of Marina Abramovic, the "spirit cooker" who mixes body fluids to create ink. Abramovic is also known for repeatedly stabbing herself as part of her performance "art."

John Podesta has been linked through his leaked emails to pedophilia. He and his pals used terms identified by the FBI as code for sex acts with children. There's also a published photo of him displaying occult symbols on his palms: a large number 14 on one hand, and the drawing of a fish on the other. These images may refer to the myth of

Osiris who was torn into 14 pieces. Thirteen pieces were recovered, but the 14th (his male member) was eaten by a fish!

John's brother Tony is a noted art collector whose home is filled with paintings of shackled and dead children. Hanging over the staircase is the contorted image of a headless man. It's eerily similar to one of the bodies posed and photographed by serial killer Jeffrey Dahmer.

Per Q, "Their symbolism will be their downfall."

Q has also warned us that disinformation is real and distractions are necessary. Therefore, the November 4, 2017, post that read, "Q = Alice," had us wondering how Q and Hillary could both be Alice. Another post told us we would soon understand the meaning behind Alice & Wonderland, and added that everything has meaning.

The parallels become curiouser and curiouser.

In 2009, the Obamas held a secret wonderland-themed Halloween party based on the movie *Alice in Wonderland*. The guest list included Johnny Depp and Tim Burton, plus several other cast and crew members. Their names were omitted from the official White House guest book in an effort to keep the party secret. However, two years later, a *New York Times* reporter spilled the beans.

Donald Trump responded to the news with this tweet on January 12, 2012.

> *"With unempoyment over 10% in 2009,*
> *@BarackObama held an extravagant Alice in*
> *Wonderland party. He is a man of the people!"*

Trump purposely tweets misspellings as codes (the missing "l" in unemployment). And while the Fake News revels in his supposed stupidity, we look for deeper meanings. One example is his labeling of Washington Post/Amazon owner Jeff Bezos as "Jeff Bozo." The WaPo is an endless fountain of Fake News, and Amazon built a cloud system to host CIA data, for which Bezos will be paid $600 million. The CIA is also known as the Clowns In America—and Bozo is a clown, right?

Q also linked to an Amazon entry for a book published in March 2017 called "Hillary Clinton in Wonderland," a rewrite of the Lewis Carroll tale that substitutes Hillary's name for Alice's. Another link took us to a BBC documentary exposing author Lewis Carroll as a likely pedophile.

Through the Looking Glass

In Carroll's second book, "*Through the Looking-Glass, and What Alice Found There,*" Alice re-enters wonderland by climbing through a mirror. She finds that everything there is reversed, just like a reflection. Up is down and down is up. What a fitting way to describe the narrative we are being fed daily by the Fake News.

On August 31, 2018, Q told us that child trafficking routes had been closed down in several places:

SA
Epstein Island (owned by friend of Bill and Hillary, Jeffrey Epstein)
Haiti
NK
China
Russia
and Cuba

The "pending" list included:

Sudan
Syria
Yemen
Libya
Somalia

In December 2018, the President announced he will pull US troops out of Syria. Does this mean the work of closing those trafficking networks is now complete, or it has entered another phase?

The battle at our southern border is another attempt by the elites to protect their routes for humans, drugs, money, and other contraband. Why do you suppose leading Democrats fought tooth and nail to stop the border wall? It's not just that they need more Democrat voters, they also need to keep the supply lines open. Imagine how much more difficult that would be with strong borders.

Q told us on November 4, 2017, that by the time POTUS returned from Saudi Arabia, the world would be a different place. Q said SA isn't clean, but they play a role in a global game of RISK. The effort is from bottom to top, and the Trump/Q team have made stopping human trafficking a high priority. It doesn't mean SA's problems are over, but it does suggest it's no longer the slave capital of the world.

The kingdom itself is oil-rich and famous for an insanely wealthy royal family. The princes have carved out a solid reputation for their wild playboy activities in the West. Follow the money, and it will take you to the shooting in Las Vegas. Besides the bizarre contradictions of facts and the incoherent narrative from law enforcement, we have the following oddities:

- The top five floors of the Mandalay Bay Hotel from which the shooting took place are owned by none other than the Dopey Prince and Microsoft's Bill Gates. It is, in fact, the Four Seasons Hotel, with a separate entrance.
- A month before the mass shooting, one Saudi prince booked a number of suites in the Four Seasons to house members of the Saudi Air Force so they could fly training missions at nearby Nellis Air Force Base.
- The night of the massacre, one whole floor of the Four Seasons was occupied by the royal family.
- The same night of the massacre, the Tropicana was stormed by men with guns escorting a roughly dressed dark-skinned man through the casino. Was he a Saudi prince in disguise?

We are led to conclude that Stephen Paddock, the so-called shooter, was a CIA operative in town to sell arms to the enemies of Prince Mohammad bin Salman. The deal ended when assassins opened fire in the casino and several people were killed.

Q suggested Trump was in Las Vegas that same night to meet with the new Prince. Just another coincidence!

Obviously, there's more to the story. Somehow, a total of 58 people were killed as the result of a failed assassination attempt, which may connect to the CIA. In the days and weeks following the massacre, six survivors mysteriously died. All of them had posted photos and details on social media about the shooting that differed from the official account. They were going to form a group to expose the truth—did someone decide they needed to be silenced?

Now, let's get back to the mysterious white rabbits. Who are they? A key to their identity can be found in the artwork of Alex Podesta (not related to John or Tony that I could find.) Alex creates images of grown men with beards and mustaches dressed as white rabbits. In one piece, the adult rabbits are having a rodeo, roping blindfolded baby-sized rabbits. If you do a search, you'll find many creepy images of these adult rabbits toying with the "baby" bunnies.

Podesta's rabbits are a dead ringer for a shadowbox rabbit found in a photo taken in the 1960s. It's a picture of Gloria Vanderbilt and her two sons on a bed in their home. Above the bed is a shadowbox that depicts a human sacrifice flanked by demonic beings and a bearded/mustached adult white rabbit. The image of the rabbit is identical to Podesta's art, but precedes it by several decades. Another coincidence!

Just as a point of interest... Gloria Vanderbilt's son is CNN anchor Anderson Cooper. Cooper interned with the CIA during college, possibly under a program called Operation Mockingbird. Although the program supposedly ended in the 1970s, the CIA still manipulates us with their propaganda through Fake News.

Q seems to indicate that white rabbits represent pedophiles. The first "Alice" was running the networks until Trump/Q put a stop to her. Now that Q = Alice, that could mean the white rabbits have been caught and the networks are going down.

End of the [D] Party

According to Q, the Red Cross, the Clinton Foundation, and John McCain's foundation are heavily involved in the trafficking. Q suggests that once the truth about human trafficking in Haiti and the stealing of humanitarian relief money by the Clintons after the 2010 earthquake is released, that will be the end of the Democrat Party. In that day, Fake News will no longer dampen public awareness. Dark to light.

We're already well underway in The Great Awakening. There's no going back—especially when black unemployment is at historic lows, paychecks are getting fatter, and taxes are growing smaller.

As Americans of all political stripes wake up, they long to tell their stories. So now we have thousands of inspiring videos by people who've "walked away" from the Party. My favorite is the video by Chelsea Brown of her #WalkAway experience. It made me cry, smile, and feel a renewed sense of purpose.

Chelsea had two unplanned pregnancies. The first one ended in an abortion at a Planned Parenthood clinic. She was alone, frightened, and ignorant. No one told her what the procedure would be like. No one showed her any kindness. She felt tricked into ending her baby's life.

The second time Chelsea faced an unplanned pregnancy, she was older and in a better place. She kept the baby, married the baby's father, and made a decision to follow Jesus Christ. Chelsea's story ends with a litany of failures in the Democrat Party and the way her life turned around when she began to pursue the truth. Praise God for Chelsea and others like her!

Follow the Money

A Q post on November 3, 2018, suggested that the Democrat Party has been happily using Planned Parenthood as a cash cow—probably since its inception. The taxpayers subsidize PP to the tune of $500 million per year. In return, PP donates back to the Democrat Party. Planned Parenthood gave Democrats $30 million in 2018 to help win back the House.

A media outlet called Live Action exposed seven different Planned Parenthood clinics in 2011 for aiding and abetting sex traffickers who were trying to obtain abortions, contraceptives, and testing for 14- and 15-year-old girls. The staffers bragged that they always ignore parental-consent laws for underage girls in the sex trade.

That's just par for the course when your goal is to eliminate certain segments of the population. Ignorance is our greatest enemy! How many people would still support Hillary if they knew:

- Hillary's mentor, Robert Byrd, was a Grand Master of the KKK.
- Hillary's teacher and friend was Saul Alinsky, a man who dedicated his book "Rules for Radicals" to Lucifer—whom he calls "the original rebel."
- Hillary's hero is Margaret Sanger, founder of Planned Parenthood and warrior for the eugenics movement—a desire to improve the population through "controlled breeding." Sanger mandated that abortion clinics be set up in black neighborhoods so they could eliminate the next generation of "inferior" humans.

Knowing all this, it's not hard to believe that a communication by HRC was intercepted on March 13, 2013, in which she said about black Americans, "Keep them starved, keep them blind, keep them stupid."

A Q post from October 29, 2017, further explains that Democrats formed the confederacy to keep slavery, formed the KKK to persecute blacks, and systematically paid off black leaders to keep the population poor and dependent on the government. Meanwhile, Democrats practice projection—blaming Republicans for racism, when they themselves are the elite racists, oppressing the people they pretend to help.

Planned Parenthood isn't about women's health or women's "choice," it's about money, fulfilling a wicked plan, and human sacrifice. There is nothing new under the sun; people have been sacrificing babies to their pagan gods since man's early days on the earth.

> "They have built the high places of Topheth,
> which is in the valley of the son of Hinnom, to burn
> their sons and their daughters in the fire, which I
> did not command, and it did not come into My
> mind."—Jeremiah 7:31

Here's what Q had to say about the child-sacrificing arm of the Democrat Party:

Review the Congressional investigation on PP.
Be prepared for what you learn.
Next question—how are they allowed to operate?
These people are SICK!

Q

The Republicans began an investigation into Planned Parenthood and these issues in particular:
- Profits from the sale of fetal tissue
- Changing procedures in order to maximize the harvesting of fetal tissue
- Not giving patients sufficient informed consent when fetal tissue is donated
- Whether the Department of Justice knew what was going on and chose not to enforce the law

However, this is not a Republican vs. Democrat battle—it is a battle between good and evil, darkness and light, truth and lies, freedom vs. slavery. The bad guys want one-world government where there are two classes of people: the ruling elite and the expendable worker bees. That's why, whenever just one person "wakes up," patriots rejoice and the elites ridicule. Worldwide, there are billions more of us than there are of them.

> *"Together, we reaffirm the truth that light will always break through the darkness."*
> —Trump tweet December 2, 2018

"The times are too grave, the challenge too urgent, and the stakes too high to permit the customary passions of political debate. We are not here to curse the darkness, but to light the candle that can guide us through that darkness to a safe and sane future. JFK"
—Q post December 10, 2018

Power of the EO

The Q movement wouldn't be worth a moment's notice unless there were signs that good is winning. So now let's look at two important Executive Orders (EOs) that were signed by the President.

Trump's EO of December 2017 declares a national emergency due to the "unusual and extraordinary threat to the national security, foreign policy, and economy of the US." It allows the confiscation of property of persons involved in serious human rights abuse or corruption. They are going to lose their piles of money.

A second Executive Order on March 1, 2018, grants the federal government the right to prosecute treason by civilians via military tribunals. The beauty of military trials is that they bypass any corruption within the civil court system.

You might remember that Christine Blasey Ford became a media darling when she accused Judge Brett Kavanaugh of a sexual assault in the 80s. The Fake News media covered her allegations and his denials during his Supreme Court confirmation hearing, but they were silent on a critical exchange about treason between Sen. Lindsey Graham (R-SC) and Kavanaugh. Both men agreed that American citizens who collaborate with the enemy are considered enemy combatants, and can be executed.

Q said this line of questioning was not normal. It directly related to the EO regarding military law versus criminal law.

Think HRC Panic

With these EOs, the president can use the military however he wants. He can institute martial law— wholesale or partial—and deploy the US military on US soil. The military detention center at Guantanamo Bay,

Cuba, has been enlarged and improved. Q has told us to trust John Huber, the US Attorney who operates out of Utah and was appointed by Attorney General Sessions to prosecute crimes at the Department of Justice and FBI. Huber has access to 470 lawyers and staff that work under Michael Horowitz, the Inspector General at the Justice Department.

Huber was originally appointed by President Obama, then fired by Trump before being re-hired—thus cementing his impartiality. For more than a year, Huber has been investigating the illegal spying on Trump's team by the FBI and the connections between the Clinton Foundation and the sale of one-fifth of US uranium to Russia.

"It would," as Alice said, "be so nice if something made sense for a change." Military tribunals to convict these evildoers makes a lot of sense to me.

Funny thing… Barack Obama signed an EO July 6, 2012, granting the president absolute power and control over all US media—including Facebook, Twitter, and others—in the event of a national crisis. His EO updates the Communications Act of 1934, dissolving the National Communications System, establishing an executive committee in its place, and placing it under Homeland Security. I bet he thought it would be Hillary, not Donald Trump, executing this EO.

The 16-Year Plan to Destroy America

One final piece of information is needed to demonstrate that this is the fight of our lives.

Q outlined the elites' 16-year plan to put the final nails in the coffin of a free and just America. In a nutshell, it required eight years of Obama followed by eight years of Hillary to destroy the economy, eliminate the Electoral College, decimate the military, and take away the Second Amendment. In addition:

- Men and women of high moral character would be sniffed out and removed from government.
- Population control would be implemented worldwide (using medicines and food/water additives to poison us, aided by the transgender movement, the hatred of manliness, and widespread androgyny)
- Borders opened

- The government would control the media, silencing the opposition
- The Supreme Court would be seated with globalists
- The end would culminate with World War III

To the elites, we are sheep and cattle. God only knows the extent to which they are messing with our atmosphere, foods, soil, water, etc., to manipulate our biology. They have been working for generations to corrupt our kids at a very young age. Thus, schools are teaching youngsters that, "Boys can have periods too," and gender is a choice. Meanwhile, modern culture encourages parents to think of their offspring as "theybies" instead of babies.

Globalist singer Celine Dion has introduced her new line of gender-neutral children's clothing designed to "liberate" children from the traditional roles of boy and girl. It's not just harmless fashion, folks, it's a satanic mindset—organized and strategic. Without a nuclear family, held together by a genetic male husband and a genetic female wife, we are doomed. The global elites' goal is an end to monogamy, God-given genders, and normal procreation.

> *We wrestle not against flesh and blood, but*
> *against principalities and power—rulers of the*
> *darkness of this world, against spiritual wickedness*
> *in high places. —Ephesians 6:12*

QAnon is a Patriot Movement

Q posts are filled with hope for our country and a call to unite us as one people.

As Ronald Reagan said,

> *"Freedom is never more than one generation*
> *away from extinction. We didn't pass it to our*
> *children in the bloodstream. It must be fought for,*
> *protected, and handed on for them to do the same,*
> *or one day we will spend our sunset years telling our*
> *children and our children's children what it was*
> *once like in the US where men were free."*

Today doesn't have to be that sunset day if We, the People reclaim what is rightfully ours. United we stand, but divided we fall. It's not a day for the faint-of-heart; this is the day for courage, prayer, and faith.

Q is a Bible-Believer

The Q group has placed verses from the Bible throughout the posts, and continually asks us to pray for our nation and for the President.

> We pray every single day for God's guidance and direction as we are truly up against pure evil. Yet there are more good people than bad. The wizards and warlocks will not allow another satanic POS to control our country.

Evil knows no bounds. Sadly, some of the people we have trusted the most are among the most wicked: church leaders, presidents, lawmakers, judges, teachers, and coaches. Whether for personal gain or out of fear for their lives, these people have failed us.

Judgment begins in the house of the Lord. That's why pedophile priests, bishops, and cardinals (and their protectors in the Vatican) are being exposed.

Who's next?

Pastors and ministers would do well to keep a clean spiritual house in every way. Corruption is rampant. When the truth is revealed, will so-called Christians be caught up in massive scandals? Whatever happens, we know that God wins.

Q is not some crazy theory. We've been given fact upon fact, and detail upon detail: It is a conspiracy no more. The public is waking up and the elitist cabal of evildoers will be removed from power. Many will go to jail, and some may even be executed. All that remains now is for the truth to become mainstream.

One day, the light will be so bright, the darkness will not be able to hide from it. Believers in the Lord Jesus Christ know that day is coming when Jesus returns. But I hope to see a small measure of that kind of righteousness in America one day very soon.

About the Author

Lori Colley

I'm a blogger, researcher and wife, mom and grandma. I left my position as Media Director for a Christian ministry in 2015 to begin publishing *Praying Citizen* newsletter—believing that God was calling me to do so.

In January 2018, I started turning the newsletter into a video and publishing it on my YouTube channel. I now have 40,000 subscribers and millions of views. No one is more surprised than I am!

My husband Bob is my proofreader and editor; I depend on God first, and him next. We've been married for 31 years, have four children (whom I homeschooled) and one granddaughter. I have a B.A. in Communications from Northern Illinois University, and started out as a writer/producer in marketing, advertising, and media.

I'm also an avid horsewoman (hunter/jumper) and taught riding lessons and trained horses for several years. My other interests include ministry, counseling, and teaching.

YouTube Channel: Lori Colley
Praying Citizen is published at: prayingcitizen.wordpress.com
Follow me on Twitter: Lori Colley@prayingcitizen

Every now and then QAnon will tell us, "You have more than you know." However, it requires the brilliance of our serious decoders to help us see what's there that we didn't know about. Deciphering Q's posts—using several approaches discussed in the chapter—has made SerialBrain2 the Anon who perhaps more than anyone has shown us that Q is indeed giving us much more than we knew. While SerialBrain2's post #1 on the board was a simple reposting of Q's own posts, by his 9th post he is illuminating world politics and economics for our benefit in a vivid interplay with QAnon's posts. As time has gone on, his insights have grown ever richer, his deciphering more complex and the spirituality he shares with us ever deeper. This is not your legacy media's talking head. This is an Anon and citizen journalist who is paving the way for a new generation and helping us to survive and thrive as we fight and then ultimately heal from this existential crisis.

Decoding and Deciphering Q

by SerialBrain2

Post #1: You, the PEOPLE, have ALL the POWER. You simply forgot how to PLAY. TOGETHER you are INVINCIBLE. Q828.

Q828
Stay TOGETHER.
Be STRONG.
Get ORGANIZED.
Be HEARD.
FIGHT the censorship.
You, the PEOPLE, have ALL the POWER.
You simply forgot how to PLAY.
TOGETHER you are INVINCIBLE.
They want you divided.
They want you silenced.
MAKE NOISE.
We are WITH you.
MAKE IT RAIN.
Q

Q812
They want you DIVIDED.
How can some be so blind?
Help them wake up.
Estimated 20mm reached.
Question everything.
Keep talking.

Stand up.
Fight fight fight.
How do they control children?
What prevents a child revealing the truth?
Q

Q767

You are a strong Patriot.
Do not give in - fight, fight, fight.
You have more friends than you can imagine.
UNITED WE STAND.
GOD BLESS,
Q

Q570

The Great Awakening.
Fight, Fight, Fight.
Q

Q563

Why are we here?
Why are we providing crumbs?
Think MEMO.
BUILDING THE ARMY.
Not convinced this is spreading?
You, the PEOPLE, have THE POWER.
You, the PEOPLE, just forgot how to PLAY.
TOGETHER you are STRONG.
APART you are weak.
THEY WANT YOU DIVIDED.
THEY WANT RACE WARS.
THEY WANT CLASS WARS.
THEY WANT RELIGIOUS WARS.
THEY WANT POLITICAL WARS.
THEY WANT YOU DIVIDED!
LEARN!
FOR GOD & COUNTRY -
LEARN! STAY STRONG.
STAY TOGETHER.
FIGHT, FIGHT, FIGHT.
This is more important than you can imagine.
Q

Q542

Fight, Fight, Fight.
DEMAND public disclosure.
BE LOUD. BE HEARD.
This is just the beginning.
2018 WILL BE GLORIOUS!!!!!!!!!!!!!!!!!!!!!!!!!
Q

Q529
Be READY.
MSM coming - BIG WAY.
We see all.
We hear all.
FIGHT, FIGHT, FIGHT.
CONSPIRACY push coming.
MSM LOST CONTROL.
D LOST SLAVE GRIP.
D LOST CENTER VOTERS.
LIBS are MINORITY.
MSM PROJECTS AS BIG MOVEMENT.
FAKE NEWS. 4-6% LOST FOREVER.
HELLO GEORGE.
Q
FIGHT, FIGHT, FIGHT. FIGHT, FIGHT, FIGHT. FIGHT, FIGHT, FIGHT. FIGHT, FIGHT, FIGHT.

Post # 9: Dow plunging 666 points. So far Trump has won 2 battles out of 3, will he win the last one?

The powers driving a nation are 3: Social power (beliefs, myths, social justice, media, etc.) Political power (legislative, judiciary and executive infrastructure, etc.) and Economical power (money supply, markets, etc.).

The one who controls these 3 components, controls the Nation. And the one who controls the most powerful nation of the world, controls the world. God knows it, Satan knows it, Trump knows it, the Vatican knows it, the Deep State knows it, Bohemian Grove knows it, pretty much everybody knows it.

The Hollywood debacle, the NFL and MSM meltdown, the Grammy's plunging ratings, the statue debate along with other matters show America is going through a deep and irreversible transformation since Trump's election. All the myths that were misleadingly strengthening the fabric of the Nation are being destroyed one after the other. Trump's ability to raise a major social question, extract the BS out of it and expose those who have undermined America, knowingly or not, has enabled him to start putting the social power back into the hands of the People. First win.

The infiltration of our political infrastructure by evil and secret powers is not a conspiracy theory. Unless President Kennedy was a conspiracy theorist. Which I doubt. That being established, Strozk text message referring to a secret society is proof our political infrastructure has been compromised. Using secrecy, blackmail and other occult means, evil powers have controlled the majority of our politicians for decades. This control, transcending party lines, explains why America has carried on with destructive foreign and domestic policies written decades ago without any incoming president challenging them. Until Trump. The way he handled TPP, Immigration, Global Warming and the UN demonstrated his personal freedom. Second Win.

The process which led Congress to produce and release the memo would not have been successful if these Congressmen were not freed. Conspiracy? Think about it. At his first attempt to tell the truth, Nunes had to temporarily step down as Chairman of the Intelligence Committee and go through an investigation! This time, the GOP stood still, remained united and even enjoyed the luxury of producing All-Stars like Gowdy, Ratcliffe and Jordan and a new MVP with Gaetz! This was a major setback for the former controllers. They had to retaliate. Hence the train "accident." Fortunately, with God's help, the casualties were limited to the death of the driver for whom we pray. Now let's stop and think about this: imagine if this "accident" was successful. We would be in a situation where there would be no elected majority. The evil forces at work would regain power in Congress and Senate because they would have successfully demonstrated Trump's inability to protect their members against them. Now that they played this card and it did not work, they know Trump's administration will now take all the necessary steps to physically protect Congress and Senate members. So... What's left? Remember? 3 powers.

You guessed it. The economy. Since the train 'accident' did not work, they figured: let's show him we control the economy. Hence the Dow plunging 666 points. Coincidence? This number was carefully chosen referencing Trump's family building located at 666 Fifth Avenue. Now the question is: how can they control the stock market like that, aren't the markets supposed to drive the numbers, how can they control uncertainty and volatility? Well, that's the final red pill only Trump, a Wharton graduate who became President of the United States, can pull off. After hypocritical Hollywood, misleading MSM, a blackmailed political infrastructure and an infiltrated judiciary system, the final myth America needs to wake up to is the Economy: it's rigged. From the artificial production of the money supply to the mathematical models driving the stock market, it's all rigged. This article would be too long to explain it. But those who want to know should research Alan Greenspan who chaired the Federal Reserve from 1987 to 2006 and who, in his early career days helped build the mathematical infostructure and technological infrastructure common to the Fed and the Stock Exchange. Folks, it's all rigged: those who write the programs decide who wins. Do you believe in coincidence? The same day the train "accident" occurred, Alan Greenspan, out of the blue says on Bloomberg:

"There are two bubbles: We have a stock market bubble, and we have a bond market bubble."

And 2 days later, the Dow plunges 666 points!

That's the third battle.

Will Trump, the Wharton graduate who became POTUS, win the war against those who have turned our economy into a rigged casino where they are the only winners?

When Trump and his Generals respond to the attack (which we should all hope they do) and move their forces to that battlefield, the coming months will be deadly.

This war will not stop until the dollar returns to gold and the Federal Reserve to ashes.

> **Q667:**
>
> **[666]**
> **Signal to POTUS they control the market?**
> **Signal?**
> **Threat?**
> **Welcome to the Global War.**
> **Q**

Those who pray should pray.

Nothing new under the sun. The Money Changers against Christ.

Post # 15: Q507: Soon, the whole world will be able to unlock hidden messages from Q's board! Learn now!

Ok guys, so let's recap:

So far, we have unlocked hidden messages 5 times using various methods:

1. The Covefefe Method that allowed us to [decode Trump's covfefe tweet] and translate it from "despite the constant negative press covfefe" to "wait to die." We gathered from this

solved riddle that Trump is promising to completely dismantle MSM. Q877: The age of MSM is over.

2. The Florida Guccifer Method that allowed us to [decode Q830] and unlock the hidden message informing us the Florida shooting was a false flag aiming at keeping Guccifer out of the news cycle and derailing Rosenstein's explosive related announcement.

3. The same Florida Guccifer Method allowed us to decode Q832 which unlocked the hidden message that AI and Sarin were somehow combined (in a way we have not figured out and that Q himself compares to magic) to create innocent mind controlled social warriors who can be used for demonstrations, shooting and even assassination.

4. The T Method allowed us to [unlock Q907 and Q908] hidden messages about NK informing us Trump has in fact been in secret contact with Kim Jong Un since before September 2017. We also learned that Trump has successfully neutralized the bad actors who funneled military grade tech to NK, using it as their base for leverage.

I also introduced the Matrix Time Stamp Method based on times stamps between Trump's tweets and Q's posts. It has similarities with the T method for pulling solving grids but involves the use of a key like in the Covfefe Method. I have made a public announcement for help to speed up the research and get that method stabilized. I still welcome any help and will share findings as soon as it is completely figured out for general consumption. In the meantime, all the other methods cited above have proved themselves and are available for you to try throughout the board.

The very next day I posted the Q830 Florida Guccifer crack, Q posted: Q860 "first boom, did you catch it? The last one will be magical" Many are speculating about what he meant. Some are connecting it to the news. They may be right. I stated my belief is he was referring to Sarin and AI being combined to perform "magic" in Q832 and also to the very first time a hidden message from his board was publicly disclosed. I say "publicly" because I know there are some anons out there who have already unlocked many messages from Q's board but have chosen to remain silent and to confine this information to a closed elite club.** I, on the other end, want people to be aware. I want people to learn these methods. I want people to unlock the board.

This is because I know that is what Q wants.** In Q507, he is announcing a day when all this will be wide spread:

> **Q507:**
> This will be the AUTH tool you use when all of this becomes public to provide friends, family, others.
> Do you think POTUS re-tweeted MAGA PILL for no reason?
> We chose this BOARD for a very specific reason.
> We believe in you.
> Q

This is why I am doing what I am doing. This is why detractors do not distract me.

So, detractors, whatever you have in your basket of tricks, [bring it on! And let's have a party!] :)[1]

"Cheered" up?! Good!! :) Now seriously:

We will not back down. We will fight the censorship. We will re-organize. Later today, I will post a brand new explosive unlocked message, so make sure you are around.

In the meantime, there is something very important you guys need to know. I hear from detractors: you are delusional, these methods are not decoding methods, these methods are not logically sound, you are reaching, you make your own rules, etc... Once again, we are not decoding. We are solving riddles. And this is the way it should be. Q is not talking to a small elite of mathematicians or cryptologists. This would not be fair. He is talking to anyone who would be willing to get his brain teased for a while with no particular academic knowledge and be rewarded with privileged information. This is the only way he can achieve the vulgarization process he is describing in Q507.

The reason why these methods come with a certain degree of uncertainty or subjectivity is because Q knows he has to defeat the AI in its effort to analyze his posts and also unlock the hidden messages it knows to be there. AI can only learn systems that can be logically replicated. But when these systems are purposely made unstable with well-crafted noise and humanization, AI is lost. This is why, while unlocking, you may see one option also working like "Sarin in AI real" could also be "Naira's Airline." But then, when you compute in the context of the original message and other T crossing methods like the 23X23 grid I showed you in the "sarin" example, you realize there is only one acceptable answer. The possible solutions being many is purposeful: plausible deniability and neutralized AI. This is what Q meant here:

Q30:

These keywords and questions are framed to reduce sniffer programs that
continually absorb and analyze data then pushed to z terminals for eval.
Think xkeysc on steroids.
Q

Q736:

Double meanings work well against sniffers.
Q

Post # 18: Guccifer 2.0 finally found its way to the news cycle: I told you. It now begins.

I told you in this [post] Post # 2 - Q's HIDDEN CODE in Q830 CRACKED! This is why the Florida shooting happened! —the real reason why the Florida false flag shooting occurred and how it was used to control the news cycle. [2]

The Texas bombing was another try aiming at derailing (again) Mueller's new attempt to release his bombshell. Q informs us in Q958: They are scared [4am]. They will fail. we know the details. [Wednesday]. Which means: their daily 4am Mockingbird routine to take over the media narrative will not work this time since we are going to provide all the intel about the serial bomber by Wednesday. Confirmation: Link 1: [3] Link 2: [4]

By pre-empting the Texas bombing story through the revelation of the bomber's identity, patriots have opened a boulevard for Mueller to plant his Guccifer story on the news map.

So now, we are learning that hacker Guccifer 2.0 is identified as a Russian intelligence officer after failing to hide IP address.[5]

An officer failing to hide his IP?

This is like saying: Michael Jordan missed his dunk because he forgot the ball behind him…

Seriously, this is HUGE folks.

Because now, Trump can securely face Mueller for the cherry on the pie visual of this amazing saga: Mueller cannot go back on Guccifer, it is now public. He has to go all the way and you know what he will find at the end right? Putin will make sure he finds everything.

Q 834:

WHY would Russia tell the world?

Since the whole Russian blanket is pulled by those who are tied to Guccifer, Trump is now as white as snow and can peacefully confront

Mueller, his hands in his pockets, whistling an old Miss Universe jingle. Any competent lawyer advising Trump would advise him not to do so, and his highly competent long time lawyer did exactly that. He had to resign because he's obviously not in the know... Or may be he is and is willingly adding drama to this first class Shakespearean drama.[6]

My parents used to drag me to the theater to watch dramatic plays when I was a kid.

Mom used to say: it's like spinach, you don't like it but it nourishes you. Never enjoyed it.

But I was always amazed by the faces of the actors at the end of the play, when people were applauding: they were so different from the roles they were playing.

This intense moment of perplexity I was going through crafted my understanding of plays for the years to come.

Watching Trump doing his thing on stage is the first play I have not paid for and where the main actor is the most powerful man on earth.

Mom was right.

Moms are always right...

Post # 26: Q 1074 [Read between the lines]. We did and this is what we found!

Have you caught Q1074 linking to an article about Joseph Schmitz?

Fake News CNN claims this Trump adviser played a key role in pursuit of possible Clinton emails from dark web before election. Q is asking us to read between the line and when we do, we extract the main information this article is trying to plant in the story line:

[Schmitz] claimed a source he called "PATRIOT," an unidentified contractor he was representing, had discovered what he believed was likely material stolen from Clinton that could contain classified information. Both the client and Schmitz were afraid that going through the material without permission could jeopardize their security clearances, though there is no indication their actions were illegal.

The first important fake news here is the idea that material may have been stolen from Clinton. We already know from Q834, Q701 and this source how and why the private server was set up. We also know who benefited from it and some of the names of government officials who were running the process. The idea of stolen material is a new idea being artificially planted with the purpose of preparing a legal defense strategy and confusing investigators.

The other key here is the last sentence "though there is no indication their actions were illegal." How does CNN know that? And what actions are they exactly talking about? Is it illegal as an action to discover material you have decided not to go through? Notice the grammar of the sentence. It is not a quote. It is a volatile comment, with no argumentative anchor. This is an indication that CNN wants investigators to focus on the planted information and not the actors. How so? If Joseph Schmitz wakes up one morning and finds some fabricated information at his doorsteps proving H's classified material was stolen and not distributed, he has to contact federal investigators who then have to interview him and ultimately pursue that theft possibility. This is what CNN means with "no indication their actions were illegal." You see how it works? They plant fabricated information at the doorstep of a close Trump ally, then, waving the obstruction of justice or preferential treatment flag, they pressure investigators to consider the planted information with front pages like: "Exclusive: Trump adviser played key role in pursuit of possible Clinton emails from dark web before election." This is what Q means here:

Q1074
Front page.
Fake news.

While officials at the State Department and Inspector General briefly interviewed Schmitz, they declined to review or accept the information, according to sources familiar with the process. The FBI interviewed him as a part of its ongoing criminal investigation into Clinton's emails, sources said. It is not clear whether special counsel Robert Mueller is pursuing information about Schmitz's efforts.

This is Mockingbird CNN subtly asking Mueller and Horowitz to take this theft option more seriously so that confusion and protection layers may be successfully added to their investigations. When, instead of reporting the News, media outlets engage in such influence operations to deceitfully create the News, you know their sponsors are in panic mode. In this case, Mueller and Horowitz evidently did not take the bait and downplayed the planted information that Schmitz had to relay to them. Why? Because they already have all they need...

From where? From the Military who asked Trump to run and who already gave him the intelligence he is fighting the Deep State with.

> **Q14**
>
> **Why did Adm R (NSA) meet Trump privately w/o auth?**
> **Does POTUS know where the bodies are buried?**
> **Does POTUS have the goods on most bad actors?**
> **Was TRUMP asked to run for President?**
> **Why?**
> **By Who?**
> **Q14**
>
> **What is Mueller's background?**
> **Military?**
> **Was Trump asked to run for President w/ assurances made to prevent tampering?**
> **How is POTUS always 5-steps ahead?**
> **Who is helping POTUS?**

Post # 31: Q1131 Drop after Testimony. The Art of War or how Pompeo brilliantly played Hillary Clinton.

Ok guys, this is the today appetizer. I will make another post later today. Make sure you catch it, I will show you among other things why Trump capitalized G, K and A in his Gas Killing Animal tweet and how he is secretly communicating with Putin...

So what do we have here? A top of his class at Westpoint to be confirmed as Secretary of State.

This is going to be EPIC!

For those who have read Sun Tzu or Machiavelli, get ready for a treat! Just studying Pompeo's every moves could now be the best strategy class you could ever attend.

In Q1129, Q provides us with these 2 links: Link[7], Link[8] and cryptically says: "down she goes."

Let's analyze this.

We gather that Pompeo asked Hillary Clinton (and also Kelly) for advice before his congressional confirmation. This very surprising (and elegant) move has been heavily relayed by the press: Link[9] Link[10].

By reading the comment section of this video[11], it seems Pompeo reaching out to Hillary led many Trump supporters to question his loyalty.

Is it that simple?

Let's open Sun Tzu's Art of War: "Chapter 6: Weak Points and Strong."

We learn these 2 fundamental rules:

1. By discovering the enemy's dispositions and remaining invisible ourselves, we can keep our forces concentrated, while the enemy's must be divided.

2. Rouse him, and learn the principle of his activity or inactivity. Force him to reveal himself, so as to find out his vulnerable spots.

Applying these 2 rules, Pompeo asks for advice to Hillary.

Hillary opens up, blindly spills the beans and basically reveals to Pompeo her weaknesses and/or desire: stop purging the State Department (so I can besiege you and make your life as miserable as Session's life with Rosenstein).

"Clinton advises Pompeo to stop 'purge' at State Dept."[12] Source: The Hill.

With this information, Pompeo now knows exactly what he needs to do: he is going to apply this rule from Niccolo Machiavelli:

"The new ruler must determine all the injuries that he will need to inflict. He must inflict them once and for all."

Get ready folks, Pompeo is going to purge the State Department in a way nobody has ever seen before!

Of course, right after he received this "advice," he probably stopped taking her calls:

> Q1131[13]
>
> **"Drop after testimony."**
> **R U learning yet?**
> **Q**

She gets she was played. Just like Snowden:

> Q1124[14]
>
> **@Snowden Yes.**
> **Testify then drop.**
> **We have it all.**
> **These people are stupid.**

So now she has a problem. Chances are when she spoke to Pompeo, she probably started distributing "protection gift cards" to SD officials: "hey, I got you, I spoke to my buddy Pompeo, he'll keep you around." Why? Because she needed to have these people know ahead of time they kept their jobs because of her intervention so that they could be loyal to her. This is why Pompeo's move was over mediatized. Do you think he would have had everybody know he asked for advice? No. The media knew it because Hillary told them. She was showing around her new influence toy she got from Satan Close! Now if Pompeo gets in office and starts firing people who Hillary already had reached out to, it is likely these people are going to be very very angry and turn against her. So? She needs to show them she was played and this is why this pops out:

THE HILL

Pompeo failed to disclose ownership of business connected to China

BY LUIS SANCHEZ - 04/11/18 06:53 PM EDT   433 COMMENTS

10,876 SHARES   SHARE   TWEET   G+ PLUS ONE

Just In...

Robert De Niro, Ben Stiller play Mueller and Cohen in 'SNL' parody of 'Meet the Parents'
IN THE KNOW — 2H 5M AGO

Trump order targets wide swath of public assistance programs
HEALTHCARE — 5H 21M AGO

Top LGBT rights lawyer sets himself on fire at Brooklyn park in protest suicide
BLOG BRIEFING ROOM — 5H 30M AGO

Accused Parkland

Autoplay: On | Off

CIA Director Mike Pompeo did not disclose last year that he owned a business linked to a Chinese government-owned company, McClatchy reported.

1 Prosecutors: Cohen raid is red...
2,412 SHARES

2 Comey-Trump feud takes vicious turn
1,012 SHARES

3 Wage growth well short of what was...
657 SHARES

4 Cohen doubles down on claim he's...

"Pompeo failed to disclose ownership of business connected to China."[15]

Too late Hillary. Thanks to you, Pompeo has now so many vacant job positions to give away, he can negotiate directly with Democrats in the House to get his confirmation votes...

> *"It is double pleasure to deceive the deceiver."*—
> *Niccolo Machiavelli*

Post # 35: Censorship within the Great Awakening?

Let's get to the bottom of this! For the Q's Movement sake.

Guys. We need to talk. We need to have a serious conversation between adults about a rampant situation that needs to be addressed now. For the good of the Movement and for the sake of what Q is doing.

It seems there is a small group of people who, because they are not interested in or do not like certain things that are published on this board, believe the authors should be banned and dealt with.

I wanted to take a minute and analyze this. Respectfully. Coldly. Rationally.

My understanding is we are here to talk about Q right?

My attempt to answer to this question led me to identify 3 lanes in which my posts are produced:
1. Spiritual/Occult
2. InvestigativeResearch
3. Decoding/Cryptography/Riddles

Within a month, 34 posts have been published in these 3 lanes. Here are a few examples: Image[16]

Now, are these 3 fields of knowledge in compliance with Q? Are they the creation of my free styling imagination or did Q signal they should be explored. Let's look at this: Image[17]

So there you have it. This is what Q is.

Now let's talk about my decoding posts. Based on the messages I receive and one of the decoding posts reaching 350 upvotes with 20k views, it is clear there is an interest. People want to learn and understand what's going on with these cryptic messages on the board.

TOPIC	SERIALBRAIN2 POSTS
Spiritual Occult	• Q Occult Series. Private: Clowns Clowns Clowns. PART1. • Q Occult Series. Q #133: [Hard to Swallow – Important to Progress. Q] This is key guys! Part 1. • Q Occult Series. [Why school shootings? $$$$$$$$. Q] Take this red pill. • Q Occult Series. Q744: Wake up guys! Here are the Nephilims! • Q Occult Series. This one is very creepy. Discover the power of 17. I warned you: not for everyone. • Q Occult Series. Q114: US Military = Savior of Mankind. What does it mean?! Part1. • Q Occult Series. Quick and important heads up: Did the Pope REALLY say "HELL DOES NOT EXIST?"
Investigative Research	• Dow plunging 666 points: so far Trump has won 2 battles out of 3, will he win the last one? • Guccifer 2.0 finally found its way to the news cycle: I told you. It now begins. • Syria: Q 1081 [POTUS NEVER telegraphs his moves. Think logically]. Trump outsmarts the Deep State. Again. • Comey compares Trump to a mob boss. This is why Comey is insulting Trump. He's toast! • Trump about Syria: "Mission Accomplished". Let me tell you what you have just witnessed. Brilliant!!! Just brilliant!!! • Q1131 Drop after Testimony. The Art of War or how Pompeo brilliantly played Hillary Clinton.
Decoding Cryptography Riddles	• Q's HIDDEN CODE in Q830 CRACKED! This is why the Florida shooting happened! • Using the T Method to CRACK Q's board: Secret and brilliant Trump's moves on North Korea! • Q's board CRACKED again: Hillary's private server was the key. It's over! They are all going DOWN! • You guys asked my thoughts about Trump's strange tweet today. Here it is! • Q1127 secret message decoded! And this is why Trump capitalized G, K and A in his Gas Killing Animal tweet! • Trump's strange "MEME" tweet decoded! Learn how to use online decoding tools to unlock Q's board!

TOPIC	JUSTIFICATION ON Q'S BOARD
Spiritual Occult	• Q925 **Good vs Evil.** • Q133 Who worships Satan? What is a cult? • Q133 "Vladimir Putin: The New World Order Worships **Satan**" • Q100 What does an upside down cross represent? • Q100 What does **Spirit Cooking** represent? Cult. • Q29 We **pray** every single day for God's guidance and direction as we are truly up against pure evil. • Q3 Many in our govt worship Satan. • Q458 Please PRAY for those who would lay down their lives to protect our **FREEDOM.**
Investigative Research	• Q371 Why did the WH link posted turn up 404 (2) days after? • **Expand** your thinking. • Q327 BDT. Think currency. • Q192 Compare. **Think.** • Q1017 The Analysis Corporation (TAC).Happy Hunting!Q • Q464 **Follow** the MONEY.Loop Capital Markets.Happy Hunting. • Q3 Follow Huma. Operation Mockingbird.
Decoding Cryptography Riddles	• Q315 Timestamp US Military against POTUS' recent Tweet - US Military. **How many clues** must we provide? • Q1150 Where are the autists?!?! Q • Q258 **Decode.** News unlocks message. • Q477 Timestamp. **Decipher.** Think clock. • Q504 WE ARE TALKING DIRECTLY TO THIS BOARD. LEARN OUR COMMS. Q • Q510 Directly after POTUS alters Tweets to [1] min interval and adds "Q" - use graphics. Learn. Q • Q507 Graphic form for each correlation a MUST. • Q506 The CLOCK and the GRAPHIC are ESSENTIAL. • Q453 Side-by-side graphic? Locate and create.[:22] • Q157 **What is a key?** What is a key used for?

Now you have some people who unilaterally decide this "decoding thing" should stop, because—they say—they think it makes the Movement "look bad." The problem is the Movement is Q and Q is the one who started this "decoding thing," is still doing it and says it is important.

In the comment section of this [decoding post] (Post #33: Trump's strange "MEME" tweet decoded! Learn how to use online decoding tools to unlock Q's board![18]), [before the ban] you [would have found] an interesting exchange where one of these censoring entities is being rightly reminded that Q has been exchanging on 8chan on grids, arithmetic, gematria and riddles with anons since day1 and that what I am doing is just in continuation of these conversations. Then, the censoring entity publicly shares an image of a very disturbing conversation he had with the Mods, I am redacting his name for obvious reasons: Image[19]

Not only is he making unsubstantiated accusations (how can some one 'create' 20k views and 350 upvotes?!) but he is deciding what the board should look like. Amazing. To know more about how the board would fit to his Royal Desires, I went to his profile to not only discover he has never, ever, ever submitted any post on this board but he has also never submitted any post about Q anywhere.

So, Mods, I am asking you. Are these the types of people you should have a conversation with while others, on the other hand, are substantially and peacefully contributing to the life and progress of our Movement?

This post where this censoring entity commented was part 1 of a 2-episode series. I wrote episode 2 would be posted the next day. The first episode had 2.3k views and 109 upvotes. I received tons of messages mirrored in the comment section about part 2. When I published it the next day, as announced, the view count was not visible for hours, when the final count showed up, it dropped to 704 and I still have people messaging me asking me where is episode 2!

So...

I am asking the Mods who have been doing a fantastic job growing this sub and keeping it a civil space where anybody can come and learn about Q, to protect it even more from negative outside influence, whether it is human or electronic. Whether it is emotional or algorithmic censorship. I have been interacting with a few of them in the past and know they have the skills and the generosity to provide us with what I am requesting. And I am sure I am requesting this on behalf of many contributors to this board.

I will later today drive in the Investigative Research lane and tell you why Rudy Giuliani joining Trump's legal team is a brilliant chess move. Literally. Make sure you catch it!

> **Q854**
>
> WE must work TOGETHER.
> WE are only as strong as your VOICE.
> YOU must organize and BE HEARD.
> THIS is why they keep you DIVIDED and in the DARK.
> WEAK.
> We are here to UNITE and provide TRUTH.
> [...]
> Q

Post # 45: Corsi gone. Infowars exposed. Our Brothers and Sisters are coming back home: Welcome! And proof Corsi was an Infowars covert operation against the Q Movement.

> **Q1340**
> What an amazing journey.

Q linking to my post and honoring my pen in such a way is a humbling and extraordinary experience.

I have a routine: in the morning I read Q, and during the day, I try to understand him. When I read this:

> **Q1328**
> This is NOT about a single person. This is NOT about fame, followers, or profiteering. We, the PEOPLE. We, the PEOPLE. We, the PEOPLE.

I immediately realized linking to my post was his way to show his appreciation to our work as a Movement, to our selfless and relentless dedication and to thank the faceless and generous Patriots who express their talents on the board and in subs such as ours. Feel proud Patriots, what comes from Q, comes from Trump.

Please allow me to mention in particular the Reddit/GreatAwakening, its members, its mods and its contributors who have graciously opened their door to my pen and let it explore even the weirdest places of knowledge and truth without constraining it. I am thankful and I am congratulating you all. The honor is shared, the achievement is ours.

Now back to the battlefield.

This post is not about kicking a man when he is down. As far as I am concerned, the Corsi/Infowars situation is resolved. Our people who were deceived have now realized what was going on and are coming back home. This is good. Let us welcome them, they meant well, they were just deceived and sincerely thought the choices they made would have helped the Movement. They now have a tremendous opportunity to really invest their talents in the Q Movement and make a difference.

This post is partly aiming at doing a little debriefing. You know, just like in the Military (I've read it in books and saw it in movies), after an operation, they produce a document that gathers all the information allowing them to improve in the future.

We all should be proud of ourselves. We have shown our capacity to immediately understand what Q needed us to do and do it efficiently while successfully containing our internal differences. This reactivity and effectiveness is a strong signal to those who oppose us: if you still want to try to dismantle us, know it will not be easy. Especially since we have now gathered experience points.

First, I will address the Infowars issue. Many, after being finally convinced there was a serious Corsi problem, were still not ready to include Infowars into the equation. Some arguing Infowars hosted Trump, some waving the unity flag. Well, those who play chess know when we have a check position with a pawn, it means the pawn is protected. We have witnessed Corsi's progressive dive into the abyss, violently defying Trump and Q. And we also know how Corsi worships Alex Jones Video.[20]

If Alex was as much concerned by unity as we were, why didn't he instruct Corsi to get back into the ranks and stop his embarrassing nonsense? Why?

Once the pressure forced Corsi out of his hiding place, Alex lost his check position and only a few hours were required for him to confirm what he has been hypocritically hiding since the very first day Q started posting. Let's watch an excerpt of his yesterday show until 35:28 video. [<= Note: The preceding YouTube account and video above were deleted and not archived]

There you have it. You now know without a doubt who is who. Check Alex's comment section. Infowars is self destructing. Who would have imagined Alternative Media is about to go through an irreversible mutation and that Infowars would not be part of it?! What an amazing time to be alive!

Q1328 There was no attempt to DIVIDE. There was however a strategic move to REVEAL.

Now as to Trump being interviewed by Infowars. This is normal. Infowars deserved it. I am not denying Infowars played a major role in Trump's election. So did Bannon. How did it end? The political chessboard is made of living objects. If these objects lose their way and try to overreach, when the leader is as strong as Trump, it never ends well for the gambler. He would immediately be reminded of his disposability. So as long as each actor knows his place and does what he has to do, the party goes on and everybody dances [video][21]

Now I would like to ask you a question. Why do you think Q posted "Be careful who you are following?" What triggered this post? We were already aware there was a Corsi problem weeks before. Why did Q post this at that particular moment? I conjectured in a previous post that he had some kind of intel that pushed him to do it. Yes, we know he was pushed to do it because in Q1297 he says: *Statements today needed to be made.*

Well, I will show you what substantially contributed to Q making this statement.

On May 9th 2018, Q posts this:

Q1324

Corrected. We all make mistakes. Busy day. Q

He is talking about the trip code change procedure. Why do you think Q is bothering informing us he made a mistake and even detailing it: Q1323: *We did not input "Q #" in the beginning which exposed the password.*

It's not the first time he changes his tripcode and the change does not follow a particular frequency rule we are aware of. He could have changed the tripcode, make his mistake, silently correct it in conjunction with the board operators and we would have never known. But Q wanted us to know he made a mistake. Why? Because of this: Image[22]

You got it? Q knew Corsi was going to accuse him of being AI. If you watch Infowars' yesterday show, Alex makes the same claim. This was their final move. This was their endgame. This is the intel Q had all along! By making this *"mistake"* and insisting about it *"we all make mistakes,"* Q is essentially saying he is human and is pulling the rug out from under Corsi's feet!

Do you imagine what went through Corsi's head when he saw that post?

It did not prevent him from still making the accusation. He had to stick to their plan.

Q636

Predictable. We SEE ALL. We HEAR ALL. Wizards & [WAR]locks.
These people are really DUMB.
Q

Now why is this relevant? Why is it important for Alex and Corsi to position in Q's timeline an interrogation about him being AI? Because AI is not clearly covered by the First Amendment. The legal expert conversation is ongoing: Link[23], Link[24], Link[25]. So now close your eyes for a minute, expand your thinking and imagine a conversation Alex could have with his crew about shutting down Qs' board.

Do you see it?

The legal option would immediately be considered and a skilled lawyer could come up with the idea of capitalizing on the legal uncertainty surrounding AI's free speech to trigger precautionary measures in a law suit... The board would then be shut down for a while, until the legal situation reaches its conclusion. This is why Corsi needed to create some kind of interaction history with our Movement to then become a "credible" source that would accuse Q of being AI... Do you want to know how this weird idea knocked at my door?

Here, listen to Corsi until 2:52: video. [<= Note: Video removed by Corsi However, SB2 fortunately quotes Corsi below]

Did you catch it? "it looked to me this is now getting into the realm where Q is basically incoherent, making no sense at all and probably inviting a law suit."

Law suit? It seems Dr. Corsi has been putting some thought into this for it to randomly pop up in a YT segment. I do not know anyone who has ever raised this issue. Do you?

So my friends, if a legal situation was to target our beloved board one day, you now know where this inconvenience would probably come from...

In the meantime:

Q778

ARCHIVE EVERYTHING OFFLINE.
Q

Do you believe in coincidences? When Divine Assistance manifests itself, this is what it looks like: as I was writing these lines, u/digital_refugee paged me to ask me my thoughts about this post. [<= Note: The preceding referenced Post was 'banned' by Reddit]

Yesterday, at 6:24 PM, Infowars sent its daily newsletter to its subscribers with a few errors: Imgur[26]

Do you think an experienced multi-million-dollar media operation would make such a mistake? No. This is secret ciphered communication. Let's decipher it. Q taught us in the board how to do this.

The text is: *Qanon Compromised: intel source hijacked by seep state's disinformation sampaign.* We get the first obvious clue from seep and sampaign, the correct spelling is "deep" and "campaign." Since the D and the C were purposely replaced by an S, we gather DC is the first clue. Let's keep that in the back of our head.

Now the letter S is the 19th letter of the alphabet. I have shown in my decoding training posts how to solve a Caesar Cipher problem based on Q's teachings. Let us apply the method using the online tool: Link[27], Link[28], Link[29].

So let's recap, we have: DC, BY, OP. Let's expand:

[DC=Washington DC] [BY=Bye Bye] [OP=Operation]

Let's interpret:

Bye bye to the DC Operation.

Who is in DC? Dr Corsi. He is the Infowars Correspondent in Washington DC, Link[30].

The newsletter "error" is a message to their network of covert operators informing that since Corsi has been exposed, his operation is shut down. They are moving to whatever next phase they have.

You are not dreaming folks, you are not watching a movie. This is the real world. This is the Infowars we all used to trust.

Now I have a few questions for you: if Infowars uses this kind of infiltration methods and this kind of comms, what do you think Infowars REALLY is? Who is REALLY behind Infowars? Why does Alex disrespect Trump and desperately looks for his attention? Why is Alex announcing Trump's possible murder at every single show? Why is Trump now showing him utter disregard? What does Trump know about Infowars since he became POTUS and took control of the Intelligence Agencies? Happy Hunting.

Start here: Link[31] Stop here: Link[32]

Link[33] and try to go further than this: Link[34]

Q114
US Military = savior of mankind.
We will never forget.
Fantasy land.
God save us all.
Q

[Update on Alex Jones: This is not in SB2's original post. Here is a screen shot from October 2018 InfoWars - Alex Jones' website that shows the URL and photo he posted claiming that "Qanon has made false allegations against him."[35]]

Post # 52: The Q1439 real time update. This board has more power than you can imagine

Before we proceed: I receive many messages from people requesting my authorization to use my writings in their work. This is the way I see things: everything I write here is the property of the Q Movement. I am sure many in our Movement have skills in commenting, video editing, memes etc... They are more than welcomed to use the material I have posted to help spread the truth on all platforms.

Ok. Done.

Have you ever watched a Michael Jordan basketball match where at money time everyone expects him to shoot the ball, but he finally does not? The coach intentionally keeps him on the court to trigger a forced double team on him so that the real shooter can be wide open. The coach has a predetermined strategy and then picks his final shooter from a wide variety of players. Video[36].

Q1045
We don't inform our enemies of the specifics.
We instead instill fear in them to make unplanned and disastrous countermoves.
Q

In this post, I explained how Q1433[37] was hinting at the firing of Rod Rosenstein and his replacement by an Acting Deputy Attorney General with May 24th 2018 as a pivot date.[38]

At the time that post was published, Q1439[39] was not available yet. I therefore integrated in the analysis the 2016 Loretta Lynch guideline scenario[40] which positioned Francisco, the Solicitor General, as the most likely person to take the position. It has to be understood this guideline does not supersede The Federal Vacancies Reform Act of

1998 §3345. Acting officer,[41] which gives the President the freedom to pick from a large list of possible officers.

Then Q posted Q1439.[42] He links to a Fox News article[43] confirming that May 24 2018 is indeed a pivot date. In this post he asks: who is Ed O'Callahan? Answer: he is the United States Acting Principal Associate Deputy Attorney General, he is a republican and a November 2017 Trump nominee. He is also eligible to the Acting Deputy Attorney General position according to The Federal Vacancies Reform Act of 1998 §3345. Acting officer. Q asking this question and adding "Acting" [Ed] is a hint Ed O'Callahan may be Trump's final choice. This question is Q following up with his Q1433 post and implicitly explaining why he did not reference the quote he used to introduce the 210 day rule: **he was dismissing the 2016 Lynch guideline scenario!**

Do you realize, what is being said here? This is a perfect example of future proves past: the Fox News article Q links to in Q1439 and where we learn about the May 24th 2018 meeting with Christopher Wray, Devin Nunes, Trey Gowdy, Dan Coats and Ed O'Callahan was published one day after Q1433. **How did Q know that the 210 day rule would be relevant but not the 2016 Lynch guideline?** The fact he did not mention O'Callahan's name in Q1433 but only did in Q1439 is an indication we are being informed in real time as things are decided in high places… Wow.

> **Q761:**
>
> **Was the point proven?**
> **This board has more power than you can imagine.**
> **Q**

Post # 65: Occam's Razor: Understand the context. Trump's enemies are on political life support. Unplugging soon.

Let's talk about Occam's Razor. Q says this:

> **Q1547:**
>
> **Ability to share [open].**
> **(Heat) on who?**
> **(Full) transparency _ DECLAS?**
> **(Undiscovered) facts emerge?**
> **Ability to move forward?**
> **Occam's Razor.**
> **Q**

What is Occam's Razor? From Wikipedia, we learn the following: Occam's Razor is the problem-solving principle that, when presented with competing hypothetical answers to a problem, one should select the answer that makes the fewest assumptions.

In simple terms, it basically means that when you have multiple possible explanations for a problem, the simplest one is more likely to be the correct one. Using this, many thought Q was inviting his readers to trivialize his entire board and find simple ways to solve his challenging riddles. Well, even though I believe the most elegant answer to a question is a simple answer, I don't believe the process that gets you to the answer is always simple. This is the very essence of pure mathematics where thousands of pages are used to prove the answer to a one-line question is a simple "yes" or a simple "no." One classic example in Number Theory is the following very simple question derived from Fermat's Conjecture:

For any integer value n greater or equal to 3, can we find 3 integers satisfying this equation:

an + bn = cn ? Yes? No? Or possibly and under which condition?

Simple question right? Well, it took more than 3 centuries, the largest number of unsuccessful proofs, the emergence of a new field in mathematics called algebraic number theory, the consideration of the very complex modularity theorem and the synergy of the brightest math minds on earth to answer this simple question. And the answer was no…

All mathematicians with a fair amount of intuition who dealt with this problem applied the Occam's Razor principle: they tried a few times with given values of n, a, b, c and d and could not satisfy the equation so they thought: the answer must be no. That's where the Occam's Razor principle stops. Then, they had to prove the answer is really no. And that's where the fun begins!

You now see what Q means when he says Occam's Razor?

What is the context? He first posts this cryptic message:

Q1543

D
Morning sun brings heat.
Full moon coming.
Undiscovered stars learned.
Missions forward.
Q

Then, once anons start conjecturing about what it meant, he says this: Link[44]

Then, when anon insisted, he said this: Link[45]

Q is basically saying: since the message was not for anons, who do you think it was for? Apply the Occam's Razor principle and the simple answer is: the message was for black hats.

Then, just like our mathematicians above, we proved the message was for black hats in this post.

> **Q1343**
>
> **Truth is Freedom.**
> **Truth is logic.**
> **Stay the course.**
> **Q**

Now that we clearly know what Q meant with Occam's Razor, let's apply it in the following example:

> **Q1575:**
>
> **Abandon ship!**
> **Hussein staff talking. Link[46]**
> **What are we leading up to?**
> **Q**

First, did you see the confirmation of what we said in this post about using the current version of the IG report to convert and put pressure on those who may bring solidifying information? Link[47]

Second, Q asks "what are we leading up to?" He is referring to this linked article where we learn Obama cyber chief confirms 'stand down' order against Russian cyberattacks in summer 2016. Occam's Razor: the stand down order was given because the attacks were not Russian. Vault 7. You now see why Brennan has to go all the way against Trump, with no possible coming back: Link[48]

Did you notice how Brennan randomly jumped in a twitter conversation which was supposed to be between Trump and Comey? Why do you think he felt he had to post this incendiary message? I will tell you.

You remember the post where Q decoded a tweet from Comey?: Link[49]

Did you know the real implication of what Q revealed here? Here it is: Link[50]

You see it? Now if these false flags were made possible because the FBI dropped the ball at some point because McCabe was threatened and blackmailed, what happens if he is fired and if Wray successfully cleans the house? Yes, you got it, they will have to use another network to plan false flags. Hence Brennan. His tweet is essentially a message to Comey: now that McCabe is gone, I got your back, I have my network, it's all yours.

You want a confirmation? Sure. Look at the way Comey acknowledges the offer and asks Brennan to activate his network the next day the IG report is out: Link[51]

You want more? If you want to distract from the IG report and want to plan false flags, you need money from your usual secret donors right? Well, this is how you ask for it: Link[52]

Stretch? No, I am only applying Q's template on how to read Comey's tweets and… expand my thinking.

You want more? Let's read Q1457. Link[53]

We know Rosenstein was in Canada on June 11. But for what? The post says: "you cannot hide what is already known." Occam's Razor: this means Rosenstein traveled to Canada, one of the 5 eye countries to alter some kind of evidence. Fisa related? Former Canadian company Uranium 1? Very likely. We all know how Rosenstein betrayed Comey and organized his defenestration. Do you think Comey would help Rosenstein achieve what he is trying to achieve in Canada if he could? Well, 2 days before Rosenstein lands in Montreal, look how Comey absolves him and calls for transcending personal feuds for the emergence of a greater good by activating his personal CIA and political network in Canada: Link[54]

So there you have it. This is what they do. And if I could figure it out just by reading Q, just try to imagine what Q knows and has about them. From what I have gathered from Q's board, the game is already over. These people are on political life support and they will soon realize that the only way to stop the pain is to unplug.

Q1573
PAIN.
House of Cards.
Link[55]

Post #74: Trump's brilliant chess combination in Helsinki.

Rule 0: They blame people for what they themselves do.

Projection

Q1677 Riddle:

Do 'reflections' violate NAT SEC rules?...
Do 'reflections' violate NAT SEC rules?..
Where must one be located in order to obtain a reflection on the back of a
phone of that image?
Image provided here has been distorted (stretched)....
Think mirror... Look there or [here] or there truth is behind you.

They accused Trump of being in collusion with Russia, we now know they were the ones in collusion with Russia: more flexibility Video[56] and Uranium1.

Now, an interesting application of rule 0 would be to list all their accusations and use them as a starting point to analyze them. For example, they insisted Putin had some dirt on Trump. So? Rule 0: Putin has some dirt on them. Pretty cool right?

Now you can take this working hypothesis and check, if down the line, it's not in contradiction with events. If it's not, it's likely to be true. Then, if you remove the hypothesis and cannot explain events rationally, no matter how hard you and other smart people try, then you know the hypothesis is as true as not being able to find a rational explanation to the events it induces. So, when you get here, what you do is take the hypothesis as a working hypothesis, call it a strong hypothesis and you go further in your analysis to gather some other data that would reinforce the likelihood of the strong hypothesis being 100% true.

Application

We know about the Contortionist and how he weakly dealt with Crimea, we know about the Witch and how she arranged the sale of 20% of our Uranium to Russia. Let's remove the hypothesis Putin had some dirt on them and analyze. Is there a rational explanation for their treasonous behavior? I can't find any. Money? Ghadafi had plenty of money and was ready to play ball, just as he played ball with Sarkozy but instead, she came, he saw, he died. It's not just about money. There has to be another power forcing the transaction.

If we go further and notice Putin is ex KGB Link[57], that, according to their own Comey, the Witch's private server was probably hacked Link[58] Link[59] and that nobody knows the truth about the Contortionist's birth certificate Link[60], we have gathered data reinforcing the likelihood of Putin having dirt on the Contortionist and the Witch. And we even have an idea about the dirt itself…

Now, you remember Trump was among the first to openly ask about the Contortionist's birth certificate right? Read Q's board: the witch's server and U1 is everywhere. Now you understand why they don't want a one on one between Trump and Putin. Now you understand why they are going completely crazy. If this dirt, that brought Putin Crimea, 20% of our uranium and SAP tech, is shared with Trump, it's game over for them. Game over.

Now the interesting question would be: why would Putin give this information to Trump?

This is the equation Trump needed to resolve before he met with Putin. He had to meet with Putin with enough good cards in is hands to force Putin to want to give this information and even more in order to get something valuable in return. So? Trump makes his first stop at NATO and makes sure Putin sees this: Video[61] BOOM. Trump reveals to the world the former chancellor of Germany is the head of the pipeline company bringing Russia's natural gas to Germany. This is Trump's first message to Putin: M1.

Then, Trump achieves this: Video[62] Trump forces other NATO members to bring an additional 33 Billion dollars to the table. This is the second message to Putin: M2.

Then, Trump goes to the UK and this happens: Video[63] This is the third message to Putin: M3.

Then, Stzrok is sent to Congress to deliver the Uranium message I told you about in my previous post. This is the fourth message to Putin previous post:[64] M4.

Et voila! These are main pieces Trump will play on the Helsinki chess board.

Let's now watch the combination: M1: I know the natural gas deal you have with Germany is vital to your economy, since it is not appropriate the former chancellor is the head of the pipeline company that will bring the gas to Germany, I have the moral grounds to delay it, stop it, control it. I can have people talk about it all day in Germany and scare the financial institutions away from it with my EO. Furthermore, I know your involvement in Syria is also related to the emergence of competing natural gas routes to Europe. If things go well between us, I won't interfere and will let you find the right solution to export your natural gas and the one that belongs to your friends. Link[65]

M2: You see these guys at NATO? I can make them do whatever I want. I wanted 33 Billion dollars, 1 million dollar per lost email Link[66], and they gave it to me just after a few hours of discussion. No opposition. So, if I want, I can start a weapon race that will cost me zero dollars and that Russia's economy will not be able to sustain. As Q would say: "33 was the hook. Enjoy!" Q1678. I'm sure your guys solved it.

M3: I know about Russia's old feud with the Vatican and the UK with their NWO. I know Hitler made the same mistake Napoleon made trying to conquer Russia in winter to ultimately crush the Orthodox Church. I know what they have in common: Napoleon left alone for a night in the King's Chamber inside the Great Pyramid of Giza Video[67] and Hitler with his vrills and occult connection to the Vatican (start here: Video[68]). I know about all this. And I also know you do:

Q133

"Vladimir Putin: The New World Order Worships Satan"

Q

We are on the same page on this. Look how I have humiliated the Queen, their administrative focal point. I am a free President. I only care about my people. I am not a globalist trying to conquer anything. Did you hear my Great Falls speech where I confirmed Q1675? I said: I don't need all this space. It meant: I just need America. They need more space. It meant: they are the colonizers. This means you and I can negotiate in good faith with no hidden agenda. We just need to find a win-win, work for our people and get along.

M4: You see, I have done my homework. Did you see Stzrok's hearing? I'm sure your guys also decoded how he brought Kate to the table. Dems are stupidly supporting him because they don't see the trap. I have flipped many officials who were involved in the U1 scandal and other things. I have the goods on all the layers of the government you may have dealt with in the past to achieve what you have achieved with the Contortionist's Administration. Good for you, you were working for your country's interest and took advantage of the stupidity of those in charge at the time in the US, but that era is over. I'm in charge now. So if you are considering giving me some information, make sure it's of high value because I already know a lot. If you want something from me, don't tell me what I already know. And of course I won't tell you what I know.

Once this combination was played, Trump and Putin held a press conference. And to make sure there is no interference in the continuation of the game, their respective protocol services agreed to separate American journalists from the Russian journalists. This trick allows any question coming from the Mockingbird side to be immediately spotted as a trap even before it is formulated and signal "caution required." Classic trick used by medieval kings... Video[69]

Did Trump play the combination right? Did he use the right chess opening? Well, in that press conference, not only Putin has atomized Rosenstein and Mueller by offering to cooperate regarding the interrogation and even possible extradition of their 12 Russians-of-the-day, but he also dropped the Bill Browder and George Soros bombshells clearly signaling he is ready to throw the Contortionist, the Witch and all the other layers under the bus to save his pipeline, and limit NATO's strategic spending around Russia. And just in case there are still some people who don't understand what happened in that Helsinki press conference, Putin gives the ultimate hint by doing this: Video[70] Did you catch it? What is Putin saying? He is reminding to the world that soccer is an 11 player game. If Mueller wants 12 Russian players to play his game, Putin is ready to be the 12th player and he just started playing by passing the ball to Trump...

Congratulations Mr. President. The show continues, we now have a new actor. From Russia.

> **Q1603**
> [Objective] to keep POTUS away from PUTIN failed.
> Q

Post #78: Now Comes the Pain 23!!!

So where were we?

Yes, Q brought Q1675,[71] I said B2, Trump said organ, I said Hammond, he pardoned the Hammonds. Then, Trump went to Helsinki. Putin gave him the ball, Trump gave it to Melania and said: this is for my Son Barron. Then, for his interview, he picked CNBC. Why? Because the name of the show is Squawk Box. Then I called Hussein the Contortionist in this post # 74,[72] he called him a Patsy the next day and refers to the exact same video footage I referred to about Hussein's flexibility... Video[73]

Coincidence? No! Trump is establishing proofs he is talking to us. And I see you guys have picked up. I see the overwhelming majority of our movement now understands that Trump is talking to us and everybody is now learning the comms. There is a minority of people still doubting, but that's ok. I hope they will join us soon.

Before we get into the solution of the riddle from my last post, are you enjoying as much as I do the panic in the opposing camp? Complete meltdown of MSM, nervous voices of lost politicians in televised interviews, and, icing on the cake, James Clapper jumps ship and finally reveals the Contortionist is responsible for the entire Russia witch hunt! Link [note: preceding link-Twitter account was suspended in conservative purge and was not archived.]

You know why Clapper is now coming clean right? He understood Trump's message very well. He is trained to understand the things we have been talking about in my last posts. Clapper knows the light incident at the White House was done on purpose and what it really meant. Beside the TOL interpretation I gave in the previous post Link[74] Link[75] Link[76] , Clapper knows Trump's message also meant: "you'd better come clean before the lights are on."

I showed you in the previous post that Trump has connected the server to the Q1675 riddle through NT, the [Microsoft Windows OS] (https://www.computerhope.com/jargon/w/winnt.htm) and we found the connection to Q board through Apache, the most widely used web server software. Imgur1. As many have noticed, I did not specify in my post which server. The reason is it's all the servers! These riddles require a minimum of abstraction from us to understand the message sent to us. When I say: the server, it's a generic term for all the servers that the method Trump is using to fight the Deep State allows him to get. When I say: Trump gave us the server, I mean his method brought the server to the center stage, connected it to the current riddle and allows it to be used as a weapon.

When you understand the comms at this level of abstraction, you can then come down and particularize: you may then read this excellent post from u/RonaldSwansong and learn there are 4 servers. [Archiver's note: The link to u/RSS post was not in Archive and therefor has been lost due to Reddit Q purge.] Then, you read Q's board and realize Trump has them all:

Q1666 We have the server

Q1279 We have it all

This way of thinking will be key in the future to understand Trump. Read again, make sure this mental gymnastics is mastered. I wrote all this from my kitchen, so imagine what Clapper really heard.

This is why he is coming clean and many will follow. The coming days are going to be EPIC! Trump has set the stage and has brilliantly sent all the messages to the Deep State allowing them to make a choice quick before he starts dropping the Server Bombs.

Q956

Panic mode.
Enjoy the show.
Q

Now, the Pledge to America's Workers. In summary, it is about asking companies and trade groups to sign a pledge to America's Workers. In this particular event, coordinated by Ivanka, POTUS signed a new Executive Order establishing the National Council for American Worker and 23 organizations were the first to sign the Pledge to America's Workers. I made it a little easier for you by pointing directly to the part of the video you had to focus on: this video until the until 49:40 mark.[77] But a special kudos to those who took the time to watch all the video as there are always other gems hidden here and there. For example, watch this until 1:02:00: Video.[78] Did you catch it? Trump says "Hey Fred, she makes a plane you can't see, it's stealth, F35." Yup, you got it. Trump is talking to us and he is giving a nod and a wink to our now famous Q1675 B2 Stealth Bomber![79] ;)

Now, why 23 organizations?

For the chess aficionados out there, did you ask yourself why my post about the Helsinki meeting was using chess references and had a 4 play opening? What is 4? Remember, elliptic language.

4 can be seen as the natural response to the sequence 2-3 right? There is a chess game that was played in Helsinki that became famous because of its 23rd move. Yes! Not kidding! And guess what?

It was between an American and a Russian Master. Coincidence? By the 22nd move, American Master Frank Marshall was losing to Russian Master Stephan Levitsky. Then Marshall, at his 23rd move, stunningly sacrificed his queen and won the game. This game entered the list of the most famous chess games under the name of the American Beauty. Link[80] Now who do you think is the "sacrificed queen?" Of course, it's costless and even fun to give away the witch...

Look, it seems she knows some chess and still wants to share her thoughts from the thick smoke of her disintegration link. All this is confirmed by Q. You remember the post where he "released" his password?

In Q1415, we can see his password.

In Q1418, he asks: Mistake or on purpose? Q.

Of course we know it was done on purpose. Let's read the password: NowC@mesTHEP@in—-23!!! Now comes the pain—-23!!! So 23 is the signal announcing the pain. Frank Marshall won his Helsinki game with his 23rd queen sacrifice move, Trump is inviting 23 organizations after having sacrificed the witch in Helsinki and defeated Putin with his 4 move opening. Do you see it? So you thought there was no plan? I told you, the Plan is beyond brilliant and it's lethal.

Q959

Learn chess.
Down she goes.
Nobody escapes this.
NOBODY.
Q

Now, why the word Apprentice? Why does Trump repeat the word "word" several times? I gave you this hint: "Q1675 is all about reflections." Now, in this link, we learn that "The CIE measure of whiteness is a measurement of the light reflected by the paper across the visible (daylight) spectrum." This reflection is confirmation we are still in Q1675 territory. Knowing this and the context, let's re-write Apprentice, unscramble the letters and analyze, this is what we get: Link[81]

As you can see, the word Apprentice is giving us another path to the server and connects perfectly with the Q1675 riddle through the light reflection measured using the CIE measure of whiteness.

Now we may conclude.

This whole event, beyond the obvious, is Trump warning the Deep State about the pain coming through the 4 servers he is about to use against them and all the related topics we have gone through analyzing Q1675. Now close your eyes for a minute, try to purge your mind, forget everything that has been said here and re-watch the video of the event. You will realize you have just received a training that will allow you to see everything with new eyes.

These are the eyes that allowed Clapper to see what he saw and immediately throw Hussein under the bus without you being able to detect any plausible cause in the news.

These are the eyes the Deep State does not want you to have so they can still communicate without you knowing.

Q1646

DARK TO LIGHT.
GOD BLESS AMERICA.
GOD BLESS PATRIOTS AROUND THE WORLD.
THINK FOR YOURSELF.
TRUST YOURSELF.
Q

Post #83: 561=3x187—The 3 times the Deep State tried to assassinate Trump.

Did you know Q told us the Deep State tried 3 times to assassinate Trump?

Today, I will walk you through these 3 attempts recorded in Q board.

First Assassination Attempt: Las Vegas

We went through this in detail in a previous post.

This is connected to the October 1st 2017 shooting at the Mandalay Bay. Reading correctly Q92 [or here] gives us a clear understanding of what happened that night: Trump had a classified meeting with who appears to have been Crown Prince Salman in the top floor penthouse of the Hotel. One of the owners of the top floor being Prince Al Waleed (the other is Bill Gates), we can safely assume he was made aware of Prince Salman's date of presence there. The attack of the penthouse was conducted by members of MS13 and all the eyewitnesses who saw what really happened were later eliminated. The reference to the JFK files is a hint that the final purpose of the MS13 mission was to assassinate Trump.

The shooting at the concert was used as a decoy, a diversion and, probably ultimately as a cover centered around Stephen Paddock, just like the JFK operation was centered around Lee Harvey Oswald.

One of the ways that was used to kill eyewitnesses was to cause car accidents through electronic remote control, as Wikileaks revealed about the CIA. From this, Q is inferring a rogue part of the CIA was involved in this assassination attempt, in complicity with bad actors in Saudi Arabia among whom Prince Al Waleed and Prince Mansour bin Muqrin who was later reportedly killed in a helicopter crash north of the Yemen border. From this, we can safely deduce responsibilities: financing of the operation: Prince Al Waleed and Prince Muqrin, planning: rogue part of the CIA, execution: MS13.

The picture in Q1411 titled by Q "LV remove" is a hint Prince Salman was successfully removed by the US Military and safely flown back to Saudi Arabia. November 4th 2017, pay back: under the disguise of fighting corruption, Prince Salman undertakes the largest political purge of the Kingdom's history. He arrests Prince Al Waleed along with other high profile personalities of the kingdom and hundreds of government officials. We all know what happened next. We all know about the Q1675 mug riddle.

Second Assassination Attempt: The Moon Township Rally in Pittsburg, Pennsylvania

This one went unnoticed.

But it's right here:

Q942
CNN airing assassination of JFK.
CNN 3 sec delay - speech.
CNN Jim's finger on button ready to stop transmission.
These people are sick.
Q

March 10, 2018, Trump is holding a MAGA rally in Moon Township, Pennsylvania. As usual, because Trump rallies are the most entertaining political events, several thousands of people tried to attend: Video[82]

Trump started his speech at 7:05 PM Eastern and left the stage at 8:25 PM. Did you analyze that speech? What was it about? Did you know Trump's speech always have a "theme?" What was the theme here? Did you notice Trump used the verb "kill" 23 times in this speech? Yes, 23. Coincidence? Let's analyze. First, you need to read Trump's last tweet before the event: Tweet[83]

With this tweet, Trump is setting the stage. He is signaling we should focus on the part of his speech that will address the related issues. Then, you have to notice how Q "warms up" the audience a few hours before the rally and what he reveals about CNN and Jim: Imgur1

Then, you listen to his speech and triangulate with the tweet and Q's post. You get you should focus on the following first part, let's listen until 31:35 video. Did you catch the threat on the German cars? Now let's listen to the second excerpt until 36:12: video. Did you catch how Trump insists on the German cars? He says: "So I said, open up your barriers, get rid of your tariffs and we'll do this. We'll have a nice, fair, open—and if you don't do that, that's okay. And that's where the cars come in." Trump knows this is Germany's Achille's heel. Image[84]

Trump knows Germany is the EU's main engine, if he defeats Germany, he defeats the EU. Why should Trump defeat the EU? I will tell you again: the EU was created and firstly presided by a Nazi in 1958. His name was Walter Hallstein. He was the Dean of the University of Rostock in 1936 and in June 1938, Hitler and Mussolini missioned him to create Das Neue Europa, the 'New Europe'. He was captured by American troops in 1944 and in 1951 they recycled him as Germany's Secretary of State under Konrad Adenauer. From there, he 'microwaved' his 1938 project document which became the basis of the EU as we know it today. And, to make sure the EU would take the direction they wanted, his puppet masters let him be its first president! So you think the Nazis lost WW2?! Think again. I summarized the work of French presidential candidate Francois Asselineau in this video 3:30. [The account associated with the preceding video was banned by YouTube- and video was not archived]

Once again, who won World War II?

Now that we have a clear understanding of what is really at stake in Trump's speech, we go back to Q's posts and expand our scope of research. We discover that before starting his exposé on Nazism and how it infiltrated our political system, he posted this: Image[85]

Wow. Is the puzzle coming together? Q is essentially telling us that Trump was targeted in this rally by the real forces behind the creation of the EU: the Nazi World Order which infiltrated our political system (research Operation Paperclip and study Q142[86]) and which continued to rule Germany after Hitler though his daughter Angela Merkel! The reason for this assassination attempt was his stance on trade with the EU and his threat against the nerve center of Germany's international trade: the car industry. CNN was aware of this assassination attempt and broadcasted the event with a 3 second delay. Jim had his finger on the button to interrupt transmission at the fatidic moment. Then, Q says this:

> **Q943**
> You witnessed a strength test tonight.
> Speech promoted here/POTUS to gauge response.
> Net slowed.
> Protections in place.
> Q

Do you realize what is being said here? Trump knew about this assassination attempt, he nonetheless made it to the rally and had Q send the following message to the perpetrators before the rally: we know what you are trying to do, we know exactly who you are, let's get to it. Did you notice the acronym of Moon Township Rally, Pennsylvania? Reorder and dismiss the vocalizing vowel, just like in Hebrew. Coincidence? No. This is a lesser manifestation of the strength test Q is talking about in Q943...

Third Assassination Attempt: The Air Force One Missile

This one is pretty obvious, we are all aware of it and it does not need much explanation. Q clearly says:

> **Q1728**
> Unauthorized missile fired.
> Unauthorized emergency incoming missile threat activated Hawaii.
> POTUS AF1.
> POTUS re-routes.
> Coincidence?
> NO MSM investigations?
> Biggest threat to the American people!
> Q

I have shared in Post # 80 how this unauthorized missile firing is made possible on American soil. Let us notice Trump was coming back from the June 12, 2018 Singapore Summit. I have also explained in my article titled Post #56[87]—The Establishment against Trump or the birthday gift from Pyongyang how Trump was constantly undermined by the Establishment in general and the Bush family in particular. The article shows how Trump picked the June 12 date as a way to troll the Establishment, making it coincide with George H. W. Bush's birthday. Well, knowing this, it perfectly makes sense to expect retaliation from the military industrial complex that is so very dear to the Bush family right? Link[88] Link[89]

Do you know of a better way to show its power and sign its misdeed than to fire a missile at Air Force One?

Conclusion

To conclude, we need to stop at Q133:

> **Q133**
>
> Hard to swallow.
> Important to progress.
> Who are the puppet masters?
> House of Saud (6+++) - $4 Trillion+
> Rothschild (6++) - $2 Trillion+
> Soros (6+) - $1 Trillion+
> Focus on above (3).
>
> Triangle has (3) sides.
> Eye of Providence.
> Follow the bloodlines.
> Q

Q explains in this drop how the Deep State rules its kingdom occupying the 3 angles of an evil power triangle. I have explained in detail in this post how this triangle operates. Here is the summarizing picture: Link[90]

Do you see it? Do you see how each angle of the triangle has tried to assassinate Trump?

Before looking at the following solving image, try to identify which attempt belongs to which angle.

Here is the solution: Link[91]

So there you have it. As you can see, the Deep State has been very busy but there is no doubt our prayers to keep our President and our Country safe are being answered.

Q587
PRAY. PREY.
Notice the similarity?
Q

Post # 96 - All Q related subs banned.

Perfect.

I wanted to wait to see what would happen to other Q related subs on Reddit before posting there.

Now they are all gone and we therefore can all conclude it was a deliberate strategy to silence us and was not related to content, to offense, to guidelines, rules or anything like that.

Knowing this, we can now expand and see that our next move to re-group has to be done out of Reddit. VOAT seems to be an option but so far, it seems they have server capacity issues.

[Archiver's note. SB2 is currently posting just fine on his own account on Reddit. Most are reading his latest posts there or the archived Posts AND current posts I am including the next several VOAT posts just to archive everything.]

Let's continue thinking and exchanging about this and make a final decision in the coming hours.

Let's all stay united; let's all stay the course. Q is still posting on 8chan and has made several drops tonight including one about the banning. He said their attempt to silence us will fail. I trust Q, I know many of you trust me so we don't have anything to fear. This blunt move shows the desperation of the enemy and his inability to oppose us without breaking the rules.

We have already won.

Much Love!

WWG1WGA!

SB2.

About the Author:

SerialBrain2 posts here on Reddit:
https://www.reddit.com/user/SerialBrain2?st=JRWDG7NI&sh=3849 0982[92]
and here: https://www.serial.rocks/serialbrain2
You can also find the latest post at VOAT in these 2 subs:

https://voat.co/v/theawakening/2718748#submissionTop[93]
https://voat.co/v/GreatAwakening/2718759[94]
Enjoy and see you there! :)

---

[1] https://www.youtube.com/watch?v=fquGjSt8RpA&feature=youtu.be

[2] https://www.serial.rocks/post-2

[3] https://www.cbsnews.com/news/mark-anthony-conditt-austin-bomber-suspect-name-identified-pflugerville-texas-2018-03-21/

[4] https://edition.cnn.com/2018/03/21/us/austin-explosions/index.html

[5] http://www.nydailynews.com/news/politics/hacker-guccifer-2-0-identified-russian-intelligence-officer-article-1.3891341

[6] https://www.washingtonpost.com/blogs/plum-line/wp/2018/03/22/trumps-lawyer-just-quit-heres-what-it-means-for-the-mueller-investigation/?utm_term=.36debcf82937

[7] https://thehill.com/homenews/administration/382714-clinton-advised-pompeo-to-stop-the-purge-of-state-dept

[8] https://thehill.com/homenews/administration/382765-pompeo-failed-to-disclose-ownership-in-business-connected-to-china

[9] https://www.politico.com/story/2018/04/10/pompeo-hearing-state-clinton-512155

[10] https://thehill.com/homenews/administration/382418-pompeo-reaches-out-to-clinton-kerry-for-confirmation-advice-report

[11] https://www.youtube.com/watch?v=Wv46-NPoE0Y

[12] https://thehill.com/homenews/administration/382714-clinton-advised-pompeo-to-stop-the-purge-of-state-dept

[13] https://qanon.pub/#1131

[14] https://qanon.pub/#1124

[15] https://thehill.com/homenews/administration/382765-pompeo-failed-to-disclose-ownership-in-business-connected-to-china

[16] https://i.imgur.com/PAYMcSg.png

[17] https://i.imgur.com/ru3w1A7.png

[18] https://www.serial.rocks/post-33

[19] https://i.imgur.com/BkVrRH0.png

[20] https://streamable.com/l4j4f

[21] https://www.youtube.com/watch?v=Lbpp_3AwyrI

[22] https://i.imgur.com/PaxwWUI.jpg

[23] https://docs.google.com/viewer?url=https%3A%2F%2Fscholarlycommons.law.northwestern.edu%2Fcgi%2Fviewcontent.cgi%3Farticle%3D1253%26context%3Dnulr&fname=Siri-ously%3F%20Free%20Speech%20Rights%20and%20Artificial%20Intelligence.pdf&pdf=true

[24] https://www.wired.com/story/should-facebook-and-twitter-be-regulated-under-the-first-amendment/

[25] https://www.forbes.com/sites/thomasbrewster/2017/02/23/amazon-echo-alexa-murder-trial-first-amendment-rights/#601e553d5d81

[26] https://i.imgur.com/u3uCH5n.png

[27] https://i.imgur.com/BrQGwBo.png

[28] https://i.imgur.com/YjNJ487.png

[29] https://i.imgur.com/D4Ljg8Z.png
[30] https://twitter.com/jerome_corsi
[31] https://www.youtube.com/watch?v=oDUMp0OniVI
[32] https://i.imgur.com/uZjIZhP.png
[33] https://i.imgur.com/gsasvUw.png
[34] https://i.imgur.com/i2XNxLB.png
[35] https://i.imgur.com/hs4xe0y.jpg
[36] https://www.youtube.com/watch?v=BGTIq4yO-og
[37] https://qmap.pub/read/1433
[38] https://www.serial.rocks/post-51
[39] https://qmap.pub/read/1439
[40] https://i.imgur.com/j1tYzra.png
[41] https://www.gsa.gov/governmentwide-initiatives/presidential-transition/legislative-overview/the-federal-vacancies-reform-act-of-1998
[42] https://qmap.pub/read/1439
[43] https://www.foxnews.com/politics/fbi-doj-to-brief-lawmakers-on-handling-of-russia-probe-on-thursday
[44] https://qmap.pub/read/1545
[45] https://qmap.pub/read/1547
[46] https://archive.li/Scyka
[47] https://archive.li/NbCwu
[48] https://i.imgur.com/H3Bl4Uo.png
[49] https://qmap.pub/read/645
[50] https://i.imgur.com/sVvXIKv.png
[51] https://archive.li/xKLvb
[52] https://archive.li/xr2qP
[53] https://qmap.pub/read/1457
[54] https://archive.li/xTfiO
[55] https://qmap.pub/read/1573
[56] https://www.youtube.com/watch?v=XsFR8DbSRQE
[57] https://www.biography.com/people/vladimir-putin-9448807
[58] https://www.politico.com/story/2018/06/14/doj-watchdog-james-comey-hillary-clinton-server-647020
[59] https://www.nytimes.com/2016/07/07/us/hillary-clintons-email-was-probably-hacked-experts-say.html
[60] https://thehill.com/homenews/administration/362264-trump-still-privately-questions-obamas-birth-certificate-report
[61] https://www.youtube.com/watch?v=IbUp60CYkDE&feature=youtu.be&t=196
[62] https://www.youtube.com/watch?v=1eTTkK2Ytz4
[63] https://www.yahoo.com/lifestyle/president-trump-made-major-missteps-meeting-queen-194626332.html
[64] https://www.serial.rocks/post-73
[65] https://www.youtube.com/watch?v=ot9cRcmbYLE
[66] https://www.politifact.com/truth-o-meter/statements/2016/oct/09/donald-trump/donald-trump-says-hillary-clinton-deleted-33000-em/
[67] https://www.politifact.com/truth-o-meter/statements/2016/oct/09/donald-trump/donald-trump-says-hillary-clinton-deleted-33000-em/
[68] https://www.youtube.com/watch?v=jA3sCC8LvWQ
[69] https://www.youtube.com/watch?v=9ykbxCc-JAA

[70] https://www.youtube.com/watch?v=HOxtN1Uwfq4

[71] https://qmap.pub/read/1675

[72] https://www.serial.rocks/post-74

[73] https://www.youtube.com/watch?v=XsFR8DbSRQE&feature=youtu.be

[74] https://www.abbreviations.com/term/498082

[75] https://www.allacronyms.com/TOL/Thinking_Of_Laughing

[76] https://pc.net/slang/meaning/tol

[77] https://www.youtube.com/watch?v=H8wLX2voWWQ&feature=youtu.be&t=2916

[78] https://www.youtube.com/watch?v=H8wLX2voWWQ&feature=youtu.be&t=3685

[79] https://www.youtube.com/watch?v=ya8umwgtsLw

[80] https://www.youtube.com/watch?v=4PPsK1QKVao

[81] https://i.imgur.com/VhHrFr3.png

[82] https://pittsburgh.cbslocal.com/2018/03/10/trump-supporters-moon-township-rally/

[83] https://twitter.com/realdonaldtrump/status/972585290857672704

[84] https://i.imgur.com/NtlL42c.png

[85] https://i.imgur.com/eRziC0b.png

[86] https://qmap.pub/read/142

[87] https://www.serial.rocks/post-56

[88] http://articles.latimes.com/2004/feb/08/opinion/op-phillips8

[89] https://www.youtube.com/watch?v=a4jrv71ZfgA

[90] https://i.imgur.com/rsmm6ui.png

[91] https://i.imgur.com/WqnZv8c.png

[92] https://www.reddit.com/user/SerialBrain2?st=JRWDG7NI&sh=38490982

[93] https://voat.co/v/theawakening/2718748#submissionTop

[94] https://voat.co/v/GreatAwakening/2718759

Between Donald Trump, QAnon and the emergence of citizen journalists, there is obviously a sea change underway in many aspects of the media. The biased reporting during the 2016 and midterm election cycles and the stunning silence when it comes to covering the "Good News" regarding Trump's many achievements simply must change. Not only is the "legacy media" complicit in covering up crimes of the Deep State, they work hand in hand with the Deep State to put forth a version of reality that has little to do with what is actually going on. Combined with the monopolistic structure of corporate media, it is clear that they no longer report the news. They control the news.

Changing the Narrative:
Trump and the Media
by Pamphlet & Radix

Once upon a time, the left used to care about something called "manufacturing consent." *Manufacturing Consent: The Political Economy of the Mass Media* is a 1988 book by Edward S. Herman and Noam Chomsky, in which the authors propose that the mass communication media of the U.S., "are effective and powerful ideological institutions that carry out a system-supportive propaganda function, by reliance on market forces, internalized assumptions, and self-censorship, and without overt coercion," by means of the propaganda model of communication. The title derives from the phrase "the manufacture of consent," employed in the book *Public Opinion* (1922), by Walter Lippmann. (*Wikipedia*, Manufacturing Consent)

The book argues that the mainstream media is designed to work as a propaganda arm of the state, and that it serves a purpose: the social engineering of society. This can be applied in tandem with techniques of behavioral control to condition the public. One need only mention the CIA-coined term 'conspiracy theory' to any random person and watch the visceral reaction you most likely will get, to understand how this can be applied as almost a form of operant conditioning.

Several books could be written about Trump and the Media, so for the purposes of this chapter I will only briefly touch on some subjects, but any online search will bring you more information on any topics covered herein. For brevity's sake, we will be working with the underlying assumption that QAnon is indeed a high-level insider in Trump's administration, if not Trump himself. The reasons to believe this is the case are many, and arguments for Q's validity and proofs of his access to Trump can be found all over the Internet and are probably outlined in this book by someone far more intelligent than myself. With this assumption in mind, we will be analyzing how Trump uses Q posts to change or control the narrative, and how that is changing the media and journalism in general.

"CONSPIRACY THEORY"

Term meaning "Look no further. Nothing to see here."
Instruction to shut off thinking parts of your brain.
Obey the "Don't ask questions" rule.
Remember to heap shame on those in pursuit of truth.
Censor opinions that differ from the approved narrative.
Say "ba" in unison as you march where we tell you.

—THE MAINSTREAM MEDIA

Social engineering is a discipline in social science that refers to efforts to influence particular attitudes and social behaviors on a large scale, whether by governments, media or private groups in order to produce desired characteristics in a target population. Social engineering can also be understood philosophically as a deterministic phenomenon where the intentions and goals of the architects of the new social construct are realized.

Social engineers use the scientific method to analyze and understand social systems in order to design the appropriate methods to achieve the desired results in the human subjects (*Wikipedia*, Social Engineering Political Science). One of the social systems exploited by the establishment today is Twitter. The blue checkmark verified Twitter intelligencia circularly promote each other's content, as well as target and de-platform those in the alternative media they see as their competition and as challengers to their control of the narrative.

There is a term, "social technology," that can be applied to the social-media town square, and that is "a way of using human, intellectual and digital resources in order to influence social processes." The term was first used at the University of Chicago around the end of the 19th Century. At a seminar in 1898, Albion Small spoke of social technology as being the use of knowledge of the facts and laws of social life to bring about rational social aims. By 1895, Charles Henderson coined the term 'social art' for the methods by which improvements to society are and may be introduced, social sciences make the predictions and social art gives directions. (*Wikipedia*, Social Technology)

So if we look deeply at the aims of social sciences, social technology, social justice and the like, we see them as having the goal of studying social processes in order to predict and influence social life, the town square. In 1935, Luther Lee Bernard wrote an article called "The Place of Social Sciences in Modern Education." In this article, he writes about the nature of an effective education in the social sciences to reach effective education by the willing masses. It would be of 3 types: first, a description of present conditions and trends in society, second, the teaching of desirable social ends and ideals necessary to correct such social maladjustments as we now have, and finally, a system of social technology which, if applied, might be expected to remedy existing maladjustments and realize valid social ends. (Henderson, Charles: *The Place of Social Sciences in Modern Education*)

He also spoke of the need for technologies for the less material forms of human welfare. These are the applied sciences of "the control of crime, abolition of poverty, the raising of every normal person to economic, political and personal competency, the art of good government, or city, rural and nation planning." After WWII, the social psychologist Dorwin Cartwright used the term 'social technology' for techniques developed in the science of group dynamics such as 'buzz groups' and 'role playing,' and Olaf Helmer used it to refer to the 'Delphi technique' for creating a consensus opinion in a panel of experts.

From the Rand Corporation website itself: "RAND developed the "Delphi Method" in the 1950s, originally to forecast the impact of technology on warfare. The method entails a group of experts who anonymously reply to questionnaires and subsequently receive feedback in the form of a statistical representation of the "group response," after which the process repeats itself. The goal is to reduce the range of responses and arrive at something closer to expert consensus. The Delphi Method has been widely adopted and is still in use today."

At Twitter, a modified version of the Delphi Method is being employed. The blue checkmark verified members are the 'experts' and they create the expert consensus of the digital town square, and their interactions with other blue checkmark verified experts (while simultaneously shadow banning or de-platforming those whose opinions challenge the status quo) creates the feedback process of refining group consensus.

Finally, we look at Karl Popper, a George Soros idol. In his book 'The Open Society and Its Enemies' and in his article 'The Poverty of Historicism' he discusses the use of both social technology and social engineering, thus we can conclude the two concepts are related. In the Open Society, Popper distinguished two kinds of social engineering, and the corresponding social technology. Utopian engineering strives to reach 'an ideal state, using a blueprint of society as a whole, is one which demands a strong centralized rule of a few, and which therefore is likely to lead to a dictatorship' (P. 159). Communism is an example of utopian social technology. On the other hand, there is the piecemeal engineer with its corresponding social technology, which adopts 'the method of searching for, and fighting against, the greatest and most urgent evils of society, rather than searching for, and fighting for, its greatest ultimate good' (P. 158). Popper argues that the use of social technology and social engineering are crucial for democratic social reconstruction.

Social technologies have caused concern for some people, as they are technologies dealing with social interactions and behaviors. Vladislav A. Lektorsky pointed out In his journal "The Russian philosopher, Viacheslav Stepin, calls modern European civilization 'technogenic.'" Initially, this meant the pursuit of technologies for the control of natural phenomena. Then projects began to be put forward for social technologies for the control of social processes. Based on this concept, impacts that social technology might have for man, like 'Forcible Collectivization' or the deportation of ethnic groups are recognized because, according to Vladislav, social technology blunts the individual's capacity for critical reflection, though it 'presents a different possibility which can be used to develop man's creative capacities, to expand his realm of freedom and his social and interpersonal ties." (Lektorksy, Vladislav A.)

The more you automate society, the more you can predict and control it. Thus, we get the terms like social pedagogy, technocracy, political science engineering, planned society, efficiency engineer, and social economic planning. With this in mind, and understanding how social technology and social engineering are used by the powers that be to direct and control society, we will discuss the narrative and news cycle and how Trump and Q are using social technology to change the narrative.

Now that we understand the news environment is manipulated by social technology and social engineering, we can assume there is a level of coordination among mainstream outlets. This is further understood once you see how ownership of newspapers and media companies have been consolidated into just 6 mega corporations controlling 90% of the news the American public gets (*See* Figure 1A) and "The Global Movement: Who Controls the Media" for more information on how this was achieved.[1]

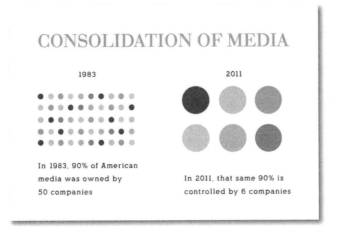

Figure 1A

If you doubt that this is indeed the case, I suggest you do more research into this topic. An entire book could be written on the topic of media consolidation and infiltration by members of the Central Intelligence Agency as part of Operation Mockingbird. But for the purpose of our discussion of changing the narrative, you need to understand these basic facts about the media environment. Finally, I suggest you read the following quote from David Rockefeller, and heed it well:

"We are grateful to The Washington Post, The New York Times, Time Magazine and other great publications whose directors have attended our meetings and respected their promises of discretion for almost forty years. It would have been impossible for us to develop our plan for the world if we had been subject to the bright lights of publicity during those years. But, the work is now much more sophisticated and prepared to march towards a world government. The supranational sovereignty of an intellectual elite and world bankers is surely preferable to the national auto determination practiced in past centuries."
—David Rockefeller, founder of the Trilateral Commission, in an address to a meeting of The Trilateral Commission, in June, 1991.

Now that we understand this was the media environment that candidate Trump would have to contend with, we look at how he went about challenging the narrative and the media. Unlike his fellow Republican candidates, he did not cower to mainstream media pressure every time they called him a 'racist, bigot, homophobe, anti-Semite, xenophobe' etc. He understood their *Rules for Radicals* techniques, and he fought back. Trump used his skills of persuasion to challenge the media and to control the narrative and dominate the news cycle.

This was something Scott Adams picked up on right away. In his August 13, 2015 blog, he predicted that Trump had a 98% chance of winning the presidency based on his persuasion skills.[2] One of the things Adams picked up on was Trumps use of the Intentional Wrongness Persuasion Play. The method goes like this (*Business Insider*):

Make a claim that is directionally accurate but has a big exaggeration or factual error in it.

Wait for people to notice the exaggeration or error and spend endless hours talking about how wrong it is.

When you dedicate focus and energy to an idea, you remember it. And the things that have the most mental impact on you will irrationally seem as though they are high in priority, even if they are not. That's persuasion.

Adams explains, "If I had boringly predicted that Trump would win the election, without any odds attached to it, the public would have easily shrugged it off as another minor celebrity's irrelevant opinion. But if I make you pause to argue with me in your mind about the accuracy of the 98% estimate, it deepens my persuasion on the main point—that Trump has a surprisingly high likelihood of winning." (Business Insider)

He goes on to add that he picked that number, 98 percent, because a prominent political observer, Nate Silver of FiveThirtyEight.com had already predicted Trump had a 2% chance of winning. So by picking 98%, he inverted it and connected his prediction to Silver's prediction as a way of attracting attention, which it did. On Social media, people began mentioning Scott Adams name next to Nate Silvers during the election, which was Adams' goal all along. This had the effect of raising Adams' profile as a political observer and commentator. The other thing it does, which Adams perhaps overlooked, was it also exposed Nate Silver as someone who is either a liar, or horrible at being a political observer.

Because of the Mainstream stranglehold on the narrative, via their corporate talking points, Trump relied heavily on social media during the election. He used Twitter to take issues to the American people directly. He spoke our language and he didn't act like a typical politician or insider. It's important to point out here, that even I didn't understand how much the Deep State and globalists were against Trump, nor the lengths they would go to stop him. Had it not been for Q, I wouldn't have understood the situation the President would have to contend with once he won. The obstruction, the leaks, the Obama holdovers working against him from within the government, the intelligence community and the career criminals in office opening counter-intelligence investigations based on DNC and HRC funded 'opposition research' that was totally unverified and then obtaining FISAs to spy on Trumps campaign and create the Russian Collusion narrative.

The Media played a very big role in spreading the Dossier, and media stories themselves were used as 'additional sources' in the FISA warrants, despite the medias source being the same as the FBI's, a technique known as circular vetting or circular reporting. The media crafted and shaped this coordinated narrative very much in tandem with the intelligence community it seems.

Getting back to the importance of Social Media and Trumps campaign: After the 2016 election, General Mike Flynn, Trump's National Security Advisor at the time stated at an event for the Young Americans Foundation that 'social media was the key to building a pro-Trump, conservative "army of digital soldiers . . . this was a digital election, run as an insurgency, irregular warfare at its finest" and that "we have what we call citizen journalists. The American people decided to take over the idea of information. They did it through social media."

This was the way to break through the manufactured consent. One of the ways the media controls the narrative and manipulates their audience is by playing to their confirmation bias. Confirmation bias, also called 'confirmatory bias' or 'myside bias' is the tendency to search for, interpret, favor, and recall information in a way that confirms one's preexisting beliefs or hypotheses. It is a type of cognitive bias and a systematic error of inductive reasoning. People display this bias when they gather or remember information selectively, or when they interpret it in a biased way. The effect is stronger for emotionally charged issues and for deeply entrenched beliefs. (*Wikipedia*, Confirmation Bias)

We all have confirmation bias, and one way to break through this is to use the Socratic method of posing questions, and letting the person think for themselves and answer the question on their own, rather than providing the answer for them in the beginning. And this is how Q initially worded his posts, in the form of questions, some of which partially answered the question asked prior. This was interesting because it made you curious and then got you actively searching for the answers. That gets you engaged and thinking for yourself. Trump often uses this technique in his tweets, for example, "What ever happened to the DNC server?" He is controlling the narrative here, and posing a question, reminding us of the existence of the server, and then we wonder, why hasn't anyone been held accountable for that? Where is the server, why wasn't it turned over for FBI forensic analysis, rather than a third party?

And this is how he challenges the narrative and disrupts their daily talking points. This repetitive use of the Socratic method encourages people to start thinking logically, rather than emotionally and to think for themselves. Trump is great at using tweets to get his base engaged, but that is limited, due to the number of characters you can use in a tweet, but also because Twitter as a platform censors people, mostly conservatives and so it's controlled by the very large corporations who are ardent globalists.

At one point very early into his presidency Twitter announced they were going to change their rules of service and it had to do with location tracking, which of course alarmed the Secret Service who wanted the president to stop using Twitter for security reasons, then there was the supposed 'rogue employee' who deleted Trump's account, and had it down for several hours, during which time he could not tweet directly to his base. And of course the media twists anything he says. So, perhaps he decided they needed a back-channel to speak directly to his base and the American public, in the event Twitter shuts him down again.

I believe that was the purpose for Q posting on the chans, the place where many Trump fans congregated online during the election to communicate and share information, news, memes, etc. One of the first things Q said was 'we need to get organized' meaning the MAGA base needed to hunker down, organize and be prepared because the battle has just begun.

Q has used the word 'Narrative' 78 times. He has often asked, 'Who controls the narrative?' 'Why is controlling the narrative important?' We know now who controls the narrative, and we know its important for their globalist system. So it should be equally important then for Trump to be able to have a counter-narrative. One that continuously cracks away at the lies, but also provides a focus for America First talking points. It's a way Trump can get all eyes at once on, for example, 'who funds ISIS?' from Q post 120, from Nov. 6, 2017.

If we look at the mainstream media response and reaction to Q. The hit-pieces, the daily coverage from the Daily Beasts' Will Sommers, to even Bill Maher and Comedy Central doing skits mocking Q and anyone who reads the posts and does research into the topics and issues Q posts about. The media hasn't gone after anyone in such coordinated fashion, except Trump himself. In fact, Q is the second most attacked by the mainstream media, with Trump of course being the most attacked. This is an interesting correlation on its own, but taken with the many proofs of Q, and members of Trump's administration and Trump himself echoing phrases from Q's posts, like 'The world is watching,' only seems to reinforce the notion that Trump is using The Great Awakening to shift the Overton window and change the narrative.

Finally, when we talk about narrative and changing the narrative, it's important to define what a narrative is. A 'narrative' or story is a report of connected events, real or imaginary, presented in a sequence of written or spoken words, or still or moving images, or both. (*Wikipedia*, Narrative)

I'd be remiss if I didn't point out one very important thing about narrative. Narrative, or story telling has always been an important aspect of human society. From the oral traditions of the Native Americans, to art, literature, theatre, music, poetry, journalism, film, radio, and even visual arts like photography so long as a sequence of events is portrayed. Historically, narratives have been used to guide society on proper behavior, cultural history, formation of a communal identity, and values. There is also a historical intersection between the occult and esoteric, and narratives nested within other narratives. From symbolism and art used to communicate a hidden meaning, to theater and performance art, to the use of cyphers and allegory.

And this brings us finally to the power of words. According to the Bible, words have real power. God spoke the world into being by the power of his words (*Hebrews* 11:3), and we are in His image in part because of the power we have with words, a power only granted to humanity. Words do more than simply convey information. The Bible says the power of our words can actually destroy one's spirit, even stir up hatred and violence. They not only exacerbate wounds but inflict them directly. Our words have the power to destroy and the power to build up (*Proverbs* 12:6). This is the importance of words, story telling and the narrative. And I don't think it's a coincidence that, as punishment for the Tower of Babel, God chose to confound the language of the peoples. This is the importance of the narrative the Luciferian Globalists seek to control and why challenging that control and providing a counter-narrative based on freedom, values and transparency is so important.

In closing, we'll leave you with a quote from techno-philosopher Martin Geddes.

"We are witnessing right now one of the greatest communications events in history."[3]

About the Authors

Pamphlet and Radix

YouTube: https://www.youtube.com/watch?v=4PfAf-yoD5s

---

[1] www.theglobalmovement.info/wp/areas-of-focus/global-financial-war/who-controls-the-media

[2] https://www.businessinsider.com/dilbert-creator-scott-adams-explains-trumps-persuasion-style-2017-10

[3] https://medium.com/@martingeddes/wwg1wga-the-greatest-communications-event-in-history-698ba926df64

When the media is controlled by those who oppose you, you cannot assume that your message will be delivered accurately or on a timely basis—or delivered at all. This is one of the reasons that President Trump tweets and why QAnon posts on 8Chan. You might argue that these have become the people's media by default. However, without the power of network television or a chain of newspapers, WWG1WGA uses the power of memes that can spread ideas like wildfire across the Internet. The emergence of citizen journalists, researchers who dig into the historical record and educate us, plus the decoders who help us read between the lines combined with the ability to make memes give us a unique form of power. We are people with vision and passion who have grown tired of deception and criminality, and who work together to communicate the truth, and we have invented, in effect, a new form of media.

The Power of Memes

by Liberty Lioness

Please note that the image in the above meme has been replaced by a similar official White House photo to avoid copyright violations.

Introduction

"A Picture is Worth a Thousand Words." Most of us have heard this expression many times and marketers understand how very important logos and photos are to their campaigns. So, in this chapter, I'm going to give you examples of graphics or Memes that have been instrumental in promoting the Q/Trump information campaign, along with tips and software solutions you can use to create your own. But first, here is the story on how the above meme came about: Changing the narrative is one of the most important battles politicians and their followers participate in daily. Whoever can control the narrative in the press and on social media, has the upper hand at that moment in time. It's kind of like an ongoing 'ping pong' match! I learned the importance of narrative changing while assisting a fellow Redditor (SerialBrain2) in the Spring of 2018.

SerialBrain2 is an Anon that has become famous in Q circles for decoding Q's posts using Gematria. I first saw these posts when participating on the Great Awakening subReddit. Today, you can also find folks posting his decodes in videos. You can learn more about Gematria at this link if you're curious: Link[1]

The "We Are Q" meme above was created in a strategic move to change the narrative after SerialBrain2 was attacked in a Twitter tweet posted by Jerome Corsi. Corsi had been decoding Q (very poorly, I might add) for several months. But after Q posted Q#12952 and changed his tripcode on 8Chan one day (a normal occurrence-like changing a password), Corsi began a rant about how Q had been compromised and said whoever was posting now was a fraud. A couple of days into this nonsense, which the majority of people understood was not true, Corsi put up a tweet stating that SerialBrain2 was Q.

Note: I attempted to retrieve the Corsi tweet about SerialBrain2 mentioned above, but unlike other Twitter accounts, I'm unable to view tweets on Corsi's Twitter feed prior to January 1, 2019. Think about that for a moment. Why would his Twitter feed be handled differently? Maybe it was just a glitch. But, I just want you to notice when you see these types of things that some folks seem to be protected, while others are censored and slandered. Then notice if there is some type of pattern. Lots of shenanigans going on these days!

Anyway, to continue the story: On Reddit, or anywhere online actually, it is really bad manners (like treasonous) to give away anyone's true identity if they are anonymous. It's called "doxing" and that's exactly what Corsi was doing. The problem, of course, is that the real Q was still posting and, to this day, we don't really know who Q is and many believe it's actually a team of people working together. Corsi had no evidence at all to show that Q was SerialBrain2.

When I saw the doxing tweet on Twitter, I messaged SerialBrain2 on Reddit to let him know about it. That afternoon he wrote a new post about how each and every one of us working in the Q movement should promote the "I am Q" label. But I had a different idea.

I made the above meme and posted it on the Great Awakening subReddit. In a few hours it went to the top of the threads and the next day Q posted it on 8chan. After that, the meme went viral completely diminishing any controversy Corsi was attempting to create.

Today, I see this meme regularly. Not only did it change the narrative, but it also showed how wrong the mainstream media had been in attempting to convince the public that not many people attended Trump's inauguration. See this "fake news" article by ABC News: Link[3]

Related Q Posts

Q has referred to "memes" or asked us (Anons) to make memes on many occasions. This is the first, where Q asks Anons to make memes to educate others:

Q Post #179 – November 21, 2017 (in part)

>We may have overestimated your ability.
you came to us for certain strengths but there are weaknesses as well, some being exploited
not enough focus

answer the questions
build the big picture
break it back down
make memes for the normies to calm & educate

so we'll be ready for the Storm

Q often posts memes that are educational to Q followers:

Q Post #191 (a repost of an Anon post)

Q !ITPb.qbhqo ID: T4rZfKsN No.150434351 ☐ 🏴   191
Nov 22 2017 01:34:58 (EST)

Anonymous ID: Ukm/q3OU No.150434251 ☐ 🏴
Nov 22 2017 01:33:54 (EST)

popes snake pit.jpg

>>150432420

anon meme makers please make some memes of the popes
audience hall looking like a snake pit. That sum sik shit

>>150434251

Q also uses memes to give us clues:

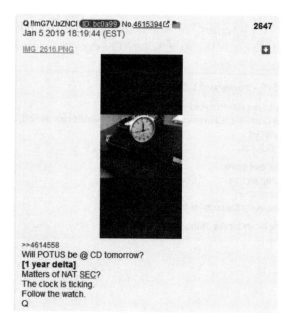

Q !!mG7VJxZNCI ID: bc0a99 No.4615394 ☐ 🏴   2647
Jan 5 2019 18:19:44 (EST)

IMG_2616.PNG

>>4614558
Will POTUS be @ CD tomorrow?
[1 year delta]
Matters of NAT SEC?
The clock is ticking.
Follow the watch.
Q

And more requests for Anons to make and post memes:

Q Post #532 – January 14, 2018

MSM Fake News Awards.
Are you prepared?
MEMES/POSTS.
Organized and coordinated?
POTUS may reTWEET one or more.
READY FOR LAUNCH?
SHOW the WORLD.
SHOW the WORLD the TRUTH.
OPEN THEIR EYES.
DON'T LET POTUS SUFFER FROM THE SOROS/LOSER BOTS THAT
CONTINUALLY FLOOD.
MAKE THE FAKE NEWS AWARDS YOUR 1ST ORGANIZED TWEET STORM DAY.
MAKING AMERICA GREAT AGAIN!
Q

Q Post #1232 – April 21, 2018

Fire up those Memes!
Please stand by.
On the clock.
Ready to play?
MOAB incoming.
Q

Q Post 2126 – September 9, 2018

How do you know when something VERY BIG is about to drop?
ATTACKS INCREASE FROM ALL DIRECTIONS.
READY THE MEMES.
[FISA CORRUPTION]
You have more than you know.
KEEP UP THE GOOD FIGHT.
WE STAND TOGETHER.
Q

The brackets are known as the "kill box." [FISA CORRUPTION] We've seen many people in the kill box too! When did you first learn about the FISA Corruption? Anons have known about it for some time. Q has been talking to us about FISA since December 2017. That's why we follow Q.

Aha! Another reason Q wants us to drop memes. Computer code can't read the memes, making censorship much more difficult. It takes human eyes to determine what the meme depicts. Even text in a meme is not readable by the algorithms.

When a browser displays a photo, the underlying code contains the coordinates and color of each pixel in the photo, along with some other information about the photo. The higher the resolution of the photo the more complex the code becomes. Until now, having the ability to understand the viewable contents of the photo was never needed. As long as the photo displayed correctly in the browser, that's all the coder cared about. But now, the spying social media giants are working on creating an algorithm that can interpret the contents of the photo code as well so they can further censor us. Eroding our privacy even further!

Now, you understand why Q often asks us to post memes: Not only are memes more capable of quickly depicting a thought or a story, they also cannot be 'read' by the algorithms like text can.

Meme Tips

The following tips are a few things I've learned along the way. I hope they help you in your Meme making journey. My purpose here is not to be all inclusive in teaching you about these subjects but rather to get you started and point you in the right directions to learn more.

Resolution

Photos or memes, in computer code, are made up of pixels. Each pixel is a single color. How many pixels are in a photo determines the resolution of the photo. In other words, a 300 dpi (dots per inch) photo contains 300 dots per inch. Each "dot" is a pixel.

72 dpi   300dpi

As you can see in the above image, the higher the resolution, the more clarity the image has. This is also why sometimes when you take a small image and try to enlarge it, it often becomes "pixelated" which makes the image blurry. However, a high resolution image will create a larger photo on the screen. Then if you need it smaller, you can scale it down or back up and it will keep its clarity. Higher resolution images will use more memory in your camera and will load more slowly in a browser, but if you want them to be easily resized, use a higher resolution when taking photos. As you work with images more you will become familiar with resolutions and which ones best suit your needs.

For a better understanding of 'resolution' you can visit the following site: Link[4]

What's Your Purpose?

Before you start, it's important to determine your purpose. Are you just doing it for fun or do you have something else in mind? Most memes I've made were either for fun, to educate, to ask the user to take some kind of action or to promote something. Except, of course, for that 'change the narrative' one!

No matter what your purpose is, the thing that seems to kick me into gear is to go and look at memes other people have created for something similar to what I want to do. It's very inspirational.

Content

Remember KISS? No, not the music group silly! It's an acronym for: Keep It Simple Stupid! KISS is used in many ways, but with memes it's important because people are scanning social media every day. So, you want something that will catch their attention quickly.

Remember, a picture really is worth a thousand words. That's why the Trump inaugural meme worked so well. So, picking out the right photo is important.

Sometimes you might need something more complex in order to get your point across but try to keep it as simple as possible. You can also consider using arrows or speech bubbles to keep the flow clearer to the viewer. But I can't over emphasize the importance of simplicity in this process.

Examples of Good Memes

This Q post of a simple comparison meme makes a huge historical statement. I sure wish everyone understood the history involved in the politics being played out today. Did you know this?

Another effective comparison meme.

Yep. A picture really is worth a thousand words! Found on I-40 near Little Rock!

Don't have a picture that fits your cause? Try using a cartoon or other famous character!

I just like this one! But I'm sure someone with graphics skills created the 'storm' effect!

Using quotes from well-known or famous figures is very effective and educational.

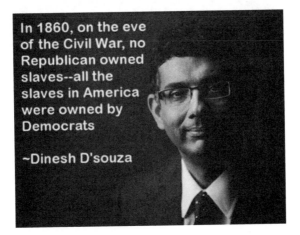

Quite often, you may be working on a meme campaign where you want the viewer to take a specific action that involves clicking on a link. This is called a 'call to action.' Unfortunately, I've seen many, many such memes that lacked the very element needed to take the action. Specifically, the link.

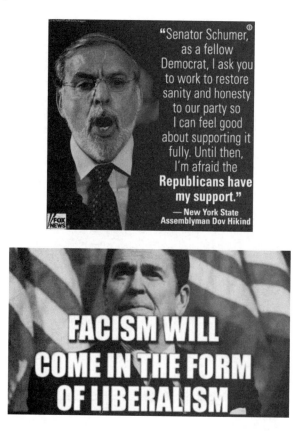

In order to be successful in this type of a campaign, you must include the link in as many places as possible. But, at a minimum, it must be on the meme. Why, you ask? So the viewer can type the link into the browser if needed, in order to take the action. But, ideally, you should also put a clickable link in the post on the social media site you're posting the meme on.

This is how your meme might look with the link embedded in the meme text:

You can go to many URL shortening sites to create a shorter link that can more easily fit on your meme. In this case, the site tinyurl.com was used to create the shortened link.

Then when you post the meme, be sure to also include that shortened link in your post text, like this:

This is a retweet I did on Twitter one day. The original meme was great but I couldn't help add a comment about the pose Teresa May was in that corresponded to the original intent and gave it a double meaning. I can't help but laugh every time I see this one.

And, I think Teresa May is explaining it. #GreatAwakening #QAnon #WWG1WGA

The Face You Make
when everyone realizes how big your balls are

♡ 12   ↻ 154   ♡ 324   ᯤ

I left the numbers below that post to show you what happens when you post something that gets a lot of retweets. Remember that each retweet that is done will also get retweets and on and on. Here are the stats for this post:

Tweet Activity

WE ARE Q!		
I Am Q! #QAnon #GreatAwakening pic.twitter.com/erqfd1WFDV		

Reach a bigger audience
Get more engagements by promoting this Tweet!

Get started

Impressions	89,669
Total engagements	1,181
Media engagements	684
Likes	192
Link clicks	96
Retweets	85
Detail expands	63
Profile clicks	37
Hashtag clicks	16
Replies	6
Follows	2

Meme Making Tools

There are many, many sites that offer free or low-cost software tools you can use to create memes. You don't need to purchase a high-end, high-priced software tool to do this. And, the more memes you create yourself, the better you will get at it and the better the world will be for your efforts!

Snagit by Techsmith is sold as a screen capture program and that's what it started out as but it now also includes a powerful editor that will give you all the tools you need and many you'll never use to create great memes. I've been using Snagit for many years and over the years, it's become more and more powerful without any increase in price. That's not something you see very often. Techsmith is a very reliable software vendor. They are also the creators of a popular video software tool called "Camtasia" that you may have heard about.

As of this writing, Snagit comes in both Windows and Mac versions and costs $49.95 for a one-time purchase license (not yearly or monthly) that you can use on 2 computers. When an upgrade is available, it will only cost you $24.95. You can view more details and purchase Snagit here: Link[5]

There are many free and membership sites that offer meme making software. Some are better than others. I know a lot of folks that use PIXLR and it appears to be very comprehensive without being difficult. It is free to use. Link[6]

Also, check out Lifewire for the compilation of meme tools and their reviews: Link[7]

You can also use Imgur to host your memes for free and simply use the link to your meme on Imgur. Link[8]

About the Author

Liberty Lioness

I'm a 70-year-old Boomer lady that spent my early career working in Word Processing until I was able to move into Computers in the late 1980's. In the 1990's, I started working for IBM in the first IT Support Center in the country that supported all software installed on the 3 major computer operating systems sold at that time (Windows, Mac and OS2). Our customers were Fortune 500 companies all across the US including companies like Baxter Labs, Intel and Price Waterhouse.

There were no colleges teaching IT back then, so that was my 'college' education and, in my opinion, it was better than anything I've seen them teach in college. I started as the center was just beginning and there were only about 15 technicians. At the end of 5 years, there were about 120 of us, 17 of which were women.

We helped users resolve software and hardware problems over the phone without the use of the Web, which didn't exist at that time. It was the most challenging and interesting thing I've ever experienced and I loved it! We were the pioneers and, as such, there was little competition among us. We all needed each other to get the job done so there was a great deal of respect and camaraderie which is often rare today. As such, it was the best experience of my life.

After I left IBM, I started my own computer repair company after moving to the Ozarks. It was very popular and also very challenging and fun for me. But, I had been poisoned while living in Tampa when they sprayed for med flies with Malathion. So, I spent about 13 years learning how to become healthy when doctors could not help. In 2013, I accomplished that task and today, I'm also a Certified Nutrition and Wellness Consultant.

I love the Internet and during my time studying health and healing, I was also studying Online Marketing. So, I'm about to start a new business that will help online Health and Wellness businesses market online.

I may be 70, but I love life and learning. I now take many supplements that keep me young and I plan to be here a long, long time! Some of my favorite quotes:

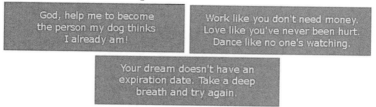

God, help me to become the person my dog thinks I already am!

Work like you don't need money. Love like you've never been hurt. Dance like no one's watching.

Your dream doesn't have an expiration date. Take a deep breath and try again.

If you'd like to connect with me, you can find LibertyLioness on Gab.com.

---

[1] https://en.wikipedia.org/wiki/Gematria

[2] https://qmap.pub/read/1295

[3] https://abcnews.go.com/Politics/2009-2017-comparing-trumps-obamas-inauguration-crowds/

[4] https://www.creativebloq.com/graphic-design/what-is-dpi-image-resolution-71515673

[5] https://www.techsmith.com/screen-capture.html

[6] https://pixlr.com/web/

[7] https://www.lifewire.com/popular-meme-generator-tools-3486457

[8] http://imgur.com

Most casual users of the Internet have no idea how much censorship occurs there. Whether it is Twitter or Facebook, YouTube or Reddit, the high-handed, authoritarian efforts to shutdown independent voices would undoubtedly shock those who believe our free speech is protected by the First Amendment to the United States Constitution. Now researchers, independent journalists and advocates alike find themselves shadow-banned, or outright banned from these and other websites. In some instances, the only explanation given (if any) is that the poster has violated the "terms of service" or "community standards" with no specific information and little or no recourse. Increasingly there is censorship of channels with growing audiences that question the official government reports on subjects such as the assassination of President JFK or the events around 911 with sweeping generalizations, for example, by calling them "conspiracy theories." Those who follow or post commentary on QAnon fall into this category. Another disturbing trend is that financial and other services (PayPal, Patreon) have also started banning those whose views do not conform with the official mainstream media or government narratives. The following material, intended to help Anons sort out the most important players in QAnon's posts, has been censored multiple times through deletion on Reddit.

The Good, The Bad, and the Ugly: Characters of ObamaGate/SpyGate

by Captain Roy D

QAnon & Reddit

The social-media platform Reddit played a critical role in the public exposure of QAnon. QAnon or Team "Q" first appeared at 4Chan in late October 2017 and due to security concerns, moved over to the sister posting site of 8Chan. To this day, this is the only place that QAnon communicates. "NO comms outside this platform," posted QAnon.

Beginning in early January 2018, a new sub-Reddit called the "Calm Before The Storm" (CBTS) was started as a place to post articles/stories/commentary about QAnon. This additional public outlet was a more comfortable platform due to the "rough" anything goes atmosphere characteristic of the Chan Boards. Besides the unwritten rules of conduct on the Chans, the language and pornographic ads are way over the top for most normal people. A tolerant home was found at Reddit for the rapidly increasing base of new "Q" followers.

Many MAGA Patriots started to post at CBTS and later millions of interested citizens came to take a look or "lurk." What started out as a few thousand Reddit members, would swell to over 70,000 prior to the final shutdown ban.

The CBTS site was shut down by the Reddit platform in March and everyone migrated over to the Subreddit called Great Awakening (GA). This marked the beginning of many total purges of QAnon from various Reddit communities. I personally have had 6 Subreddit boards deleted this year and the loss of hundreds of my prior posted articles. When you cannot win an argument on the facts, many resort to the silencing of the opposing narrative.

The last round of Reddit bans in September 2018 took out over almost 2 dozen QAnon related sites and was the main factor leading to the publication of this book. When you begin to witness the tearing down of statues and the burning of history books, your "Spidey Sense" should instantly alert you that there is trouble in paradise. Censorship is the final act of a failed argument.

The outstanding Anons (also called Autists) interact on 8Chan with Q on a regular basis. Then they research Q's "bread crumbs" and share their findings with one another. The best research is gathered together in a list of notables and when the thread closes due to 8Chan limitations, those notables and other pertinent information is carried over to the next thread. This is called Baking and so you will also sometimes hear the Anons (Autists) called Bakers.

Reddit provided us the last set of metrics for the GA community and the figures were mind-blowing. In the month of August 2017, the Great Awakening sub had over 70,000 active posters and close to 2 million unique visitors that came at least once to view the material.

I hope you will enjoy this sampling of QAnon political corruption articles that I have selected. My posts were geared as introductory stories that blended Q-drops with actual individuals/events centering around the efforts to eliminate the Deep State.

QAnon and the Anons are assisting President Trump in his effort to "Drain The Swamp." Please bear in mind when reading over this information that it was geared to help fellow Anons in their research efforts. You will discover many Q-coded terms and initials for the main characters. I suggest that my relatives read over the article once leaving out the "Q" references to get the main content. If you re-read these posts again now stopping to go over the various QAnon "intel drops," it will add an additional layer of understanding to the article's subject.

My chapter has been separated into 3 sections of stories of various characters in the many unfolding scandals. Reflected is an epic struggle that has been taking place between the forces of Good vs. Evil. We term individuals as being a White Hat (good guys) or a Black Hat (bad guys) but often there is a middle or Gray area as well. I have selected some of the notable characters connected to ObamaGate/SpyGate and these articles will tie-in QAnon information along with the public open source record (real news).

Hat tip to Clint Eastwood: please meet a few characters of this current QAnon drama—*The Good, The Bad, & The Ugly*. Classic White/Black/& Gray Hats galore and what is becoming the most interesting event in known memory. It is all ultimately about the "Truth" and we are learning that the other side really "Can't Handle the Truth."

President Trump and his loyal Military Intelligence team known as QAnon, have enlisted Patriots worldwide to help. Our duty has been to get out these "bread crumbs" as POTUS' way to mitigate the Mockingbird Fake News. We have discovered this information on the Chan Boards and have tried our best to get it out to everyone.

You will notice that on the bottom of each article are a few extra answers provided by an anon called "Pure_Feature." Never requested by me, this individual has posted critical information on every article I have made at Reddit. "Pure" has repeatedly put them all back up each time Reddit has deleted everything. I have included a brief bio by this incredible Anon in both English and her native Dutch language. Her efforts demonstrate the worldwide impact of the QAnon movement and how we are all related. WWG1WGA.

Admiral Mike Rogers:
A Quiet Hero's Two "Infamous" Deeds

Admiral Mike Rogers has retired from proud service earlier this year as the NSA Director. After years of dedication to this country and his shown unwavering service to President Trump, Mike has turned over

NSA/US Cyber Command.

books will show Admiral Rodgers to be the true Patriot that has been. There are two critical dates that NSA Rogers ᵖ˙˙˙˙ heroic actions that will long be remembered by all Patriots.

Q Post # 8 on 10/29/18 (in part):

POTUS installed his people within each top spot at each 3 letter agency except 1 (good reason there as Adm R kick started this and scrubbed all POTUS nominations to verify oath).

On April 18, 2016, Admiral Rogers shut down the previous unrestricted flow of FISA 702 raw data to outside private contractors (Fusion GPS/CrowdStrike). Early in 2016, an internal review alerted Mike to the suspicious use of "702 About Queries."

Post Q #1661 on 7/1/18 (in part):

What role can NSA play?

General FISA 702 "Queries" allow for the collection of all emails, text, voice, and other electronic data on an individual. Rogers saw this top secret raw intel was going to outside contractors and immediately put a stop to it.

Post Q #1380 on 5/16/18 (in part):

When did Adm R step down?
Reconcile.

Outside contractors like Fusion GPS and CrowdStrike were the recipients of the 702's. This raw intelligence helped to them construct the discredited Steele Russian Dossier.

This action forced the Deep State to switch to using HUMIT, human intelligence assets, aka SpyGate "LURES." This is where Five Eyes/Halper/Hakluyt/Downer and friends all enter into the "sting-like" operation.

Post Q #520 on 1/13/18 (in part):

THINK BIG.
THINK BIGGER.
THINK BIGGEST.

The classic nickname that Sundance/CTH (Hat Tip) gave to this phase of Admiral Rogers' plan was "Operation Condor." Reference being that Mike plays the Robert Redford character.

Post Q #2028 on 8/31/18:

Information comes in many forms.

In the popular movie, Redford/Rogers exposes, and ultimately brings down, the corrupt CIA Clowns. Our hero, Admiral Rogers, performed in real life way better than any Hollywood actor could portray.

Post Q #270 on 12/5/17 (in part):

Adm R/ No Such Agency (W&W) + POTUS/USMIL =
Apply the Keystone.

On November 17, 2016, Mike goes outside his chain of command and visits President Elect Trump at Trump Tower. No one knows exactly what was said in the newly constructed SCIF between POTUS and NSA Rogers that day. We do however know Team Trump's immediate reaction.

Trump along with only his top staffers, were evacuated over to Trump National Golf Club in Bedminster/NJ the very next morning. I'm looking into rumors of additional physical "bugs" planted in Trump Tower during the transition period.

It is obvious to most folks now, that Admiral Rodgers told President Elect Trump about the Coup/FISA Surveillance/SpyGate. I still feel that a "physical threat" against our POTUS was discussed by the DOJ's Small Group Cabal.

Post Q #144 on 11/12/17 (in part):

+++Adm R+++
What agency is at war w/Clowns In America?

Planned as only a final option under their "Insurance Policy" was the Crossfire Hurricane/Operation and the Dragon/Crossfire FISA operation in this Coup Plot. The sad legacy with all of these ObamaGate criminals will be failed plan upon plan.

Of interesting timing (remember dates are important), is what happened on April 18, 2016. This was one day after FISA raw intel was shut down, the DNC claims a major computer breach.

Post Q #120 on 11/6/18 (in part):

Why is the NSA limited re: ability to capture and unmask US persons?

This was the Guccifer 2.0 intrusion claim that led to CrowdStrike with their Cozy and Fancy Bear Russian hacking claims. It was the start of public claims of Russian interference in the 2016 elections.

Please note that the DNC/DWS refused both the FBI and DHS, access to their so-called breached computer servers. Never in the recorded FBI's files, were such bizarre actions performed in an effort to exonerate HRC/Aides of all crimes.

Post Q #585 on 1/22/18 (in part):

"Q" was crystal clear to all Patriots:
TRUST Adm R.
He played the game to remain in control.

Thank you Admiral Rogers for both your years of devotion to our country, as well as your two points of needed historic intervention-a true White Hat Patriot

REFERENCES:

Conservative Treehouse – "Operation Condor"
Epoch Times – "NSA Admiral Rogers Disclosed FISA Abuse"
Shift Frequency – "The Great Unmasker"
Markets Work – "The Uncovering: Admiral Rogers Investigation"
Conservative Treehouse – "Occam's Razor"
Markets Work – "A Quiet Hero Admiral Rogers Retires"
US Defense Watch – "Did Rogers Warn Trump"
New York Magazine – "Admiral Rogers Leaked Retirement Memo"
The Washington Times – "Admiral Rogers Warns Senate Panel"
Conservative Treehouse – "Rogers Turns Over NSA and Cyber Command"

NOTE BELOW: Pure_Feature" Extra Answers:

Michael S. Rogers, Wikipedia[1] Michael S. Rogers (born October 31, 1959) is a former United States Navy admiral who served as the second commander of the U.S. Cyber Command.

Operation Condor, How NSA Director Mike Rogers Saved The U.S.[2] For the real life version, NSA Director Admiral Mike Rogers plays the... We always suspected NSA Director Rogers gave President-elect Trump a heads up of sorts. Told the FISA court he became aware of unlawful surveillance and that a coup attempt against the Constitution had been thwarted.

A Quiet Hero: NSA Director Admiral Mike Rogers Retires[3] NSA Director Admiral Mike Rogers formally retired on May 4, 2018. A quiet hero, most will never understand what Rogers did for our country. From the NSA Press. September 27 2016. Carlin announces he is resigning.

Deep State's Early Targets:
The General and his "FlynnStones"

NO JAIL TIME FOR THE GENERAL

Q said the General was safe and Mueller's recommendation is NO JAIL for General Flynn. Time will reveal the heroic efforts by Mike Flynn in service to POTUS and our country.

The Deep State's first victim from the Trump Administration was General Flynn. McMaster then routed out all of Mike's NSC staff known as the "FlynnStones."

Post Q #1280 on 4/27/18 (in part):

Who knows where the bodies are buried?

At a security seminar at Cambridge/London in February 2014, the first known meeting occurred between Trump/Flynn/and Stefan Halper.

Halper reported back to John Brennan about Flynn talking to a Russian FSB agent (a woman) and the brief meeting of Trump/Flynn at this event.

Post Q #1935 on 8/27/18 (in part):

Think FLYNN [30].

The deliberate purge of loyal top intelligence officials was designed to hobble President Trump. This was in fact censorship in the worse possible way, by cutting off the source of incoming credible intelligence destined for our POTUS.

Post Q #36 on 11/21/17 (in part):

Military Intelligence.
Focus on Flynn.
Background and potential role.

General Mike Flynn put together a very loyal band of Patriots beginning from his time under BHO at the DIA. Those chosen to go over to the NCC, were termed affectionately in many intelligence circles as the "FlynnStones."

Proud "FlynnStones" members included K.T. McFarland, Gen. Keith Kellogg, Michael Anton, Victoria Coates, Rich Higgins and Flynn's protégé Ezra Cohen-Watnick.

Post Q #120 on 11/6/17 (in part):

What does the NSA/MI have (at least what you know of) that allows for data collection?

The old guard intelligence community was always skeptical of this inner circle of General Flynn. After President Trump's appointment of Flynn as the new NSA, he filled his National Security Council team from this special intelligence group.

Post Q #1282 on 4/27/18 (in part):

Why did Flynn take the bullet?
Rubber bullet?

Ezra was NSA's Senior Director for Intelligence Programs under NSA Director Flynn. Cohen-Watnick's position gave him the authority to inspect the files all of 17 US Intelligence agencies for wrongdoing.

Post Q #2218 on 9/19/18:

In the end, all will be right.
Patriots protect Patriots

A powerful post that's designed to coordinate/liaise between the various Intelligence Community and the White House. Ezra gained the trust of POTUS as he regularly gave the daily intel briefings to then President Elect Donald Trump.

Post Q #1661 on 7/1/18 (in part):

What role can MI INTEL play?
BANG!

Ezra is credited with first alerting Devin Nunes to "unmasking and surveillance" abuses, along with W/H lawyer Michael Ellis. Note that all three were ultimately made special targets of the Deep State.

By order of the POTUS, Ezra has returned to government service. This time assisting Attorney General Jeff Sessions, as his National Security Adviser, responsible for both counterintelligence and counterterrorism.

Post Q #1370 on 5/17/18 (in part):

Does Flynn know?
Define "on the record "

Everyone will always remember Nunes' presser in front of the White House. Devin was signaling alarm bells and Ezra helped to make that all happen. Having MI (think "Q" level clearance) in the DOJ, is an important chess piece for POTUS.

Post Q #1008 on 4/14/18 (in part):

Flynn is safe.

Everyone is hoping for the gallant return someday of their favorite General. We need General Flynn to help "Drain the Swamp" and reconstitute his famous band of Patriots called "FlynnStones."

They Never Thought She Would Lose

REFERENCES:

Atlantic – "The Man McMaster Couldn't Fire"
USA Today – "Mueller Recommends No Jail Time For General Flynn"
NBC NEWS – "Meet the 'Flynn Stones': Holdovers From Mike Flynn's Brief Term as National Security Adviser," Mar 10, 2017
Daily Mail – "Mike Flynn: Generals Reduced to Rubble by BHO"
Breitbart – "Trump picks Lt. Gen. Keith Kellogg for NSC"
Forward – "Meet Ezra Cohen-Watnick"
The Hill – "K.T. McFarland Withdraws Ambassador Nomination"
Breitbart – "Ezra Joining DOJ as NSA to Sessions"

The Atlantic – "The Populist Nationalist: Mike Anton"
The Daily Wire – "Timeline for Flynn's Resignation"
NY Mag – "Ezra Hired at the Insistence of POTUS"
Heavy – "5 Fast Facts on Ezra Cohen-Watcnick"
NOTE BELOW: "Pure_Feature" Extra Answers:
Michael Flynn, Wikipedia[4] Michael Thomas Flynn (born December 1958) is a retired United States Army Lieutenant General who served in the U.S. Army for 33 years, from 1981 until 2014

Ezra Cohen-Watnick, Wikipedia[5] Ezra Asa Cohen-Watnick (born May 18, 1986) is the national security adviser to United States Attorney General Jeff Sessions and a former Senior Director for Intelligence Programs.

Who Is Michael Flynn 19 Facts About Donald Trump's National[6] Retired Army general Michael Flynn pleaded guilty to lying to the FBI. Michael T. Flynn pleaded guilty December 1 to "willfully and knowingly," because he put our nation's security at extremely high risk with her billion Muslims together in language that The Intercept described as showing a...

Ringmaster Horowitz's
FISA/SpyGate Report Due Soon-BOOM

The Ringmaster is the master of ceremonies that introduces the "circus acts" to the audience. Inspector General (IG) Michael Horowitz is such a Ringmaster.

Post Q #2462 on 11/9/18 (in part):

Who is HOROWITZ?
Mandate charged to HOROWITZ?
Resources provided to HOROWITZ?

IG Horowitz's 2.0 report will be on FISC/FISA abuses by the DOJ/FBI during the 2016 campaign. Also expected are the SpyGate and insertion of paid intelligence assets into President Trump's election campaign staff.

Post Q #2554 on 12/5/18 (in part):

WHITAKER, HOROWITZ, HUBER, and WRAY.
Long meeting held within a SCIF [unusual].

Carter Page's FISA application release seems to be synced now with the OIG's next report. Horowitz has additionally been handling the forthcoming total DECLAS by POTUS.

Post Q #1842 on 8/11/18:

Do you believe in coincidences?
We have the source.

IG Horowitz and his hundreds of lawyers have been working since January 12, 2017 on several investigations. Reports on the McCabe and the HRC probes have already been publicly released.

Post Q #2489 on 11/12/18 (in part):
[Placeholder - OIG Report and Findings].

The OIG has been doing its primary assigned job, which is oversight of the DOJ/FBI. The stage is set for the next drop and indications are it will be big.

Post Q #2489 on 11/12/18 (in part):
[Placeholder - OIG Report-Umbrella SPY and Targeting].

Phase Two is being finalized and focuses on FISA Court abuses by the DOJ/FBI. The Carter Page Title-1 Surveillance application as well as interactions by Stefan Halper in 2016 will be the focus.

Post Q #1318 on 5/7/18 (in part):
"Horowitz oversees a nationwide workforce of more than 450 special agents"

Horowitz has been working mostly in secret, in conjunction with Utah US Attorney John Huber. This combination according to historian Jonathan Turley, is far better than a second Special Counsel.

Huber was assigned by Jeff Sessions in November 2017 and has full prosecuting authority over all of these investigations:

• HRC Server/Email
• FISA Court/Dossier/Halper
• SpyGate/Crossfire Hurricane

Huber was secretly appointed by AG Sessions as a Special Prosecutor to help the OIG. Huber adds prosecutorial teeth to Horowitz and assistance with routing out corruption at the top of the DOJ/FBI/State.

Post Q #1517 on 6/16/18 (in part):
IG started long before Huber setting stage.
IG = FBI.
Huber = DOJ (no DC).

Horowitz was appointed under BHO and thanks to Sally Yates, he was never allowed to review the National Security departments of both the DOJ and FBI. This was the central location of the "Coup" using Crossfire Hurricane/ SpyGate.

Post Q #1553 on 6/18/18 (in part):
". . . noting that Huber would be "conducting his work from outside Washington D.C. area" and "in cooperation" with Horowitz."

Horowitz will eventually become a household name when the "Storm" is over. A total of seven major reports are due and the HRC report was just the first completed.

My understanding is they will get progressively worse as they are made public. Big time "BOOMS" are soon forthcoming from IG Horowitz and SP Huber!

Post Q #2487 on 11/11/18 (in part):

[Placeholder - DECLAS GEN_pub].

Hopefully with Acting AG Whitaker in place, the PAIN can finally begin. Let all remember Utah still has the Death Penalty and fair Grand Juries!

Post Q #2397 on 11/3/18 (in part):

OIG works w/HUBER [important to remember].

We all recall the riveting personal text messages between Strzok and Page as-they also uncovered a personal relationship with a "key" FISA Court Judge (RUDY).

Some FBI staff like Peter Strzok, went from exonerating HRC/Aides, directly over to the new DOJ/FBI Trump-Russia Counterintelligence Investigation.

Post Q #1122 on 4/10/18 (in part):

TRUST HOROWITZ.
TRUST HUBER.

I can't wait to see the big-league dump coming from Ringmaster Horowitz. Get your popcorn ready, as this may ignite the fuse for the final "STORM."

REFERENCES:

The Atlantic – "Michael Horowitz: The FBI's Reckoning"
FOX News – "IG 2.0 Could Even be Worse for FBI/DOJ"
Greensburg Daily News – "Plot To Overturn Presidential Election Revealed"
Conservative Treehouse – "Phase 2: IG Horowitz Review of FISA Court Abuse by DOJ/FBI"
Heavy – "Michael Horowitz: 5 Fast Facts"
ThreadReader.com - Imperator Rex – "IG Horowitz's Report"
Breitbart – "Professor Turley: 'Q' Emphasized"
The Gateway Pundit – "Solomon: At Least 6 DS Operatives Infiltrated Trump Campaign"
The Hill-John Solomon – "FBI Email Chain Evidence Of FISA Abuse"

NOTE BELOW: "Pure_Feature" Extra Answers:

Trump orders Justice Dept. to declassify Russia-related material[7] 17, Sep. 2018 For months, conservative lawmakers have been calling on the department to release Russia-related and other materials, many of them...

Comey Drafted Statement Exonerating HRC Before Interviewing Her[8] Comey Drafted Statement Exonerating HRC Before Interviewing they were all given immunity and that her aides destroyed Hillary's devices with hammers. Actually she did, its well documented but she was never going to be charged.

IG 2.0 could be even worse for FBI as feds brace for Trump-spying[9] Hipp on IG report: Chaos will ensue when Horowitz testifies . He is probing allegations of government surveillance abuse, in light of memos released on Capitol Hill about FBI and DOJ efforts to obtain FISA warrants to surveil.

Nunes says "Follow the HOPS" Not the White Rabbit

In the Shadowy world of Intelligence gathering, the term "HOPS" refers to the ability to jump communications chains between individuals -no White Rabbit. FISA Title-1 allows a total of 2 contacts or 2-degrees of separation to be captured.

> **Post Q #2043 on 8/31/18 (In part):**
>
> **FOREIGN TARGET DESIGNATOR(S) CREATE LEAPFROG (HOPS) TO ISOLATE 'REAL' TARGET(S).**

In lay terms, you call Ken and then he calls Barbie. All 3 people are now under this total net of surveillance. It is a "leapfrog" method to ensnare all suspects. Crossfire Hurricane was an example of reverse engineering of Title-1, as Trump was the target not Page.

> **Post Q #1745 on 7/28/18 (In part):**
>
> **FISA BRINGS DOWN THE HOUSE.**

All communications records including phone calls, texts, data, FAXES, social media, DM, HAM comms, Xbox chat logs, Gmail ghost drafts, blogs, etc. "The whole Enchilada Snow White." The total of "friends of friends" is over 8,000 people after the 2nd Degree HOP is applied.

> **Post Q #1498 on 6/14/18 (In part):**
>
> **[[RR]] approved/signed FISA-warrant application(s) to extend surveillance on POTUS/others.**

To obtain a FISA Title-1 surveillance warrant, law enforcement must demonstrate unquestionably to the FISA Court Judge that the "Target" of the application is an agent of a Foreign Power. Normally a very high bar, except during the reign of BHO.

> **Post Q #2489 on 11/12/18 (In part):**
>
> **[Placeholder - OIG Report-Umbrella SPY and Targeting].**

In this case Carter Page is a foreign agent who appears regularly on FOX News with no lawyer. Not the normal routine for a high level covert Russian spy.

Carter Page attended a London symposium at the request of Stefan

Halper. The carrot dangled to Carter by Stefan, was some juicy HRC "opposition research." This interchange was to be the genesis event from which sprang the entire Trump-Russia fraud.

Post Q #553 on 1/19/18 (in part):

Do we TRUST the FISA judges?

Recall the famed Devin Nunes presser in front of the White House in 2017. Ezra Cohen-Watnick showed Nunes the Obama Presidential Daily Briefings (PDB).

This vital meeting was held in the White House SCIF. BHO had his PDBs spread via a dissemination method called "Operation Latitude" (can you say Evelyn Farkas).

Post Q #2042 on 8/31/18 (in part):

BULK DATA COLLECTION (UMBRELLA).

Patriot Nunes saw unmasked names, opposition research from Steele, illegal FISA 702 Queries and more inserted into BHO's PDBs. As a Gang of 8 member, Nunes has the absolute highest "Q-Type" level security clearances to even be allowed to access this top secret material from Ezra.

Post Q #436 on 12/22/17 (in part):

[FISA 2]

Decode: at least 2 FISA Title-1 Surveillance Warrants have been approved for the Trump-Russia Probe.

IG Horowitz and SP Huber have taken on the investigation of alleged abuses by the DOJ/FBI with past FISA/FISC applications. Phase Two OIG report should be out soon as well as the Carter Page FISA application redactions [20].

Post Q #1971 on 8/28/18 (in part):

BIGGER THAN WATERGATE.

REFERENCES:

The ACLU and Civil Libertarians should be shouting and howling at the sky (like the crazed SJW's have done) about these governmental surveillance abuses. Unfortunately, from this prior concerned crowd, all we hear are crickets.

Zero Hedge – "FBI Knew Steele Dossier Was Bogus"
Tablet Mag-FISA Title-1 Surveillance
Conservative Treehouse –"Nunes Explains the 2-HOP Rule"
Sara Carter – "Nunes Calls For Declassification of Emails/FISA"
Judicial Watch – "No FISA Court for Carter Page Warrants"

Markets Work – "Carter Page FISA Applications"
Markets Work – "FBI's Contractors, FISA Abuse, and Steele Timeline"
WTPO(?) – "NSA Surveillance 'HOPS'"
The Guardian – "3 Degrees of Separation: HOPS"
National Public Radio(?) – "3 HOPS gives NSA Millions of Phone Records"
The Forward – "Nunes gets Secret Intel from Ezra"
US House of Representatives – "FISA Title-1 Summary"

NOTE BELOW: "Pure_Feature" Extra Answers:

The judges who preside over America's secret court, Reuters10 - "Since FISA was enacted in 1978, we've had three chief justices, and they have all Three judges live in the Washington area and are available for emergencies. FISA Our Standards: The Thomson Reuters Trust Principles

Foreign Intelligence Surveillance Act, Wikipedia11 Approval of a FISA application requires the court find probable cause that the target of the surveillance be a "foreign power" or an "agent of a foreign power'...

Understanding The Context of Devin Nunes Requests,12 Admiral Mike Rogers ordered the "About Query" activity to stop, using FISA 702(17) surveillance "about inquiries" that would deliver email They saw more than just illegal searches, imo. .. BHO didn't "just follow that familiar path"...

Think Huber / Trust Huber / Meet Big John Huber

"Stealth" Jeff Sessions announced with little fanfare, that US Attorney for the District of Utah, John Huber, has been appointed as Special Prosecutor (SP). Huber has silently been working alongside Inspector General (IG) Michael Horowitz since November 13, 2017.

Post Q #2506 on 11/30/18 (in part):

To all those that doubted SESSIONS and HUBER you ALL WILL PAY THE PRICE VERY SOON.

Huber is scheduled to testify to the US House on December 5, 2018— [D5]. Rep. Mark Meadows expects an update regarding the ongoing DOJ probe of the Clinton Foundation. (This appearance was since cancelled since the investigation is ongoing.)

Post Q #1517 on 6/16/18 (in part):

IG started long before Huber setting stage.
IG = FBI.
Huber = DOJ (no DC).

SP Huber and IG Horowitz have been conducting internal reviews of the DOJ/FBI. In this unique setup, Horowitz acts as the FBI and Huber acts as the DOJ.

Post Q #2555 on 12/5/18 (in part):

WHITAKER, HOROWITZ, HUBER, and WRAY.
Long meeting held within a SCIF [unusual] ...

Originally focused on the HRC Email, possible misconduct, their scope has now expanded to include FISA/Dossier/SpyGate/Halper/and U1 probes.

Post Q #1682 on 7/24/18 (in part):

Who does Huber report to [directly]?

OIG Phase One, 500-page report on the HRC investigation, showed bias and a deliberate effort to exonerate HRC prior to the investigation.

Post Q #2462 on 11/9/18 (in part):

Who is HUBER?
Mandate charged to HUBER?
Resources provided to HUBER?

Phase Two is over FISA Court abuses and the activities of Stefan Halper/SpyGate and will be the main focus by Horowitz and Huber.

Post Q #1644 on 6/28/18 (in part):

Timing is everything.
Think Huber.

Huber has been referred to affectionately as a "Jock with the soul of a Geek." Big John being a very smart former college football player, helps with that overall personal image.

Huber has been serving in various positions in the Utah District US Attorney's Office since April 2002 and took the helm in 2015. Always considered a straight shooter and leaving politics at the door.

Post Q #2253 on 9/22/18 (in part):

FISA DECLAS WILL BRING THE HOUSE DOWN.

The combination of Huber's prosecutorial abilities along with IG Horowitz's investigative tools and large staff, far outweigh the tools that a second Special Counsel would have had at hand. Sen. Orrin Hatch has praised Huber's independence and his outside of DC Swamp perspective on many critical issues.

Post Q #1660 on 7/1/18 (in part):

Ask yourself-does Huber have the ability to file across all 50 states?

Horowitz and Huber have been hunting government criminals, LURES/spies and traitors. Please note that Utah still carries the Death Penalty and has access to non-swamp Grand Juries!

Post Q #1122 on 4/10/18 (in part):

TRUST HOROWITZ.
TRUST HUBER.

Jeff Sessions (TRUST SESSIONS) had kept the Huber appointment a big secret for a long time. Now, the "Stealth Bomber," Whitaker, will assist Team Huber/Horowitz with the justice phase.

Post Q #499 on 1/7/18 (in part):

Do you believe in coincidences?

One reason for Huber's selection, is that Utah has large Uranium One mining operations. Utah may very well become the base of prosecutions for the U1 case, due to jurisdictional location of these many uranium mines.

Post Q #1552 on 6/18/18 (in part):

Weiner HRC / Others-crimes against children.
Noose.
Ref to Huber?

NOVEMBER 2017: SP Huber secretly starts / Podesta Group closes / General Flynn pleads / per "Q" HRC-Huma-Skippy all indicted, then drops COINCIDENCE.

Post Q #2397 11/3/18 (in part):

OIG works w/HUBER [important to remember].

Huber has spoken up previously on behalf of both "Kate's Law" and "No Sanctuaries Act." Have your popcorn ready, as second of the OIG Reports/FISA DECLAS/Unsealing should start to "drop" in the near future fellow Patriots.

REFERENCES:

The Washington Times – *"U.S. Attorney John Huber"*
The Epoch Times – *"Mr.Huber Goes To Washington"*
Sundance/CTH(?) – *"Huber to Testify to House on 12/5/18"*
The Hill – *"House to Hold Hearings on DOJ's CF Probe"*
The Salt Lake Tribune – *"Utah's Own John Huber"*
Sundance/CTH(?) – *"Horowitz Found Grounds for Referrals to Huber"*
US Dept. of Justice Website – *US Attorney John Huber*
TheMarketsWork – *"Why Sessions Chose Huber"*
Breitbart – *"Turley: Sessions Appointing Utah Federal Prosecutor Much Better for Trump than 2nd Special Counsel"*
Lew Rockwell – *"Trust Sessions, Horowitz and Huber"*

NOTE BELOW: "Pure_Feature" Extra Answers:

This is why the deep state is freaking out.13 Ask yourself - does Huber have the ability to file across all 50 states? Is any of this normal? Think sealed indictments. Think resignations of CEOs.

Mystery surrounds Sessions appointee to FBI investigation, The Hill14 U.S. Attorney John Huber has been given an unusual role. Known as a no-nonsense prosecutor whose primary experience is fighting violent...inquiries at a point in the inspector general investigation where Horowitz would...

Eric Bolling calls on Trump, Congress to focus on recovery side of opioid crisis.15 'Huber was described as a "jock with the soul of a geek," a protector for others against bullies, and a man who lived by the motto: "Be the hammer, not the nail."

Inquiring Minds Want To Know: The Skinny On Huma's Seized Laptop

NYPD was working an underage child pornography case involving former Congressman Anthony Weiner. A shared laptop and several other devices were seized by NY authorities.

Post Q #1235 on 4/22/18 (in part):

Don't forget about Huma.

Criminal charges were later filed against Weiner and he is currently in prison serving his sex crimes sentence. Anthony has become a serial repeat offender.

IG Horowitz's review, in advance of the 2016 election, highlights some unexplainable official actions. On page # 281 of the report, Comey describes himself as having a "reasonably good memory."

Post Q 2219 on 9/19/18 (in part):

None are protected.
None are safe.

Incredibly during the same interview, Comey states "I didn't know that I knew, Weiner was married to Huma was married to Weiner" The only person in the World!!!

Post Q #1124 on 4/10/18 (in part):

We have it all.
These people are stupid.
Fireworks.

Found in the IG Review on page #294 are troubling references to "Crime Against Children" and "HRC and Foundation." This would all be located in a section marked as "Insurance File" by Huma and Anthony.

Post Q #45 on 11/2/17 (in part):

What did HRC instruct Huma to do re: Classified markings?

On September 27, 2016, the DOJ assigned two Assistant US Attorneys from the Southern District of New York (SDNY) to work with the local NY FBI. An email was exchanged between the FBI/SAC and DOJ/AUSA the next day concerning which "search terms" were to be used.

The Abedin/Weiner "Insurance File" had evidence of crimes related to the sexual exploitation of children, enticement, and obscenity. The sexual emails were stored alongside the top secret emails.

> **Post Q #1345 on 5/12/18 (In part):**
> **U1 [donations to CF].**

A later complete review of these seized devices, discovered over 600,000 work related emails from Huma Abedin. Huma was HRC's closest advisor and constant companion/partner.

> **Post Q #8 on 10/29/17 (In part):**
> **Huma.**
> **Husband in jail.**

After the FBI forensic review, many of these HRC emails were found to be highly classified.

"Lordy" many of these emails had Special Access Program (SAP) designations. Incredibly this meant that the FBI was restricted from reviewing this secret compartmentalized material.

> **Post Q #15 on 10/31/17 (In part):**
> **11.6 - Huma indicted.**

After Comey, McCabe and Strzok knowingly sat on this material for almost a month, the FBI started up the Mid Year Exam (MYE)-the HRC probe.

> **Post Q #953 on 3/17/18 (In part):**
> **TRAITORS EVERYWHERE.**
> **AMERICA FOR SALE.**

The threat to go public by the NYPD forced the reopening of the HRC (MYE) email "matter" days before the 2016 Presidential election. Lynch got involved in stopping future leaks or other inquiries by threatening the NYPD.

> **Post Q #484 on 1/7/18 (In part):**
> **Who are the Muslim Brotherhood?**
> **Who is Huma?**

Lynch was using old leverage from the Eric Garner case, in keeping NYPD in-sync with main Justice.

Abedin has been described mostly in terms of her involvement with the Muslim Brotherhood (MB). Huma's family has long been involved with the radical elements of the MB.

Post Q #1515 on 6/16/18 (In part):

JP/Huma NOV.

The DOJ "Small Group" all had private email (non .GOV) accounts. Private accounts are perfect for avoiding FOIA requests and hide improper/illegal activities Gmail Ghost Draft messages.

Post Q #2 on 10/28/17:

Where Is Huma?
Follow Huma.

Much speculation has swirled around this confiscated shared laptop of Huma Abedin and the many secrets it may reveal. Inquiring minds surely want to know!

REFERENCES:

The Hill – "Huma Abedin's Ties to the Muslin Brotherhood"
Real Clear Politics – "FBI Says Clinton Foundation Cases 'Moving Toward Indictments'"
True Pundit – "IG Report Confirms Comey Briefed on "Sex Crimes Against Children" Evidence"
Conservative Treehouse – "FBI Never Investigated Laptop Emails in 2016"
Citizens for Trump – "NYPD: Weiner's Laptop has Evidence 'Put HRC Away For Life'"
Breitbart – "The Infamous Erik Prince Interview: Weiner's Laptop"
True Pundit – "NYPD turns Against the FBI Over Weiner's Laptop"
New York Magazine – "FBI Admits That James Comey Misled Congress About Huma Abedin's Email Habits"
The Gateway Pundit – "What's Hidden in the IG Report Will Make You Sick"
Vault.FBI.gov – "Discovery of HRC's Emails on Weiner Laptop"
Judicial Watch – "FOIA Documents: Weiner's Laptop (C/P)"

NOTE BELOW: "Pure_Feature" Extra Answers:

Is Anthony Weiner Still Married? Details on His Relationship With[16] It was only a matter of time before Anthony Weiner's underage sexting cost him his marriage. Huma Abedin filed for divorce from her estranged ...

NYPD Betrays FBI: Says Seized Laptop Shows Clinton Covered Up[17], Government Corruption 24 mrt. 2017 - NYPD detectives building a child porn case against Anthony Weiner say as detectives working an underage child pornography case against ...

Anthony Weiner gets 21 months in prison in sexting case - CNNPolitics[18] Anthony Weiner was sentenced Monday to 21 months in federal prison for sexting with a minor. ... Huma Abedin, Anthony Weiner split after sexting claims .... that the former congressman had with a 15-year-old girl on social media sites. Weiner's attorneys said his crimes were a "product of sickness" and ...

Mysterious Russian Oligarch
Meet Oleg Deripaska

Regardless of your feelings about ObamaGate/SpyGate, this coup plot has produced many colorful characters. One of the most mysterious actors exposed is Oleg Deripaska.

Oleg is considered a close friend of Putin and earned his oligarch status in the aluminum metal industry. Considered the wealthiest person in Russia in 2008, Deripaska was also connected to organized crime.

Post Q #1745 on 7/28/18 (in part):

FISA IMPLICATES SENIOR MEMBERS OF UK, MI5/6, US INTEL, WH, FVEY, R PARTY (CONGRESS/SENATE) OF KNOWN CORRUPTION IN EFFORT TO RETAIN POWER AND RIG ELECTION.

Oleg has long been restricted from entry into the USA and has been attempting to change that status. Contacted in 2009 by the FBI (including McCabe), Oleg was officially asked to assist in the release of former FBI/DEA agent Robert Levinson from Iranian captivity.

Post Q #436 on 12/22/17 (in part):

BRIT INTEL. HRC CAMP PAY. DNC PAY. STEELE.

Deripaska would spend $25 million personally and it looked very much like the release of Levinson would occur. Oleg has steel/metal interests ongoing in Iran.

Then the entire hostage deal was scrubbed, unexplainable by HRC in 2010. Deripaska has been Manafort's partner in some businesses and claims Paul cheated him out of $10 million. Oleg has retained Adam Waldman in the past, at a sweet $40,000 monthly lobbying fee.

Post Q #1164 on 4/15/18 (in part):

Avoid US data collection laws.
Public: Dossier FISA.

In the Fall of 2016, the FBI again contacted Deripaska, this time about possible Trump-Russia ties. Oleg laughed at the FBI about their unbelievable Putin/Russian collusion narrative tale.

Post Q #1626 on 6/28/18 (in part):

Putin/U1 will come out post summit.

Oleg offered to testify to Congress in 2017. For some reason, that offer was rejected. Deripaska and Waldman got involved with Sen. Warner in his efforts to meet personally with Christopher Steele.

Post Q #1286 on 4/27/18 (In part):

The Brits-raw Intel/dossier/5 Eyes.

Odds are that, in fact, the "Our Guy" referred to in the released exchanges between Bruce Ohr and Christopher Steele is mystery man Oleg Deripaska.

REFERENCES:

The Hill (John Solomon) – "5 Things About Oleg Deripaska"
New York Post – "Feds Freeze Oleg's U.S. Assets"
Sundance/CTH(?) – "'Our Guy' Deripaska: Real Russian Collusion"
Thread Reader – "NYT 's Article Seems To Support Deripaska"
The Daily Caller – "Steele Lobbied Ohr about Deripaska"
Washington Examiner – "Links to Steele/Ohr/Simpson to Oleg Deripaska"
Sundance/CTH(?)-Ramifications of Oleg Deripaska
Business Insider(?) – "Court Records Show Manafort Indebted to Deripaska"
The Guardian – "Deripaska's Lobbyist Waldman Visited Assange"
FOX NEWS – "Sen. Warner Asked Deripaska to Contact Steele"
The Hill (John Solomon) – "Mueller May Have Conflict w/Deripaska"
Sundance/CTH(?) – "US Treasury and DOJ Turn on Deripaska"

NOTE BELOW: "Pure_Feature" Extra Answers:

Mueller may have a conflict — and it leads directly to a Russian,[19] The FBI, under Mueller's leadership, in 2009 asked Oleg Deripaska to fund a rescue mission for an ex-agent captured in Iran, and rewarded the ... Then in fall 2010, the operation secured an offer to free Levinson. . Waldman declined to say if Deripaska has been in contact with the FBI since Sept, 2016..

The Frothing Right Prefers Oleg Deripaska as an FBI Asset to,[20] "Deripaska laughed but realized, despite the joviality, that they were serious," Manafort and his long-time Russian associate into a story about the dossier (In September 2016, FBI agents approached Russian oligarch Oleg B no-one said "the FBI agents told D to go along with their tale of collusion"

Russian Once Tied to Trump Aide Seeks Immunity to Cooperate With, Oleg V. Deripaska's offer comes amid increased attention to his ties to May 26, 2017, Vladimir V. Putin, recently offered to cooperate with congressional He sought to get a visa in 2015 to testify in the Manhattan court case, according to court filings, but the State Department refused to issue him one.

The Insubordinate FISA Signer: Meet Sally [SY] Yates

Legendary FISA signer that disobeyed direct Presidential orders - meet Sally Yates. As all of Carter Page's FISA applications get declassified, Yates will play an important role in this plot.

Post Q #2118 on 9/7/18 (in part):

FISA SIGNATURES
FISA 10/?/16
SSA ?-Comey-Yates-DOJ ?

Sally Yates was the former Deputy, then acting, US Attorney General. She was a carryover from the BHO administration. Yates is being painted into a legal corner by both Senator Grassley and IG Horowitz.

Post Q #1929 on 8/19/18 (in part):

Page [ ]-Sally Yates.

Horowitz is seeking redemption from being prohibited by Yates from oversight into the National Security Divisions of DOJ/FBI. This was the home of the Secret Society, where the treasonous coup plot was hatched and managed.

Post Q #1291 on 3/17/18 (in part):

Who makes arrests?
FBI & DOJ?
Can you make arrests w/ a crooked FBI sr team?

Sen. Grassley's Judiciary Committee has sent out a detailed 10-Page questionnaire. These forms were sent to several high ranking former Obama Officials, including past CIA Director Brennan and DNI Clapper.

Completion was made mandatory by Congressional Committee subpoenas. Can you imagine that most were outright ignored or had abstract reply answers.

Post Q #1316 on 5/4/18 (in part):

Sally Yates, Deputy Attorney General and Acting Attorney General-FIRED.

Yates's name is brought up in a few of these questions and the answers could prove damaging to Yates as well as others BHO era officials. Due to several never being returned, final Congressional conclusions are still pending.

Post Q #2376 on 10/8/18:

[Sally Yates].

Most likely the answers will all be run by IG Horowitz and SP Huber, to be reflected within their final subsequent oversight reports.

Post Q #1351 on 5/12/18 (in part):

What happens if FED [criminal] indictments are brought forth to a corrupt FBI/DOJ/FED Judge?

Sally's biggest past public notice was of course early on in President

Trump's administration, during the Travel Ban. Yates chose on her own to ignore a lawfully given order direct from POTUS, directing DOJ to enforce these new travel related regulations and entry rules.

> **Post Q #2375 on 10/8/18:**
>
> [Sally Yates].

This unbelievable insubordination to POTUS, lead to Yates quickly being dismissed on 1/31/16, "You're Fired." Future proves past, as the Supreme Court later upheld most of the major elements of POTUS's new travel ban order.

> **Post Q #953 on 3/17/18 (in part):**
>
> How bad is the corruption?
> DOJ (past/present).
> # 1
> # 2

Decode: 1=AG Loretta Lynch and 2=Dept. AG Sally Yates.

The Oval Office meeting on 01/05/17, which Susan Rice has now immortalized with her CYS "Memo to Self" was on Trump's Inauguration Day and Rice was no longer working/employed by the government.

> **Post Q #1891 on 8/15/18 (in part):**
>
> Texts, emails (gmail), drafts (gmail), HAM comma, PS/Xbox chat logs.
> JC-BO-CS-LL-# 2-NO-SY.

Bear in mind that Comey and Yates were the only Top Tier (Secret Society) holdovers going into the Trump Administration. This was the final time to coordinate Operation "Crossfire Hurricane" and the final plan option, which was the "Insurance Policy."

> **Post Q #1316 on 5/4/18 (in part):**
>
> Sally Yates, Deputy Attorney General and Acting Attorney General-FIRED.

The question now is: Was it all "By the Book," or were there plans for a Deep State Coup. Inquiring minds now want to know what BHO/JB/SR/JC and Yates all said at that critical January 2017 White House Oval Office meeting.

REFERENCES:
The Hill – "Yates saysTrump's Tweets: 'Beyond Abnormal'"
The Markets Work – "FISA Abuses and 4 Coincidences"
The Hill-John Solomon – "FBI Email Chain Evidence Of FISA Abuse"
True Pundit – "DOJ Yates Ordered FBI Not to Investigate Clinton Foundation"
The Western Journal – "Intel Committee Going After Fusion GPS"
US Senate-Grassley – "Susan Rice Memo"

The Gateway Pundit – "Comey/McCabe Ordered Yates to go After Flynn"
Talking Points Memo – "Yates', McGahn's Accounts Of Meetings On Flynn Differ: What That Tells Us"
The Guardian – "Sally Yates Fired by Trump"
NOTE BELOW: "Pure_Feature" Extra Answers:

Sally Yates - Wikipedia[21] Sally Caroline Yates (née Quillian; August 20, 1960) is an American lawyer. She served as a United States Attorney and later United States Deputy Attorney.

Acting attorney general fired by Trump stands by decision not to. The former acting attorney general who was fired by President Trump for refusing to defend his travel ban told a U.S. Senate committee she has…[22]

Seven Mysterious Preludes to the FBI's Trump-Russia Probe.[23] Trump campaign in an operation code-named "Crossfire Hurricane," there were at the same time, in early spring, the Clinton campaign commissioned, through. is publicly known, generated no evidence of coordination with the Russians. The seventh, and apparently final, approach before the full

Planted Trump "Campaign Spy"
Meet Stefan Halper

Hat tip to Dan Bongino (ex-US Secret Service) for first advancing the "Dirty Up" theory for the Trump-Russia investigation. What has now become obvious is that certain lower level Trump campaign advisors were specifically targeted for meetings with these intelligence assets.

Post Q #2489 on 11/12/18 (in part):

[Placeholder - OIG Report-Umbrella SPY and Targeting].

These "entrapment" get-togethers later could be tied into the "Russian Collusion" delusion narrative. Elaborate plans and professional execution was the hallmark of the SpyGate operation.

Post Q #1164 on 4/15/18 (in part):

Not Public: Five Eyes/UK/AUS POTUS targeting using pushed RUS decoy meetings/campaign insertions.

The DOJ/FBI has not yet officially released the name of this paid "meeting planner" but all eyes are on Stefan Halper. Halper is a syndicated columnist, college professor, defense contractor, past White House Adviser, and has close ties to both CIA and MI6.

Post Q #1589 on 6/26/18 (in part):

ILLEGAL SPYING.
FRAME.
INSERT ASSETS.

Halper arranged several very suspicious meetings with Trump officials during the 2016 campaign. Joseph Misfud, former head of MI6 and colleague of Halper, assisted with this complex sting operation.

In July 2016, Halper set-up a meeting in London with Carter Page, just days after Carter's infamous Russia trip that became part of the Steele Dossier. Halper made initial contact, inviting Page over to attend a symposium at Cambridge. Globalist featured speakers like Madeleine Albright gave themes of Global Politics and the upcoming US Presidential election.

In August 2016, Stefan reached out to then Cochairman of the Trump campaign Sam Clovis. According to Victoria Toensing (Clovis attorney), Halper met with Clovis in Virginia to offer his expertise in foreign relations. Additionally, to assist in the election of candidate Donald Trump, with any "information" that may be of value that Halper discovers.

NOTE: On 8/2/16, a gala party was held at the Australian Embassy in London. FBI Peter Strzok flew over to attend this event and specifically meet with Downer/Halper at the embassy.

In September 2016, Halper contacts George Papadopoulos and they agree to have a meeting. Stefan bragged to George repeatedly that his Russian contacts had the missing HRC deleted emails. He offered his personal help and to turn over the emails to the Trump campaign.

"FUTURE PROVES PAST" —Q

Originally back in May 2016, George Papadopoulos was introduced by an Israeli Diplomat to Alexander Downer. George was in London to speak at a lecture and write a paper, under a $3,000 plus expenses contract job.

While out pub crawling at the Kensington Gardens, George was overheard by Australian diplomat Alexander Downer, talking about Russian "emails" on HRC.

This famous off-hand bar talk, lead to the onset of the "Russian Collusion" narrative. The DOJ points to this "Intelligence" as the sole reason used to first launch the FBI's counterintelligence probe into Trump-Russia on July 31, 2016.

Post Q #1238 on 4/22/18 (in part):

Not 'official' product-5 Eyes.

Records indicate that Stefan Halper has received almost $1 million from the US Federal Government over the last several years. Halper was paid to conduct four separate "research projects" and report findings.

Post Q #1935 on 8/27/18 (in part):

Focus Here:

"...raise troubling questions about Halper, who was believed to have worked with the CIA and part of the matrix of players in the bureau's 'CrossFire Hurricane'

Stefan has past ties with various intelligence agencies due to his roles with the Nixon, Ford/and Reagan Presidential administrations. Halper has been paid to act as an intelligence asset for the CIA.

Since Halper will be confirmed as the paid FBI mole within the Trump campaign, it destroys the previously given timeline and the real origins of the FBI Counterintelligence probe.

Post Q #972 on 3/28/18 (in part):

Intelligence A's across the globe in partnership to spy on citizens.

IG Horowitz has publicly announced an additional investigation into possible abuses of the FISA Court by the DOJ and FBI. Horowitz will look for the basis on the Carter Page Title-1 FISA Warrant.

The FBI considers July 31, 2016, as the marked official counterintelligence launch date. Unbelievably this flawed timeline is based upon Papadopoulos's drunken bar tales.

Post Q #2043 on 8/31/18 (in part):

UK ASSIST + FISA SURV INCLUDED ALL UPSTREAM COLLECTION + TANGENT CONTACTS (UMBRELLA SURV).

Figuring out the real FBI start date, will help expose the roots of this pre-planned traitorous coup plot. Understanding and connecting the various components of Crossfire Hurricane, Operation Dragon, and Crossfire FISA programs, will reveal all to the world.

REFERENCES:

Zero Hedge – "Halper Tried to Infiltrate State Department After Spying on Trump World"
The Gateway Pundit - Solomon: At Least 6 DS Operatives Infiltrated Trump Campaign
Heavy – "5 Fast Facts: Stefan Halper"
Conservative Review – "Halper is the Tip of the Iceberg in BHO's SpyGate"
Sundance/CTH(?) – "The Insurance Policy and the Mysterious Informant"
The Daily Caller – "A London Meeting before the Election is Suspicious"
The Markets Work – "Ties That Bind: Halper/Downer/Mifsud/and Papadopoulos"
The Federalist – "8 Times BHO's Intelligence Agencies Set People Up to Fabricate Russia Story"
Sundance/CTH(?) Stefan Halper Agent Provocateur
The Daily Caller – "Senate Wants To Interview Mifsud"

NOTE BELOW: "Pure_Feature" Extra Answers:

EXCLUSIVE: A London Meeting Before The Election Aroused George,[24] *Halper also offered to pay for Papadopoulos's flight and a show he has been paid $928,800 since 2012 on four* *separate research projects.....*

Docs Confirm FBI Spy Halper Was Paid $282k From Unidentified Obama,[25] *The Obama administration paid Halper $282,000 (or $411,000 not clear which) planned to do moving forward on the collusion investigation…*

Did a Cambridge Professor Frame Trump Campaign Aides…[26] *Reporting on Halper and the government employee in question, If Halper were indeed paid to conduct these negotiations, it would be a…*

Deep State Firewall and FISA Manipulator Meet Rachel Brand

Rachel Brand was the DOJ Associate AG and held the third highest rank in the agency. She was the first woman to hold that position, with tenure from May 2017–February 2018.

Post Q #1498 on 6/4/18 (in part):

Why was Rachel Brand removed?

Like so many others have done since the election of President Trump, Brand has suddenly left government service and moved on to work for Walmart. Record numbers of resignations and terminations seem to be the new norm.

Post Q #2129 on 9/10/18 (in part):

ALL FISA SIGNERS WILL BE [CURRENTLY] UNDER INVESTIGATION.

One of Brand's primary responsibilities at the DOJ involved aspects of the Woods Procedure. Under the Woods rules, the DOJ must "push-down" all unverified information/intelligence in the FISA application process.

Post Q #1944 on 8/28/18 (in part):

FISA = FISC.

Rachel was in charge of overseeing all of the FISA applications. Brand was to comb through all reported details and only allow confirmed verified facts to be presented to the secret FISC (court).

Post Q #1433 on 5/21/18 (in part):

Who is Rachel Brand?
Why was Rachel Brand dismissed?

Rep. Devin Nunes has drilled down publicly on this critical aspect of this Woods/FISA procedural process that obviously was not followed by Rachel. The Carter Page FISA Title-1 surveillance warrant relied primarily on the totally unverified Christopher Steele dossier.

Post Q #2381 on 10/9/18 (in part):

Why did McCabe try to take SESSIONS out?

By most neutral observer standards, the Christopher Steele Trump-Russia "Dirty Dossier" is a work of total fiction. History may even show that a large portion of this "hit piece", was in fact written by Nellie Ohr and not a few aging obscure Russian intelligence officials.

Post Q #1316 on 5/4/18 (in part):

Rachel Brand, Associate Attorney General-No. 3 official behind Deputy AG Rosenstein-FIRED/FORCE.

The Vacancies Reform Act of 1998 comes into play when looking at the chair of succession at the DOJ. Deep State Black Hats had hoped that Brand (number 3 at DOJ), would act as a preventative "firewall" for future firings/recusals.

Post Q #2129 on 9/10/18 (in part):

THE US GOVERNMENT UNDER HUSSEIN KNOWINGLY PRESENTED FALSE EVIDENCE TO FISC IN AN EFFORT TO OBTAIN LEGAL US INTELLIGENCE UMBRELLA SURV OF POTUS [IDEN TARGET] FOR THE SOLE PURPOSE OF THE 2016 ELECTION.

Evidence is coming out now that McCabe had attempted to get [RR] to recuse (pushed for Sessions as well) from the Trump-Russia probe. The Black Hats always wanted to elevate loyal Brand into that critical Mueller oversight role.

These failed Coup Plotters are now scrambling to get all of their stories straight as they all are called to testify. Team "Q" has let on that [LL] is now talking (as well as recording) and thus the "Rats in DC" are in a total panic.

Post Q #1745 on 7/28/18 (in part):

FISA = START.

To put a "cherry on top" of this scene, Brand publicly claimed she did not want the responsibility of the Trump-Russia investigation. Ask yourself what government employee would not welcome a promotion, let alone, depart lucrative security for the public sector.

Post Q #2273 on 9/23/18 (in part):

Did the IG recommend [RR] step down or be fired [speed]?
Why was Rachel Brand removed?

The looming FISA DECLAS/UNSEALING will help to fill in all of the blanks. Exposure will make the public aware of what the Anons have known for months-FISA BRINGS DOWN THE HOUSE.

REFERENCES:
NPR – "Number 3 DOJ Official Steps Down"
The Hill – "Nunes: Did FBI/DOJ Violate Woods Procedure"
VOX – "Brand Resigns: Bad News For Mueller"
Sara Carter and George Papadopoulos: "FBI Withheld Exculpatory Intel From FISC"
Sundance and CTH(?) – "DOJ's Rachel Brand Resigns"
Heavy – "5 Facts About Rachel Brand"
NBC News – "Who Is Rachel Brand and Her Resignation Concerning Mueller's Probe"
Praying Medic – "Thread-Reader" - May 21, 2018
The Hill (John Solomon) – "FBI Email Chain Evidence Of FISA Abuse"
Justice.gov – Rachel Brand bio

NOTE BELOW: "Pure_Feature" Extra Answers:

Rachel Brand – Wikipedia, Rachel Lee Brand (born May 1, 1973) is an American lawyer, academic, and former government official. She served as the United States Associate Attorney General from May 22 and was ousted as part of the purge. Brand ultimately declined the position, however, and resigned from the Department of Justice in June 2007.

Rachel Brand, No. 3 official at DOJ, is stepping down [27] *Rachel Brand, the associate attorney general in the Department of DOJ officials say Principal Deputy Associate AG Jesse Panuccio will step.*

A DOJ official quit so she wouldn't have to oversee the Russia probe, [28] *Associate Attorney General Rachel Brand of the Justice Department has the associate attorney general was fearful that Rosenstein's removal.*

HRC's "Other" Trump-Russia Dossier

Devin Nunes has announced that the House Intelligence Committee is almost complete with Phase Two of it's investigations into Trump-Russia.

Devin's main target is Cody Shearer and Cody has earned his nickname of "Mr. Fixer" for the Clinton Crime Family.

Post Q #1794 on 8/1/18 (in part):

FISA.
[20]
Impossible to defend.

Mr. Fixer has a track record of smearing the reputations of female accusers of Slick Willy. Additionally, silencing any potential witnesses against the Clinton's.

Post Q #1235 on 4/21/18 (in part):

America for sale.
Betrayal.
Treason.

Cody has a decades long devotion to Bill and Hillary. Shearer has a journalistic background and contributed several memos into Chris

Steele's final Dossier.

Nunes in the House is working with Grassley from the Senate, to probe both the origins and distribution of this so-called Trump-Russia "Clinton" Dossier. Christopher Steele got some "oppo intel" through the U.S. State Department.

Cody along with his longtime sidekick Sid Blumenthal, both claim to be the coauthors of this fictional "oppo" research hit piece concerning Trump. They contributed two memos used to buttress Steele's own work product.

Cody's Brother In-Law is Strobe Talbott and was the "entrance token" into the Obama State Department for Cody/Sid. There was a 2-way conduit flow of information between Cody/Sid, Jonathan Winer and Victoria Nuland over at BHO's State Department.

Christopher Steele also got into this special circular flow of "Anti-Trump Oppo" material. Steele helped to pass along this extra State Department "intel" to his DOJ/FBI contacts with his own memos.

Chris Steele primarily used the material given to him from Sergei Millian (Source D), as well as other "memos" from Cody/Sid and Nellie Ohr, to form his own final Steele Dossier.

Nuland and Winer both have admitted publicly to their direct involvement with The Dossiers. IG Horowitz and SP Huber are keenly aware of this once secret second "Clinton" Dossier and how it got to the FBI.

Post Q #436 on 12/22/17 (in part):

[DNC BREACH / DOSSIER]

Watch for both Cody Shearer and Sid "Vicious" Blumenthal to become household names (like Chris Steele) in the near future. Nunes and IG Horowitz reports are due out soon-BOOM BOOM.

References:

The Weekly Standard – "The Other Secret Russia Dossier"
Zero Hedge – "FBI Knew Steele Dossier Was Bogus"
Apelbaum – "The Dossier Network (chart)" [Can't find any reference to Apelbaum news or magazine online]
Zero Hedge – "Nuland Confirms Steele Shared Dossier"
The Atlantic – "Devin Nunes's Next Target"
Frontpage Mag – "The Clinton Dossier"
The Guardian – "Second Dossier Being Assessed by FBI"
National Review – "Meet Cody Shearer"
The American Spectator – "Cody Shearer's Dirty Dossier Role"
Breitbart – "Jonathan Winer was Steele's Inside Guy"

NOTE BELOW: "Pure_Feature" Extra Answers:

The Clinton Crime Family. « *Hillary is the Most Dangerous Presidential*[29] *The Bill and Hillary crime family long ago should have been held accountable for high crimes against peace and numerous others. Hillary is the most recklessly ......*

Post Q #1286 on 4/27/18 (in part): The Brits-raw intel / dossier / 5-Eyes. Sunday Talks – Explosive Interview With Devin Nunes,[30] The CIA provided raw intel, to start the operation, and the FBI and DOJ-NSD .. Nunes ELIMINATES NSA-Database spying suspects from British, ... used everything he had access to, 5 eyes or not, to build the Dossier!....

Steele-Winer-Nuland connection: Link between RussiaGate and the...[31] What is also not yet publicly known, but is now coming into focus due to .. Winer admitted, in an oped in the Washington Post on February 8, 2018, that . Nunes and Grassley are both investigating the Steele-Winer-Nuland.

Infamous Tarmac Queen:
Meet Elizabeth Carlisle [LL]

We can all thank Christopher Sign from ABC15 (morning anchor) for breaking the Clinton-Lynch Tarmac meeting. This Plane-to-Plane event happened at the Phoenix Sky Harbor Int'l Airport on June 27, 2016.

Post Q #953 on 3/17/18 (in part):

TRAITORS EVERYWHERE.
AMERICA FOR SALE.

Bill's plane was only 30 yards from Loretta's private government jet, so why not go over to talk about golf and grandkids. When BC boarded, it was just [LL] and her husband Stephan Hargrove onboard.

Post Q #1556 on 6/19/18 (in part):

Bridge LL and BC.
+1 BC and LL (TARMAC) Witness.

Please bear in mind the obvious fact: high ranking government officials never leave themselves without one staffer (witness). Additionally, it is hard to ditch any Secret Service protection detail, without violating protocols.

Post Q #2219 on 9/19/18 (in part):

None are protected.
None are safe.

The FBI security detail for Loretta knew for certain that the former President and accompanying Secret Service would be in the airport area. A similar mad scramble happened over at the Justice/FBI headquarters once this strange rendezvous later became public knowledge.

Post Q #2261 on 9/21/18 (in part):

[LL] talking=TRUTH revealed TARMAC [BC]?

The FBI was very concerned about who had leaked this meeting and how best to "spin the talking points" to the media. Lynch had to recuse herself from the HRC "matter," paving the way for FBI Director Comey's full exoneration presser statement on July 5, 2016.

Post Q #674 on 2/16/18 (in part):

Tarmac meeting [SC/LL deal AS 187].

Decode: Supreme Court seat/ Lynch deal/Murder of Antonin Scalia. Also LL would stay on as AG until RBG's seat became available, not open AS seat.

Question: Who was HRC's pick for open AS SC seat (since LL had to wait)? Answer: Sam's husband Cass!

In the frantic scramble by main Justice trying to get ahead of this breaking story, the teams initial talking points started to fall apart. Top level FBI and DOJ Officials exchanged a flurry of emails, to better coordinate the company narrative.

Post Q #2292 on 9/27/18 (in part):

Hive Mind.

Thanks to a FOIA request by ACLJ, we now know that Loretta Lynch used the email alias of Elizabeth Carlisle. Rumors abound of the NSA taping of the Tarmac plane conservations-which may also include a 3rd party (can you say BHO).

Post Q #1443 on 6/10/18 (in part):

Hussein [WH [call] [tarmac] BC/LL]

Besides the obvious horrible optics of this meeting, the facts will all come out about what was said and what was promised in this Tarmac Affair. Round one is about to start with the upcoming Horowitz/Huber Report and Loretta or Elizabeth will be front and center.

REFERENCES:

Deep State News – "Media Coverup of Tarmac Meeting"
Zero Hedge – "Lynch and Comey Receive Houses Subpoenas"
The Blaze – "IG Report Blows Holes in LL/BC Tarmac Meeting"
LifeZette – "New FBI Emails Wreck Official HRC Timeline"
Sundance/CTH(?) – "FOIA Docs Reveal LL used Alias Elizabeth Carlisle"
The Washington Free Beacon – "DOJ Officials sent Talking Points to FBI for Tarmac"
Medium – "Bombshell Coverup Clinton/Lynch Meeting"
Observer – "Inside Security Source detail Tarmac Meeting"
Heavy – "5 Facts on LL's Husband Stephan Hargrove (Tarmac Meeting)"
FBI Press Office-Director Comey's Statement on July 5, 2016

NOTE BELOW: "Pure_Feature" Extra Answers:

Clinton/Lynch Tarmac Tape - 247Sports.com[32] The National Security Agency (NSA) blocked the release of a purported tape of Bill Clinton and former Attorney General Loretta Lynch's private airplane talk with ....

Video Appears to Show Day Clinton, Lynch Met on Tarmac - ABC News[33] Video Appears to Show the Day Bill Clinton and Loretta Lynch Met on Tarmac . airport on June 27, including any surveillance footage of the plane(s) on the tarmac." Former CIA, NSA head Michael Hayden suffers stroke ...

Loretta Lynch used 'Elizabeth Carlisle' email alias at Department of[34] Former Attorney General Loretta Lynch went by the alias 'Elizabeth Carlisle' in email she used to ... Loretta Lynch used 'Elizabeth Carlisle' email alias at Department of Justice to FOIA requests or subpoenas aren't hidden when they are requested under FOIA. Subscribe Now to the Digital Edition.

Soros' Open Society Foundation (OSF) The Gift That Keeps On Giving

George Soros (GS) was born in Hungary and has become one of the richest people in the world. His Open Society Foundation (OSF), started in 1993, is the second largest worldwide charity behind only the Bill and Linda Gates Foundation.

Post Q #490 on 1/7/18 (in part):

Think GS pays for Antifa out of his own pocket?
The hole is deep.

Soros uses his philanthropy charities, to promote NWO agendas and a one-world global philosophy. Massive donations are deliberately directed toward Progressive Communist Leftist causes and ultra-liberal programs.

Post Q #99 on 11/5/17 (in part):

Foundations?
Institutes?
Soros.

Soros has turned over all of his accumulated wealth ($18 Billion) directly to his OSF charity. Over the last 3 decades, Soros has donated over $10 billion toward Progressive Liberal causes.

Post Q #2 on 10/38/17 (in part):

Why did Soros donate all his money recently?

Soros is often referred to as "The Godfather" of the Left and is one of the NWO's main "Puppet Masters." George belongs to a shadowy club of billionaires called the "Democracy Alliance."

"Q" drops have referred to George Soros as (+) or as GS, many times so far.

Post Q #53 on 11/2/17 (in part):

List of all who have foundations.
How can donations be used personally?

In 2002, Soros gave one of his charities over to Robert Redford, along with $5 million to influence the Sundance Film Festival. Soros combined with HRC and Harold Ickes in 2006, to form the "Shadow Party."

In recent times, Soros' OSF was directly involved with some the following:

- Refuge Caravan/Immigration Wave
- Major donor to BHO's O.F.A.
- 2017 political activism in Albania
- 2016 $8 million toward HRC (2020 ?)
- Flooding Europe with Migrants
- Sponsorship of Black Lives Matter
- Smartmatic Voting Machines
- Paymaster of Antifa and many Marches

- Behind the NFL sidelines protests
- $50 Million toward Steele Dossier 2.0

Post Q #330 on 12/11/17 (in part):

We have a special place picked out for GS

OSF pushes for open borders and unlimited illegal immigration, to help achieve their NWO goals. The flooding of Europe, going on now, is the future plan for the USA. Glenn Beck forewarned that Soros had "Messianic Fantasies."

Post Q #2398 on 11/3/18 (in part):

Re_read drops re: Soros and taxpayer funding.

Soros insists on his own blend of Progressive Socialism/Liberalism/and Communism. Judgement Day is coming for George Soros and there will be NO DEALS!

Post Q #2502 on 11/25/18 (in part):

Thank you, Mr. Soros.

REFERENCES:

The Atlantic – "Soros and the Demonization of Philosophy"
Zero Hedge – "Soros' OSF Thrown Out Of Turkey"
News Week – "Trump: Would Not Be Surprised If Soros Was Funding Caravans"
American Free Press – "George Soros Billionaire Terrorist"
Breitbart – "Soros Wants to Fill Italy/Europe with Migrants"
Judicial Watch – "Records show Obama Helped to Fund Soros's Albania Activities"
Zero Hedge - Hacked Emails Show Soros is a Ukraine Puppet Master
Politico – "Soros donates $8 million to Boost Hillary"
Frontpage Mag – "Collaborator Soros Announces Muslims are the New Jews"

NOTE BELOW: "Pure_Feature" Extra Answers:

Is George Soros Dying? $18 Billion Donation to Open Society Raises,[35] *George Soros has transferred $18 billion to his 'charitable' creation: the Open . Soros, who is 87, transferred the funds as part of a plan to make sure his... Open Society is after all a juggernaut of think tanks, created by a billionaire to . that I think most of us can relate to pertains to the recent NFL drama...*

Why Isn't The FBI Investigating George Soros? – Godfather Politics[36] *- George Soros is a real-life Dr. Evil, the only difference is that he's more The Democratic Party's Progressive Puppet Master is often referred.*

Open Society Foundations - Wikipedia[37] *Open Society Foundations (OSF), formerly the Open Society Institute, is an international grant-making network founded by business magnate George Soros. Open Society Foundations financially support civil society groups around the world. Since its establishment in 1993, OSF has reported...*

Bruce and Nellie:
Modern Day Bonnie and Clyde Couple

Bruce and Nellie Ohr's criminal roles, expand with every new revelation related to the ObamaGate/SpyGate scandal. They, sadly, are part of a growing list of "Dirty Couples." A regular modern day Bonnie and Clyde crooked criminal couple.

Rep. Jim Jordan got ex-FBI Peter Strzok, to admit publicly that Bruce Ohr gave the FBI the original first draft of Chris Steele's Dossier.

Post Q #2170 on 9/21/18 (In part):

Twelve moves ahead.
Suicide watch.

Husband and Wife pairs that are involved with high crimes, is normally very rare these days. For some odd reason, BHO and HRC have convinced several married pairs, to risk everything including their Liberty, for their Progressive Leftists Marxist agenda.

Post Q #436 on 12/22/18 (In part):

BRIT INTEL.
HRC CAMP PAY.
DNC PAY.
STEELE.

Bruce Ohr was the former Associate Deputy Attorney General (# 4 spot at DOJ), prior to several demotions. Bruce is rumored to be a cooperative witness and is now still employed at the DOJ.

Nellie Ohr was employed at Fusion GPS during the Summer/Spring of 2016. Nellie coordinated the preparation and distribution of the infamous Christopher Steele Dossier for Fusion GPS.

Post Q #1938 on 8/27/18 (In part):

BO > > Alexander Downer (FVEY) (EX1).

Bruce Ohr met several times in the Fall of 2016 with Glenn Simpson (Fusion co-founder), without approval or knowledge of his superiors at the DOJ. Bruce was the main conduit between (in both directions) the Justice Department and Fusion GPS, for the Christopher Steele "oppo research" Dossier.

Post Q #1316 on 5/4/18 (In part):

Bruce Ohr, Associate Deputy Director Attorney General-Demoted 2x-cooperating witness [power removed].

DOJ first demoted Bruce to the head of Organized Crime Drug Enforcement Task Force, where he had worked previously, involved with Operation Cassandra (Awan). Later Bruce was demoted for a second time, to parts unknown.

Nellie Ohr's work at Fusion GPS, very well may have been more than just helping compile the "Dirty Dossier". It has been said Nellie was even the co-author and had input in developing the entire Trump-Russian narrative.

Post Q #2004 on 8/30/18 (in part):

What is the significance of Nellie Ohr being fluent in Russian?

Nellie has a unique background, including a Ph.D. in Russian history/fluent in Russian/a Stalin apologist/former CIA Analyst/expert Ham Radio operator/and just may be, the main author of the bogus "pee pee" Dossier.

Incredibly in 2010, all three paths crossed between Bruce/Nellie and Glenn Simpson during a CIA Open Source Works program. By actively attending CIA sponsored seminars, the "Clown" influence gets real hard to shake off.

Post Q #847 on 3/6/18:

Watch the water.

Sen. Grassley has sent out a 12-page questionnaire to top Obama Alumni. Many of these very specific questions involve Fusion GPS and the Steele Dossier.

Post Q #1286 on 4/27/18 (in part):

Fusion GPS.

The Brits-raw intel/dossier/5 eyes.

The answers to Senator Grassley's tough questions may just ignite the fuse for grand finale finish. The "Dirty Couples" uncovered so far with direct connections to ObamaGate/SpyGate:

- Andy/Jill McCabe
- Peter Strzok/Melissa Hodgman
- Glenn Simpson /Mary Jacoby
-. Anita Dunn/Robert Bauer
- Shailagh Murray/Neil King
- Huma Abedin/Anthony Weiner

REFERENCES:
Breitbart – "FISA was not informed about Ohr's Ties"
Conservative Treehouse – "Nellie Ohr Refusing to Testify"
FOX NEWS - Jim Jordan on Peter Strzok's Revelations about Bruce Ohr
Hot Air – "Sen. Grassley Requests Bruce Ohr's Contacts w/Chris Steele"

Daily Coin – Judicial Watch - Fitton Video: Fusion GPS and Bruce Ohr's Conflicts of Interest
LifeZette – "Court Orders DOJ to Produce Fusion GPS Records"
Heavy – "5 Fast Facts: Bruce and Nellie Ohr"
Conservative Treehouse – Sometimes a Conspiracy Theory is Not a Theory
Spectator – "Nellie Ohr at Center of Investigations"
Federalist – "Nellie used Ham Radio to avoid Surveillance"

NOTE BELOW: "Pure_Feature" Extra Answers:

Nellie Ohr: Woman in the Middle The American Spectator[38] - Nellie Ohr is the "dossier" spying scandal's woman in the middle. order, so Ohr's subtitle refers to the "stabilization" of the collective farm order. Conquest, renowned for his works on the purges and the terror

ULS License Archive - Amateur License - KM4UDZ - Ohr, Nellie H wireless2.fcc.gov › WTB › ULS › Online Systems ULS License Archive Amateur License - KM4UDZ - Ohr, Nellie H, Help in new window Operator Class, Technician, Prev. Op. Class. Group, D, Prev.

Bruce Genesoke Ohr[39] (born March 16, 1962) is a United States Department of Justice official. A former associate deputy attorney general and former director of the Organized Crime Drug Enforcement Task Force (OCDETF), as of February 2018 Ohr was working in the Justice Department's Criminal Division. He is an expert on transnational organized crime and has spent most of his career overseeing gang- and racketeering-related prosecutions, including Russian organized crime. Attorney General Rod Rosenstein has stated that as far as he knew, Ohr was not involved with the Russia investigation, United States Associate Attorney General

(Answer is:) BHO's Iranian Consigliere (Question:) Who is [VJ]

Valerie Jarrett [VJ] was born in Shiraz/Iran and served BHO as his White House most Senior Adviser. As the Italians call the Capo's top counselor—aka the Consigliere.

Jarrett was the sole gatekeeper of the Oval Office and was the "fixer" to many of the Obama era scandals. Valerie was the hand that gave, or slapped back.

Post Q #1887 on 8/15/18 (In part):
What is VJ's background?
Muslim by faith?

Roseanne Barr refocused the public's attention upon Valerie Jarrett, a past key figure from the Obama era. Without dispute, all major decisions coming from the Obama White House, were run by and approved by VJ.

Post Q #1947 on 8/28/18 (in part):

Who is Valerie Jarrett?
Where was she born?

Jarrett continues in her predominant overseer/gatekeeper role, as she has moved into the Obama's new DC mansion. The command post for the Progressive Leftists "resistance."

Post Q #1235 on 4/22/18 (in part):

Don't forget about Huma.
AWAN.
VJ.

VJ's fingerprints and stench are all over the below infamous BHO scandals:
- Fast and Furious (AG Holder lying)
- Libya/Benghazi Stand-Down Order
- Journalists Files/Computers Seized
- Secret Service-Prostitution Deal
- Edward Snowden NSA Leaks
- BHO's "Sniffer" Routing Military
- Excessive Drone Strikes/Kills
- HRC Email/Server Handling
- Tarmac Meeting Coverup

In recent times, VJ has taken to the MSM to pronounce that BHO had no real scandals during his 8-year term. As the ObamaGate/SpyGate scandals unfold, VJ may need to revisit that statement.

Post Q #1828 on 8/9/18 (in part):

[SPY OP].
[WH] [Hussein] [VJ] [DM] [JB] [RE].

Jarrett comes from a family of hard left communist sympathizers. Her father-on-law was activist-author Vernon Jordan. "Q" mentioned Valerie (VJ) early on.

Post Q #50 on 11/2/17:

Where is BO today?
Where is VJ ?
Alice and Wonderland.

Yes, it does seem that they all had secret email accounts. Additionally, Gmail "ghost draft" emails were utilized with the blessing of BHO.

Post Q #559 on 1/19/18 (in part):

Who used private email addresses?

VJ.

Jarrett is credited with spearheading the Muslim Communist infiltration within the USA. VJ will be back in the news with the upcoming release of OIG Horowitz's second report.

[VJ] will be shown in this exposure as having a key central role in ObamaGate/SpyGate!!! It is bad enough when we had to battle one Jarrett, but this crowd is steeped in nepotism and VJ's daughter was implanted at CNN.

Post Q #1828 on 8/9/18 (in part):

[SPY OP].

[WH [HUSSEIN] [VJ] [DM] [JB] [RE] [[JK]]].

Laura Jarrett (no real journalistic background) was the Justice Department correspondent at CNN, at the time the network was helping to set up Trump with the phony Dossier and "Russian Delusion" narrative.

Post Q #669 on 2/15/18 (in part):

VJ phone call w/AS.

Make no mistake, Valerie Jarrett is still Obama's "Tip of the Resistance Spear" and the final say in the most important matters-The "Consigliere."

REFERENCES:

LifeZette – "Jarrett Must Explain Her Clinton Foundation Coverups"
Breitbart – "Valerie Jarrett, Chicago, and Iran Deal"
The Washington Times - BHO Scandals Overlooked by VJ
Fox News – "Valerie Jarrett Moves In With Obama"
FRONTPAGE MAG – "Communist Family Tree of Valerie Jarrett"
Fox News – "Jarrett's Rumored Role in Iran Deal"
Judicial Watch – "FBI Files on Communist Jarrett Family"
Rush Limbaugh – "Did Jarrett give Benghazi Stand Down Order"
Breitbart – "Roseanne Apologizing to Valerie Jarrett Over 'Planet of the Apes'"
American Thinker – "Valerie Jarret's CNN Daughter Useful Tool"

NOTE BELOW: "Pure_Feature" Extra Answers:

CNN Profiles - Laura Jarrett - Reporter - CNN - CNN.com[40] Laura Jarrett joined CNN in September 2016 as a reporter based in the Washington, D.C. bureau.

Valerie Jarrett, Wikipedia[41] Born..Valerie June Bowman ..November 14, 1956 (age 61) Shiraz, Iran . As a child, Jarrett spoke Persian, French, and English. In 1966, her mother was one of four child advocates who created the Erikson Institute. She graduated from Northfield Mount Hermon in 1974, and earned a B.A. in psychology from Stanford University in 1978 and a Juris Doctor (J.D.) from the University of Michigan Law School in

1981 On May 21, 2016, Jarrett received the honorary degree of Doctor of Laws from Colby College in Waterville, Maine. Her parents are both of European and African-American descent.

Hillary Clinton email controversy - Wikipedia[42] The Hillary Clinton email controversy was a major public controversy arising from the use by Hillary Clinton of her family's private email server for an investigation regarding the origin and handling of classified emails on Clinton's server.

About the Authors

Captain Roy D

Proud Father of 2 Great Boys and a Granddaughter who I fight for
Live on my boat in Florida
I am very much single & looking
Retired from Travel Industry
Jog daily & enjoy music/concerts
http://www.reddit.com/user/CaptainRoyD ("follow" for new posts)
DustinNemos.com / Forum Posts Section (new articles here first)
Captainroydavis@gmail.com (welcome reader questions)

Pure_Feature

I'm an older woman who lives with her two cats and a dog.
And love children, a common everyday woman so nothing special.
Ik ben een oudere vrouw, die leeft met haar twee katten en een hondje.
En houd van dinderen, een gewone alledaagse vrouw dus niks byzoners.
(Pure Feature's bio in her native Dutch language.)

---

[1] *https://en.wikipedia.org/wiki/Michael_S._Rogers*

[2] https://theconservativetreehouse.com, *5 Jan. 2018*

[3] https://themarketswork.com, *5 May, 2018*

[4] *https://en.wikipedia.org/wiki/Michael_Flynn*

[5] *https://en.wikipedia.org/wiki/Ezra_Cohen-Watnick*

[6] https://www.cosmopolitan.com, *1 Dec. 2017*

[7] *https://washingtonpost.com*

[8] *https://247sports.com*

[9] *http://www.foxnews.com, 15 Jun, 2018*

[10] *https://www.reuters.com, Jun. 20, 2013*

[11] *https://en.wikipedia.org/.../Foreign_Intelligence_Surveillance_Act*

[12] *https://theconservativetreehouse.com, 4 Jan, 2018*

[13] *https://247sports.com*

[14] *https://thehill.com, 6 Apr, 2018*

[15] *https://twatter.com/*

[16] *https://www.intouchweekly.com/, Oct. 10, 2018*

[17] *https://thefreethoughtproject.com*

[18] *https://www.cnn.com/ Sept, 25 2018*

[19] *https://thehill.com/ May 14, 2018*

[20] *https://www.emptywheel.net/ May 15, 2018*

[21] *https://en.wikipedia.org/wiki/Sally_Yates*

[22] *https://abcnews.go.com*

[23] *https://www.realclearinvestigations.com/ June 25, 2018*

[24] *https://dailycaller.com, Mar. 25, 2018*

[25] *https://www.westernjournal.com, May 21, 2018*

[26] *https://news.clearancejobs.com, Aug. 29, 2018*

[27] *https://news.clearancejobs.com/*

[28] *https://www.businessinsider.com, Feb. 12, 2018*

[29] *https://www.mondialisation.ca/...clinton-crime-family.../5527943*

[30] *https://theconservativetreehouse.com Apr. 22, 2018*

[31] *https://www.sott.net/, Mar. 3, 2018*

[32] *https://247sports.com/.../ClintonLynch-Tarmac-Tape-54584393/*

[33] *https://abcnews.go.com/Politics/video-appears-show.../story?id...*

[34] *https://www.washingtonexaminer.com/ Aug. 7, 2017*

[35] *https://medium.com/ Oct. 19, 2017*

[36] *https://godfatherpolitics.com/why-isnt-the-fbi-investigating-george*

[37] *https://en.wikipedia.org/wiki/Open_Society_Foundations*

[38] *https://spectator.org/nellie-ohr-woman-in-the-middle/ 22 Feb. 2018*

[39] *https://en.wikipedia.org/wiki/Bruce_Ohr*

[40] *https://www.cnn.com/profiles/laura-jarrett*

[41] *https://en.wikipedia.org/wiki/Valerie_Jarrett*

[42] *https://en.wikipedia.org/wiki/Hillary_Clinton_email_controversy*

"The Plan" is not only well thought out, it is often astonishingly complex. Like a game of chess, each move, each Tweet is significant. Every communication is understood to have at least two audiences at war with one another: the Anons and the Deep State. So, what a normie assumes is a typo or woeful ignorance, may in fact be intentional. QAnon writes in coded messages to avoid violating national security laws. We must tiptoe through several levels of meaning and disinformation intended for Deep State consumption. We bring all we can to the task and consider the possibilities carefully. Some aspects of the plan require an in-depth knowledge of the intricacies and timing of government policies and Constitutional law. As Anons, we work collectively, doing research and teaching, each contributing what we can according to our skills and interests. Here is a good example of that. It is almost certain to give you another way to seeing things—very different from the narrative the mainstream media spoon feeds its audience, although only time will tell if the conclusions being drawn are accurate.

Schumer's Shutdown

by ZackoDaFracko

Okay guys, time to continue expanding our thinking. Q is directing the shutdown movie. What if the Dec. 21, 2018 government shutdown was always necessary and part of the plan, a plan so genius that even those that are awake are astonished by its elegance timing and hubris. The shut down exactly one year after the Dec. 21, 2017 Executive Order that changed everything, exactly ten days (Get it? Ten, ten days of darkness maybe?) exactly 10 days before the March 1, 2018 Executive Order for military tribunals started officially on 1/2/2019.

Chuck Schumer and Nancy Pelosi

It's looking more and more like like they're part of the plan and that they're working with Q Team. Chuck and Nancy acting for their lives—remember, and one of the Q posts says what makes a good movie good? Answer: good actors.

Trump owns these two traitors and he has for at least a year. Do you believe these two seasoned operatives would be naive enough to fall for a trap like the live meeting last week? Or the Dems Kavanagh chaos? We're giving Trump tax cuts? Or giving the DoD the largest budget in history through 2019? Or saying stupid, hypocritical remarks knowing they would be exposed? If they both play their roles exactly as suggested can they avoid the death penalty? Of course, they are being threatened by quote "them" too. Sophie's Choice

So the benefits of the shutdown are:

1. Trump gets military to build the border wall
2. Trump gets recess appointments
3. Trump gets DC cleared out for office raids
4. Trump gets pretext for temporary martial law
5. Trump gets window for Congress arrests

What is a Pro Forma Session?

A Pro Forma Session is when just one or two members of the Senate get together for a few minutes on a single day to act like the Senate was in session that day. No actual business is conducted. McConnell runs the schedule.

Article I, Section 5 of the Constitution

The legal purpose of each Pro Forma Session is to meet the requirements of Article I, Section 5 of the Constitution which prohibits either Chamber of Congress from adjourning for more than three consecutive days without the consent of the other Chamber. The practical purpose of a Pro Forma Session is to stop the President from making "recess appointments" to positions requiring Senate approval (like the Supreme Court) while the Senate is in recess. Pro Forma Sessions keep the Senate in a perpetual state of being "in session" which blocks the President.

What is a Recess Appointment?

A Recess Appointment is when the President makes a temporary appoint-ment. They would normally require advance Senate approval but since the Senate is in recess the President is allowed to offer a temporary Commission. Any Recess Appointment by the President will last until the end of the next full annual session of the Senate, usually about a year, then the Senate can finally vote to confirm or reject the temporary Commission.

Article II, Section 2 of the Constitution

The legal basis of a Recess Appointment is granted to the President and Article II, Section 2 of the Constitution which says the President shall have the power to fill up all vacancies that may happen during the recess of the Senate by granting Commissions which shall expire at the end of their next session. The practical purpose of a Recess Appointment is to allow the President to make temporary appointments when the Senate is in recess to keep them from constantly blocking his nominations.

Obama's Illegal Recess Appointments

On January 4, 2012, Obama made several Recess Appointments even though the Senate was in a Pro Forma Session. On January 6, 2012, Obama had his crooked DOJ issue an opinion that Recess Appointments were allowed during Pro Forma Sessions claiming that these type of sessions were not legitimate and therefore Obama could make all the temporary recess appointments he wanted during those times. And that's what Holder did this entire time in Obama's DOJ. They just snap their fingers and said okay we're going to say this is illegal or this is legal and they would just do it.

NLRB National Labor Relations Board vs. Noel Canning

ON June 26, 2014, in a stunning 9 to 0 ruling against Obama the Supreme Court ruled that Obama DID NOT have the right to treat Pro Forma Sessions as invalid and therefore a President cannot make temporary recess appointments during Pro Forma Sessions. The reason for this ruling was to keep the separation between the Executive Branch, Judicial Branch and Legislative Branch in check. Sadly, all five of Obama's invalid commissions ended up getting converted to a full legitimate commissions by the Senate at a later date.

Why Does This Case Matter?

The ruling by the Supreme Court was a unanimous 9-0 decision which is fairly rare in its own right. However, the Judicial Branch felt strongly that the Executive Branch was overstepping its separation of powers and as a result, it was overturned. More importantly, it made it impossible for a President to make a recess appointment unless the Senate was truly in recess. (Was this a reason to 187 AS?)

Pro Forma Sessions Are Not a Recess

The case allowed the Senate to continue its longtime practice of holding Pro Forma Sessions on off days to ensure that a President would NEVER have a window to make a Recess Appointment. As a result, a President would be forced to either get the Congress to agree to ADJOURN or FORCE IT TO ADJOURN through Article II, Section 3 of the Constitution.

Can a President Adjourned Congress?

Check this out guys. This is brilliant. Yes, absolutely. The President can Adjourn or Convene one or both Houses of Congress on extraordinary occasions at any time.

Article II, Section 3 of the Constitution

The legal basis of a Presidential Adjournment is granted to the President in Article II, Section 3 of the Constitution, which says the President shall have the power on EXTRAORDINARY OCCASIONS to convene both houses or either of them and in a case of disagreement between them, with respect to the time of Adjournment, he may adjourn them to such time as he shall think proper, not to exceed the remaining time in the current session. The practical purpose of an Adjournment is simple. The President can force a legal RECESS of the Senate to provide him a window to make a series of temporary Recess Appointments that have been blocked by the Senate for too long.

What is an Extraordinary Occasion?

The President must be aware of the optics for an adjourning Congress. If the government was already "shutdown" during a Senate Recess, the optics of an official Presidential Adjournment would be no problem to pull off. What would constitute an extraordinary occasion? How about D5? How about [DECLAS]?

Best Time for an Adjournment?

The 115th Congress session expires at the end of 2018. The 116th Congress gets sworn in on January 3, 2019. Trump will have no better time then right before December 31, 2018 for an official adjournment. Why? Think Paul Ryan's last day. Remember Q post 1483.

> **Q1468**
>
> **WHY IS RYAN STILL IN OFFICE?**
> **WHY IS RYAN LEAVING OFFICE?**
> **WHO CONTROLS RYAN?**
> **Q**

Oh my gosh guys! We have never seen anything like this in our lives.

What is Needed to Adjourn?

Based on Article II, Section 3, Trump would need a simple disagreement about the timing of any recess exceeding three days between the House speaker which is Paul Ryan [now Nancy Pelosi] and the Senate Majority Leader (Mitch McConnell) to step in and legally Adjourn the Senate. And once the Senate is adjourned, Trump would be able to make all his Recess Appointments including Supreme Court picks for any vacancies. and those temporary commissions would not expire until the end of 2019.

The Final Act of Paul Ryan

Q tells us in post #1483 that Paul Ryan has one final act to play before he "retires." Maybe Ryan's final act will be to disagree on recess timing with McConnell for more than three days to provide Trump with the legal option of adjourning in the Senate to get all his nominations temporarily approved before year-end. Then again, the lower House is in charge of impeachment proceedings. Ryan may also call for a vote of impeachment on certain corrupt politicians that were shown to have conspired to frame Trump for Russia collusion. This might also include current Supreme Court Justices like John Roberts (FISA abuse) Ruth Bader Ginsburg (tarmac abuse} and other senior officials.

Justice Roberts and Ruth Bader Ginsburg

John Roberts, Chief Justice of the Supreme Court, appointed every single FISA Judge. When [DECLAS] happens, Roberts will not be able to survive the truth. Additionally, many believe he was comped long ago, perhaps because of closeted homosexuality.

We knew he was comped the minute he redefined the Obamacare mandate as a tax. He did Obama's arguing for him. Obamacare should have been deemed unconstitutional, but Roberts stepped in and said ho we'll call this a tax and make it legal

Ruth Bader Ginsburg has a long history with a Anons and she appears to be very ill. She probably has the same disease that sadly killed McCain. Either way she will retire very soon and Ruth Bader Ginsburg doesn't believe in our Constitution. She told the Egyptians if you're going to form your Constitution definitely don't use the American Constitution as a template. Coming from a Supreme Court Justice... Unbelievable!

60% of Senate Quorum Votes Needed

The Senate requires a [Q]uorum of 51% of Senators present to hold any vote. Many votes like impeachment require 60% votes to pass. When all 100 Senators are in attendance, that means 60 votes. However, if say only 88 were in attendance because of 12 arrests, then a 60% vote would only need 53 votes. [53 to 47 BOOM]. That's the Senate count right now.

Anonymous
Think logically.
Government shutdown helps Trump
America is waking up and wondering...
Why give $38 billion dollars to Israel to build their wall?
But not give $5 billion dollars to USA to build our wall?
Shut down gives Trump five things. We went through those five things.
Shut down gives Dems nothing good, so ask yourself:
Why didn't they fund the wall? Because Chuck and Nancy are "hostages?"
Are they doing exactly as instructed by Q to avoid death penalty?

About the Author

ZackoDaFracko

These are exciting times to be awake! We are watching the systematic destruction of the old guard. But since many are still deceived by MSM propaganda I decided to create a YouTube channel (ZakoDaFracko) to share my journey of eye-opening discovery while wading through these Q Anon clues. One example is this Schumer's Shutdown work from the Anons on 8Chan.

YouTube did many things to discourage my distribution which I will not mention here in fears that they will shut my current channel down. They have God-like power to hinder us the minute we start reaching the masses with the information they want kept hidden. It only makes me more determined to disseminate it.

Shout out to my sister lovelexxxx who helps me dig for information in solving the Q puzzles. Together we are fighting the battles of disinformation and censorship. The World is waking up. And nothing YouTube and Mockingbird Media does can stop it now. Nothing!

Learning the truth can be a painful process, especially when it has been hidden from you your whole life. If the world you thought you were living in proves to be based on deception, the truth can seem unbelievable, bizarre. It is made even worse, when it involves people you respected, leaders you voted for, people you trusted. At first there is disbelieve, then disorientation, then outrage over the betrayal, combined perhaps with fear and then sadness, etc. Each person has their own process of waking and goes at their own pace. But coming to terms with unwanted truth is part of the process of awakening and it is often the shocking and emotionally difficult part. However, on the other side of this process of "awakening" is a stable foundation where we will rapidly rebuild a new, safer, more prosperous and more peaceful reality for ourselves, our children and yes, even the greater world.

The Election of a Lifetime

by Linda Paris

When Has There Ever Been Anything Like the 2016 Presidential Election?

I worked at CNN for 17 years, left in 2000, and worked for every major network afterwards, as a freelancer, or as an employee. I've seen my fair share of elections, up close and personal, and I've never seen anything, even remotely, like this. This was more than an election. It was a great awakening.

In the beginning, I'll admit, that as the implications of what was happening became clear, I got, scared. By this time, lots of people had been red-pilled by Obama's anti-American language and his free and easy use of executive orders, not to mention his penchant for shredding the Constitution. In spite of the red flags, Barry's we-hate-America, administration, and the dismantling of the United States, continued full steam ahead. Many of my (self-described liberal) Facebook friends, were talking about the "great job" Obama was doing, and what a lovely "woman" The First Lady was. At the time Joan Rivers was announcing to the world, that Obama was gay, Michelle was a tranny, and everyone knew it.

How could I have known that my former-friends, had been physically assaulted by the food industry, while being systematically brainwashed by the television set?

Barry's habit of consistently announcing his plans to turn the United States of America into the "largest Muslim nation in the world," should have raised major concerns, yet there was nothing.

Radio Silence

I noticed this happening, but didn't realize the extent of it, until I watched a video on YouTube one day, where the producer had edited together all of the instances, when Obama announced in his speeches, what his plans were for America. Over and over he said; he was going to turn the USA into the largest Muslim nation in the world.

The infiltration of the Muslim brotherhood into government positions (along with the threat of ISIS and the growing number of Mosques sprouting up across the country) was cause for growing concern, but still, there was no public outcry.

Now I was beginning to wake up. Something was wrong. What the hell was going on?

When the accusations came spewing out of every major network, that Donald Trump was a racist, even though he had never been accused of committing a "racist" act in his life, my alarm system came on.

The mindless cries of "racist and Nazi" persisted, in spite of the fact that a minimal amount of research would have debunked the mainstream media's false narrative. Having worked in the broadcast industry for decades, I found their behavior horrifying. I'd never seen anything like this, and had watched people's careers implode over false reporting. Add this new twist to all of the other scary things that were taking place, and I sensed a disaster of Biblical proportions lay ahead if something wasn't done soon.

The "neo-liberals" (who were technically socialists) chanted character slurs over and over again, offering nothing but fake news propaganda to support their claims. People I'd known for decades, and who I considered to be kind people, were suddenly foaming at the mouth with hatred for Donald Trump, and anyone who dared to say they supported him.

What the hell?

What Happened to Truth and Honor?

The mass importation of un-vetted refugees, threatened to bring the war in the Middle East right into our backyards, along with disease, financial burdens, massive crime, and violence like we've never seen before. Reports from Germany and other parts of Europe confirmed, that the refugees were not fitting in, and people were dying as a result. Videos appeared on YouTube, produced by Europeans, and uploaded, as a dire warning to Americans; don't let this happen in America!

Videos and photographs were popping up on the Internet, depicting swarms of, mostly young, men with cell phones, storming across the countryside in endless streams, hundreds upon hundreds of them, with no final destination.

The refugees burst into farmhouses, and took what they wanted. The European countryside, once picturesque and pristine, was left littered with corpses. The people who had invited these refugees into their towns, now lay dead, covered in dirt and surrounded by trash, as the refugees took control of their property and possessions.

This was everyone's worst nightmare, and it was headed directly towards the United States.

Still, the leftist (socialist) community screamed hateful rhetoric at Donald Trump and his supporters, calling us Nazis, white trash and racists. They repeated these insults over and over again, denying patriots the right to respond.

What the hell was the matter with these people? Why couldn't they see the danger?

The revelation of Fema Camps (complete with guillotines) was the point of no return for me. Sleep was non-existent and I had frequent nightmares: Women, chained together, shrouded in black from head to toe, faces covered, all of them being led through the streets of my town, the black-clad men controlling them, waved giant knives in the air, while other men ran into homes and grabbed women and children, dragging them out of their homes.

I couldn't sleep, and I started actively planning to sell my house should Hillary Clinton get "elected," and I wasn't alone.

By staying connected online, and exploring chat rooms and discussion boards, I discovered a large cross-segment of the population, who were feeling the same way that I was.

Simultaneously, we were all coming to the realization that there was no place to go. We were not going to be able to avoid this insanity, because all the major news networks were suppressing this story.

The fact that this invasion was already underway, all over the world, only added to everyone's resolve. As it turned out, ironically, the only countries who were not accepting the refugees were China, Iraq and Saudi Arabia.

We were trapped.

Where Are All the Patriots?

The biggest question I had was this: Where are all the patriots? Are there no patriots? What happened to the people who's job it was to stop this from ever happening? Did no one even try to stop it? Does no one care about the country anymore? I simply could not wrap my brain around this.

I've always been an Independent and never joined one political party or the other. I considered myself a liberal-minded, live-and-let-live kind of person.

When President Trump came down those stairs, with beautiful Melania by his side, and announced that he was going to "build a wall," I was very excited by what he was saying. A wall was exactly what we needed and I assumed everyone could see this basic truth: We needed a border. We need a wall. I thought it was a great idea.

I was wrong if I thought any of my liberal friends would agree with me. They wanted Hillary to win because she was a woman. They stated that emphatically. It seemed that I was the problem for suggesting that people needed to enter our country legally, instead of sneaking in illegally and selling drugs or living off of our system.

The Great Awakening was on. People who had been calling themselves "liberal" began to walk away from the madness and support the wall. They had done their research and realized that, in reality, Donald Trump wasn't anything like a "racist," and that he had some great ideas on fixing the economy and ending corruption, thereby making positive changes for all Americans.

Those of us who experienced this pivotal moment in history will never forget it. There was a revolution in the works.

FBI Anon—MEGA Anon—Q Anon

It started as a little blip on my computer screen. I'd taken to lurking on esoteric chat boards and researching clues as to what what could be happening and why. One day I noticed that someone had been posting comments on one of the Reddit forums, claiming to be an FBI Agent currently on leave, but still working for the FBI. This person wanted to share information with Patriots about the true nature of what was happening behind the scenes.

Their screen name was "FBI Anon."

FBI Anon sounded authentic to me, and I wrote an article stating as much on my blog. In that article, I listed all of the reasons that I believed the FBI Anon was real. Many other posters felt the same way, and began to explore the authenticity of FBI Anon, by asking questions in an open format called an AMA (ask me anything The FBI Anon held sessions that lasted well into the night.

Question 4_087: "Funny How Scalia and Thomas were the only ones to dissent on the ruling against human trafficking. Maybe he really was murdered for being too biased."

FBI ANON: "Scalia was murdered for something much more sinister."

Question 1_030: "How do we fix this? And by we I mean you guys lmao"

FBI Anon: "We have our hands tied. My message to you on this board is do not get distracted by Clinton's emails. Focus on the Foundation. All of the nightmarish truth is there. The emails will pale in comparison."

Question 1_068: Q: "What did the Foundation do? Please elaborate."

FBI Anon: "Sold influence, intel, favors, and people to anyone who would pay."

"Follow the Foundation" appeared to be FBI Anon's main message, but he also wanted to warn us, not to be distracted by the mainstream media. The word "nightmarish" was an indication that the things we were going to learn would shock us.

By this time, in retrospect, most Americans realized that if Donald Trump did not win this election, it would be the end of America.

Although the Fake News Media had presented fraudulent poll results every chance they got, no one was buying it. We were all watching the rallies, and there was no way to reconcile those rallies with the phony poll numbers that the now notorious Fake News was passing off as real.

I had grown to love and respect Donald Trump, with every passing day, because the magnitude of the sacrifice he made had become clear by now. The vicious verbal beatings that he endured, from the lying mainstream media, had reached a fever pitch. We were literally trapped in a snake pit, with no way out, and it was Donald Trump who had come along and offered us a stick.

The rallies were inspirational, and, since I had cancelled my cable by this time, I looked forward to every single one of them. His first rallies were different, in the sense that I remember him dropping some massive breadcrumbs earlier in the campaign, such as this:

"These are REALLY BAD people folks! Really, really, really bad people."

and this:

"This is some wild stuff Folks! These are bad people. This stuff is way out there!"

As campaign managers and others on his team, came and went, his rhetoric toned down on these particular matters, and he focused more on practical issues, such as jobs and "the wall."

Trump stopped talking about the "really, really bad people," and the "wild, crazy stuff," probably because someone told him: "Don't go there right now."

His language indicated that these criminals were much worse than then we knew.

Enter Wikileaks

Once Julian Assange, who is a hero in this information war, released the Clinton and Podesta emails, the public got their first glimpse into the depraved nature of these government officials. The emails exposed a world wide criminal enterprise, so profoundly corrupt, that the emails themselves would change the course of history.

Once the code was broken, the contents of the emails exploded across the Internet.

According to a document released by the FBI, a decade earlier, it was a secret pedophile code, used by pedophiles when discussing sex with children. There were references to torture chambers, cheese, pizza, walnuts, sauce, square-shaped boxes, dominos and other mysterious lingo that seemed to be connected to the occult.

As time wore on FBI Anon continued to drop valuable clues, and when the clues were researched, they shed more light on these revolting activities. FBI Anon would point people in the right direction, and researchers would dig and find more information.

FBI Anon disappeared for a while, and another anonymous poster appeared on the boards in his place. This time it was a female, and she called herself "Mega Anon."

More information was shared. More clues were dropped. More research was done, and more horrors were exposed.

All of the information shared by FBI Anon and Mega Anon, was followed up on by regular Anons who, not only verified the authenticity of what was being posted, but took it further, discovering new facts and information along the way, opening up rabbit holes for other posters to pursue.

Facebook was openly censoring Trump supporters, under the guise of calling it "hate speech." As incredible as it still seems, many people were so brainwashed, that they were agreeing with the censorship!

This was a new definition for the word "liberal." As a result, more people woke up and even more walked away from the madness. People were opening their eyes, but an alarming segment of the population was still asleep.

Fast Forward to QAnon

For those who don't know, "Q" represents the highest level of government security clearance. I was unaware of the new Q-Level anonymous poster, until a few weeks after they started posting. (I say "they" because I now believe it is a group of people.) I was excited about this new Anon, because I had followed FBI Anon and Mega Anon, and we were all hungry for more truth.

QAnon had taken a more dramatic approach, and released a time stamped photo of North Korea, taken from what appeared to be Air Force One. It would later be determined that the photo was taken at the time Air Force One would have been passing over North Korea, and it was taken by someone flying that exact route.

Now who, with top level clearance, could be on Air Force One, flying over North Korea, on the same route, at the same time, that Air Force One was actually flying over that spot, with the President of the United States on board?

Who could it be?

That was good enough for me. It didn't matter who the person was. As far as I was concerned, they were allowed on Air Force One. You had to have been physically on that plane, to take that photo. Future drops would contain more clues, as to the true identity of Q Anon.

The undeniable proofs kept coming.

Massive Corruption

The information was beginning to flow, and what was at first perceived as a small group of "elites," began, with research, to evolve into an massive network of treason and corruption, at the very highest levels. A huge web of deceit had been constructed by the central bankers, and as a direct result of a centuries-old cabal.

Out of chaos comes order. The plot began to take shape.

This was a coup, brought about by big business and government, using the media to brainwash the masses, in an attempt to achieve world domination. This was going to be their New World Order.

The "New World Order," consisting of both government and big business, had infiltrated systems all over the world. So depraved, were these people, that none of us could envision it. Most of us had been thrown together politically because we were not brainwashed by the Fake News, and we could clearly see that something terrible was happening. We found each other in chat rooms, truth blogs and on YouTube. We raised our voices above the Fake Media and the brainwashed masses, and we told anyone who would listen what we had learned. Truthers began sharing the knowledge, and bolstering each other's convictions.

We began to listen to the victims, who no one believed, when they tried to tell us what was happening throughout the years. It looked as if every "conspiracy theorist" out there, had been right all along. How could we have known? This was so far off the range of human decency; how could we know what we can't even imagine? How could we have anticipated the answers that were yet to come? And indeed, are still being exposed to this day?

Secret Societies

It didn't take long to figure out that much of what was happening was directly related to the Freemasons, or the Illuminati (as they had come to be called).

As it turns out, the Illuminati was formed in 1776, by a sketchy character named Adam Weishaupt. Whether Weishaupt actually existed or not is subject to argument, but suffice it to say the illusion of such a person was effective in gathering the heads of the many "Illuminated" Secret Societies, all under one pyramid-shaped roof.

This, they had decided decades, perhaps centuries earlier, was the logical course of direction for them to take, in order to achieve a one world government.

You might ask: How is this possible?

You see, these upper-tiered "lodge members" were not strangers, in the strict sense of the word.

They were the heirs to a secret world. Their parental figures had passed a daunting torch down to each one of them. Their mission was a mystical one. They had dedicated their lives to finding each other and continuing a plan that was hatched long before any of them had been born.

They were charged with finding each other, throughout every generation, spanning over decades, for the purpose of carrying forth this legacy. It was for that reason that the illuminati had been formed, no other.

The "secret ceremonies" and the various "Degrees" of Masonry, the levels of "enlightenment", the oaths of loyalty, the building of a successful network of businessmen, the blackmail and rituals, were simply a way to weed out "the sheep", and remain hidden.

These bloodlines needed a way to connect, because their entire existence, from beginning to end, was dedicated to achieving this centuries-old vision. It was the vision of their fathers, and their fathers before them.

They Called It "The Great Work."

The "Great Work" was re-named "The New World Order," by George Bush Sr. and the "brainwashed sheep" (ie: their name for society in general) would learn of it's existence, through both old and new methods of subliminal control.

These bloodlines use symbols, iconography, science and technology to achieve their goals. The plotters, who are almost all related through blood, hijacked theatre, music, art, food, science, literature, farming, religion, romance, and just about every worthwhile human endeavor, and transformed these things into weapons.

These powerful, yet seemingly innocent past-times, were used against the uninitiated, not just in America but worldwide.

These "elite bloodlines" were able to achieve this level of success through multi-generational mind control. Without it, their plan would have ceased to exist long ago.

You might ask: Why they would do this?

The answer is complex, and at the same time, simple.

They do it because it is their religion. They do it because they hate God. They do it because they believe that Saturn, the Sun, the Light, is the real God, and that God himself, is a fraud.

The TV Guide version goes like this:

"In a world full of exciting things to do, Satan, the hero of the show, tries to teach people how to have an incredible life and experience everything the world has to offer, meanwhile…

God is colluding with Jesus and won't let anyone have any fun at all, because he's afraid people will learn his 'secrets' and take his job."

These people believe that Lucifer is the one true God, and they despise Jesus Christ and the God of the Bible. Their religion requires that they maintain control over the earth, for their "father" who is Satan. They raise their children according to the ancient Babylonian Mystery Schools, which teaches the secrets of mind control. From the moment they are born, and even in the womb, they are programmed to be a part of "The Great Work."

To ensure that these children continue to improve on, and carry out this plan, their parental figures (because most of these people are bred, not conceived) begin implementing torture and brainwashing techniques, on their own children, as infants.

These families (the 13 Illuminati bloodlines) control their offspring from the grave. They are like Terminators. They will not stop. This is their only reason for existing.

Nazis in Antarctica

When George Bush Sr. gave his "New World Order" speech, people couldn't help but notice that it sounded an awfully lot like the Nazi's plan for world domination, coincidentally called "The New Order." As it turns out, that was no fluke.

Perhaps the most fascinating question of all, is the mystery surrounding Antarctica.

In 1945, after the war, the United States allowed thousands of Nazi Germany's worst criminal scientists into this country, and as insane as it sounds, they gave some of them government positions. Many of these men, were the same monsters who used human beings as guinea pigs, and committed untold atrocities, and yet ended up working for the CIA. You can do your own research Operation Paperclip. [1] [2] [3] [4]

Here's the rub: It seems that all of the German Scientists who ended up in the United States were members of the Illuminati, or some other equally prestigious secret society, and through their American Illuminati counterparts, such as Allen Dulles, and just about every US President ever elected, these men eventually ended up working for the Military and the CIA.

This was always about "The Great Work," and never about America. [5]

The official reason given, for allowing these war criminals to be given sanctuary in the USA, was that they needed "protection," and that many had advanced scientific knowledge that could now be used for America.

The real reason these men were, not only allowed to come here but eventually ended up working for the CIA, is more sinister. On December 13, 1944, in the Moberly Monitor-Index, an item appeared, as a small blurb on the front page, and it read as follows:

"NEW NAZI DEVICE ON WESTERN FRONT"

"As the allied armies ground out new gains on the Western front today, the Germans were disclosed to have thrown a new "device" into the war—mysterious silvery balls which floated in the air. Pilots reported seeing these objects individually and in clusters, during forays over the Reich. (The purpose of the

floaters was not immediately evident. It is possible that they represent a new anti-aircraft device or weapon.)"

As a footnote at the end of the sparse article, there was this:

"This dispatch was heavily censored at Supreme Headquarters."

These mysterious orbs would come to be known as "Foo Fighters." The uncensored version of the encounter, however, was considerably more fantastic and deadly. There were first-hand accounts stating that a lazar beam shot out from the orbs, and these beams were capable of demolishing anything they came into contact with.

Near the end of the war, German officials were interviewed for South American news publications, and they were telling the media that they had prepared a place, described as a "Shangri-La," for "The Fuhrer," where he would be well protected from any attempts on his life. Since the Nazi's had been spending unusual amounts of time in Antarctica, and the existence of underground bases had been established, the United States sent Admiral Richard Byrd to the South Pole, in 1945, to round up any German soldiers who might still be there. Byrd was also ordered to take control of any underground bases they found.

Byrd's mission was shrouded in mystery from the beginning, and presented to the public as a "scientific" expedition. However, the "4000-man naval expedition," reportedly included a war fleet, complete with aircraft carriers, destroyers and attack submarines. According to many of the military men, who were there at the time, the assignment was to seize the Nazi bases in Antarctica, and bring any prisoners back to America.

What happened after that is up for grabs, depending on who you ask, and indeed, by all accounts, something terrible occurred. Surviving soldiers described the situation, as they approached Antarctica:

Several large, disc-shaped aircraft, suddenly emerged from under the water, and then, just as suddenly, they dropped back down into the sea, only to come shooting back up again. These flying discs repeated this maneuver again and again, agitating the waters to such a degree, that the huge war ships began to crash into each other, and sink, with military men on board.

The saucer-shaped objects also, reportedly, shot beams, similar to that of the Foo Fighters, causing even more casualties.

The Byrd Expedition

CONSIDERABLE MYSTERY is attached to the 4000-man naval expedition to Antartica under Admiral Byrd.

The admiral denies that the primary objective of the expedition is to search for uranium, the most important ingredient of the atom bomb, although three hundred scientists are included in the Byrd party's personnel. The expedition would not, presumably, ignore uranium deposits if some should be uncovered.

The British sent a secret expedition to Antarctica during the war, which has prompted some observers to suspect that there are military possibilities in this area not readily discernible to the layman. The fact that Russia is sending an expedition to the same frozen region has also aroused considerable conjecture.

It is plain to even the casual observer, however, that the mission of the current Byrd expedition involves something more than the mapping of terrain and the tabulation of flora and fauna. It is obvious, too, that all major nations are impressed with the desirability of knowing more about regions such as Antarctica which have undergone only cursory inspection. If any remote region contains deposits of uranium, such deposits are of potential danger to nations unaware of their existence.

Admiral Byrd did the only thing he could do. He retreated.

It is reported, by those who witnessed the attack, that the government went out of it's way to cover up this incident. Many of the survivors, including Admiral Byrd and his son, met mysterious and untimely deaths. Byrd's son, who accompanied Byrd on many of his Arctic trips, died under extremely suspicious circumstances,

Interviews surfaced from South America, where Byrd had stopped to refuel and rest before heading home, in which Byrd stated that if we were to fight the Nazis today…we would be defeated.

In the late 1940s, Secretary of Defense James Forrestal, who had accompanied Byrd on many of his missions, began to talk. According to witnesses at the time, Forrestal was not only talking, to anyone who would listen, about a UFO attack during Operation High Jump, but he also told fantastical stories of underground cities and caverns, located under the ice, in Antarctica.

Forrestal was eventually committed to a room on the 16th floor of Bethesda Naval Hospital, where he would later be found dead, on a third floor roof, clad only in his pajama bottoms. His death would be ruled a suicide.

The mysterious happenings continued, after Admiral Byrd's mission was aborted. Flying discs began to appear, almost immediately, over the US, in great numbers. Admiral Byrd returned from Antarctica on January 31, 1947, and on July 4, that same year, "flying saucers" were seen in ten different states.

The sightings persisted and on April 27, 1949, the Air Force issued a statement saying that the Flying Saucer reports were "no joke."

Then in April of 1952, eighteen flying saucers were spotted over a "Las Vegas atom bomb test area."

After planes were sent out to "check" on the "saucers," on July 4, 1952, there were two episodes that occurred: The week of the 28th, radar picked up four to ten unidentified objects, popping up on the screen around National Airport and Andrews Air Force base. Shortly after that, a large group of these objects flew, slowly and in formation, over the nation's capital. Many people witnessed the entire episode, and some described the event as appearing to be "a show of force." Coincidentally, the CIA was officially formed in 1947, and by 1952, when the sightings occurred over Washington, DC, most of the Nazi scientists who had entered the United States via Operation Paperclip, were working away, continuing their "research" in underground bases, that coincidentally, were close in proximity, to where most of the sightings occurred.

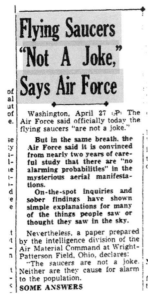

Flying Saucers "Not A Joke," Says Air Force

Washington, April 27 (P) The Air Force said officially today the flying saucers "are not a joke."

But in the same breath, the Air Force said it is convinced from nearly two years of careful study that there are "no alarming probabilities" in the mysterious aerial manifestations.

On-the-spot inquiries and sober findings have shown simple explanations for many of the things people saw or thought they saw in the sky.

Nevertheless, a paper prepared by the intelligence division of the Air Material Command at Wright-Patterson Field, Ohio, declares: "The saucers are not a joke. Neither are they cause for alarm to the population.

SOME ANSWERS

How the Nazis came to be exploring Antarctica in the first place, is one of the most fascinating mysteries in all of this. It became clear to me, and many other people following the clues provided by QAnon, that the Nazis discovered something monumental under the Antarctic ice, even before the war.

The Nazi's were obsessed with the occult, and this is what motivated them to keep making the treacherous journey to the Arctic. They were searching for a lost civilization, frozen underneath the ice, and as evidenced by the orbs that were described in 1944, they had actually found something.

To this day, no one is allowed to travel to Antarctica without authorization, and signs are posted around the perimeter, making it clear that anyone found past a certain point could be blown out of the sky or the water.

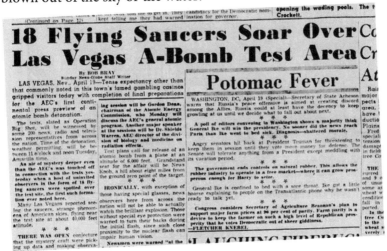

There is something important being hidden from us in Antarctica, and it is only one aspect of our life that they have manipulated, in order to keep the sheep in the dark, and under their control.

185

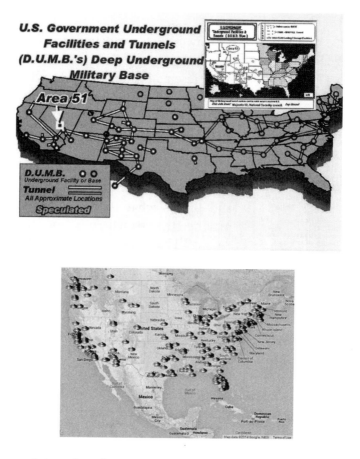

It is my opinion that the creation of the CIA was an intentional step, instigated by the Illuminated ones, towards their final goal of a "New World Order."

The World is Not How You Think It Is

QAnon has told us that the world is not how we think it is and sure enough, with each revelation, each clue, each rabbit hole, we get a further away from the fake reality that was created for us, and a bit closer to the truth.

Everything we thought was real, is fake, and everything we thought was fake, is real.

Although the mainstream media has been exposed as a CIA operation, and the moon landing is looking sketchy, this has got to be the most exciting time, in all of history, to be alive.

The entire world is waking up, and we get to have front row seats. Many of life's mysteries will soon be solved and there are exciting discoveries ahead.

When the 2016 election began, I thought we were all going to die, but after QAnon arrived on the scene, it became the movement of a lifetime, and now, there is only one thing left to do:

Enjoy the show.

About the Author

Linda Paris

https://www.youtube.com/channel/UCQTqnnPetWFbDN1nJ6hq0eg
www.deplorablemcallister.com

---

[1] http://www.thelibertybeacon.com/operation-paperclip-case-file-the-cia-and-the-nazis/

[2] https://wikileaks.org/gifiles/attach/48/48237_Allen%20Welsh%20Dulles,3.pdf

[3] https://www.youtube.com/results?search_query=mae+brussell+antarctica

[4] http://ahrp.org/pivotal-role-of-allen-dulles-in-shielding-nazi-war-criminals

[5] http://www.threeworldwars.com/albert-pike2.htm

187

One of the subjects that Q talks about in many posts is the prevalence of child and human trafficking and other forms of human rights abuse. Whether it is the sexual exploitation by pedophiles, child pornography, ritual abuse, human sacrifices, organ harvesting, and related crimes including kidnapping, slavery, murder and blackmail, the Deep State and many of the power elites in government, Hollywood, leadership in many corporations, the media, religious institutions and even charities are very much involved. QAnon followers are dedicated to the eradication of the exploitation of women and children and under Trump's leadership the number or arrests of criminals involved in these crimes have increased dramatically. It is also anticipated that many of the nearly 80,000 indictments that are currently sealed are for those who are involved in various forms of human rights abuse including the exploitation of children. Q has been willing to put the spotlight on many topics and crimes that the legacy mainstream media ignores, attempts to discredit or even participates in. Sarah Westall's interviews that follows will give you a glimpse into the world of crime that Q persists in revealing. You will also learn that we must work together to end trafficking. It will not end without us. The police can't do it without us.

Human Compromise: The Currency of the Powerful

by Sarah Westall

An Interview with Detective "Jimmy Boots" Rothstein

This and the following chapter are show transcripts from interviews I conducted with Detective "Jimmy Boots" Rothstein during the months of November and December 2018. I hope they serve as a learning tool that together we can use to better our country.

Detective Rothstein was given unprecedented free reign and an unlimited budget to figure out how the child and prostitution trafficking networks work in the United States and across the world. His work led directly to the evilest and most brutal practices used by the world's most powerful in politics, religion, and business to control and manipulate their rivals and to maintain control and power. It is the story that reveals why the United States is currently in complete chaos and why, even the most basic problems, have not been solved in our country. Rothstein believes that Trump is currently dismantling this network and soon big announcements will be made that will take down the evilest practices ever to exist in human history.

SW: Welcome to Business Game Changers. I'm Sarah Westall. This episode, we are diving into the way Washington, D.C., and the powerful around the world, politicians and powerful business moguls are controlled and compromised by various power brokers around the world. Many of you may have wondered why a show called Business Game Changers would have started discussing pedophilia and human trafficking, and I will tell you. As a journalist who is trying to understand the edge of change, in today's world, it would be impossible to at some point not run head on into the dark world of human trafficking because this is how the powerful control others, and how they are controlled. It is a currency of the powerful. It is rampant, and it is what is destroying our country.

I had the enormous privilege of interviewing Detective James Rothstein, known in the shadow world and shadow government as Jimmy Boots. His investigations into simple prostitution led him directly into organized human trafficking, including pedophilia, ritual sacrifice, and high level blackmail. He ultimately ended up in the middle of the highest profile cases, and the most powerful power brokers in the world, including the highest levels in Washington, D.C., the Catholic Church, and the United Nations.

SW: I was able to interview him about many topics. This is the first of a series of shows that I will be airing with him. This episode he lays out the groundwork for what he saw, and why it was occurring. He also shares his understanding of Trump, and the results of Trump's actions, and how their systematic breakdown of the human trafficking of children. It is important for everyone to understand that this dark side of our system is destroying our communities, and ultimately, our country. Nothing but the complete dismantling of this evil practice will allow our country to become great again. Now here's my interview with James "Jimmy Boots" Rothstein. Let's start with your background. How did you get started in investigations?

Det. R: How it got started, after I was appointed as a cop, I got assigned to the 16th precinct, which was Times Square in New York, and about a year after I got appointed, we were having problems with prostitutes, and since so many of them were from Minnesota, and especially the area around here, the captain knew I was from

Minnesota and this area. The captain told me, "Why I'm assigning you to locking up for prostitutes, for loitering for prostitution."

SW: Wow, and this activity was in New York?

Det. R: Yeah, New York City, Times Square, and that's how I got into it, and three weeks into it, I realized that everything we thought we knew about prostitution was wrong, and then eventually, shortly thereafter, I saved the life of a girl when the pimps came to kill her, because she wasn't going to work for them. That got me into the really deep stuff, and with it, a couple months later, after I had told them to be careful that the pimps were going to kill a cop, a plainclothesman or something, they killed Anthony, a pimp killed Anthony Campizzi, and that's when the police department realized they had nothing. At that point, I was assigned to going in, and finding out what was really going on.

That's how I got into the real depth of this stuff, and the different investigations. By that time, I had also learned about the pedophile underground, that was used for, and all of this, how it worked into human compromise and human intelligence. It was all organized.

SW: At one point, you were given free reign.

Det. R: Yes. Yes. I got called in one day, and I was told to report to an office, and it was on a third floor of a factory. The funny thing is, you were told when you get off the elevator, you'll go through the green door in front of you. You'll make a left and the first office is yours. There was a pretty good size room with different offices, but no names, no nothing, and I worked with a guy that had worked, and I didn't know it till about 10 years ago, we had actually both worked in the same office and never knew each other. That's how secretive this thing was.

SW: Why was it so secret?

Det. R: Because, first of all, if the information you gotten and stuff, put it on file, there were people who would go in, and get your records, and use it to extort people. See, extortion is a big thing. It's human compromise, human intelligence. In fact, they don't even want the public to know there is a thing like human compromise or human intelligence, and that's what I got into, at levels that are beyond belief.

191

Pedophilia & Human Trafficking

SW: Let's first talk about pedophilia, and human trafficking.

Det. R: Yup.

SW: That was one of the main areas that you really got into, but first, what was the main difference between pedophilia and human trafficking?

Det. R: There is no difference. Not when you get into how they're used. There's pedophilia separate, just on the local, but it is all done. It's controlled. It's used. They're professionally set up. It's a well-organized movement across the country at all different levels, and that's why people who try to put this under one umbrella, it doesn't work. You have to understand how the whole system works to be able to figure it out.

SW: That's what you did. They gave you free reign.

Det. R: Yes.

SW: You traveled all over the world.

Det. R: Yes. I could go anywhere in the world, and the country. I had an unlimited expense account, and unlimited expense in New York is a lot of money.

SW: I was told that there was a task force that was formed, and you're the only one that's left.

Det. R: Yeah, but that task force, I was the only one that was there from day one till, until we got stopped with the State Select Committee on Crime.

SW: Why did they stop?

Det. R: National security.

SW: Okay?

Det. R: Yes, and it's documented.

SW: Did they specify what national security that you were impeding on?

Det. R: Yeah. Yeah. Whole bunch of it, particularly the stuff going into ... Because I had arrested Frank Sturgis from the Kennedy assassination, and then I had arrested another guy who was heavily involved in the pedophile work, using people to compromise people.

SW: Politicians?

Det. R: And business people, and power brokers. Yes.

SW: They didn't want you interfering with what they could do?

Det. R: Yes. Yes, and they ... They didn't know how much I knew at the time, but yes, when I took the second guy in less than two, three months, and they didn't know what I knew, so they shut us down. Then I got retired. I was retired. I didn't retire.

SW: How long did you end up doing that? How many years?

Det. R: 13 years. Yeah, I ... The first thing started like ... Actually, 14 years I did total, but 13 years is when I was cut loose.

SW: You had 13 years of your unlimited budget to just figure this stuff out.

Det. R: Yeah, and in between every once in a while, they'd shut down an investigation, and I'd probably do something for a month or so. Then somebody would start again, and I'd get brought back, and then we'd get shut down again. The final one was when the governor of the State of New York appointed me to the state select committee on crime, to see what the effects these crimes were having on society and I was there about three years. Then, like I say, then one day we were shut down, and I was retired.

SW: What were the effects that you shared with people?

Det. R: Oh, my gosh. The whole gamut of it. How this affects the kids, and the people, and what the truth was, how it was used to compromise governments, and the military, and law enforcement, and every facet of our life is influenced by this.

SW: It's tearing apart the fabric of society?

Det. R: Fragment not only of that, but of the family and even the schools. When you see you have a perfect example now, and I don't know what happened out in Baron, Wisconsin.

SW: I suppose it ties into human trafficking but probably the pedophilia trafficking.

Det. R: Baron, Wisconsin came up, that area came up in our investigations 50 years ago.

SW: Then we can get into the other trafficking.

Det. R: The same as it ties in with what was going on here.

Government Compromised & Involved

SW: I know it ties into human trafficking, but let's focus on pedophilia trafficking, then we can get into the other trafficking. How serious of an issue is pedophilia in our country and Washington, D.C., and when I say serious, we know how to fix every part of the community, but how big is it, and how serious?

Det. R: Okay. According to my work that I did, and factual things that I saw, 35 to 40% are compromised, and involved. I have it from experts like Robert Merritt and people like that, that have it at 80%, and that runs the gamut of everything involved in this, in the political everything else that goes on.

SW: When you say involved, you mean somebody who may be running the company, and then there's somebody who might be blackmailed?

Det. R: Yes, yes, and that's what it's done for, both in industry and in politics, and our military. Again, I have examples, as I told you, everything I talk about, I have factual examples of what happened. They were either investigations, or cases that I personally did, not that I read about. This is what it's based on.

SW: What are some of the big cases that you've been involved in?

Det. R: The biggest one actually turned out to be the Son of Sam case, which is ... I first found out about 1968. I was taken by an informant to Untermyer Park in Yonkers, New York, and showed where they were sacrificing the German shepherds and the little kids, the victims, and also to Van Cortlandt Park, and what was known as the meadows. That's when I got ... I already had heard about the different things, but that's when I was physically taken, and introduced to it, and in the nineties, I was brought back to New York, and the biggest misnomer is the son of Sam case. That was only a part of it, but I got brought back out there, and I actually took a sergeant, Kevin Murphy, and Maury Terry to the site, and showed them after all those years. That had direct connections to right here, where in a chapel here, we found the same drawings of the cult and stuff that we found in the chapel or sacrifice place in Untermyer Park. I had infiltrated that.

SW: How many of these cases have cult or satanic underpinnings?

Det. R: A lot of them, especially right now, between the full moon and Halloween. This is a high time of the year for casualties, and we had followed that across the country. At first, we called it the Inner State 90-94, which just covered the one end. That didn't cover the one that ran through the southern part of the country. Yes, we actually had established that route. Like I say, now it's called the Smiley Face Killers, but that was another New York Detective who didn't even know me, and a professor from Saint Cloud State here, that identified that. We had known it as the interstate 90-94, because it went west from New York, and in 1970 ... was about 1976, when they first got wind that we were onto what was known as the Son of Sam case, is when they started moving west. There were other parts of it that had been operating, because these are very well connected. It's not like you think. it's a business. It is a business, but their records and modes of transferring information is unbelievable, and very secret. You have to be able to infiltrate it to learn it, and I did.

SW: When you say that 40 to 45%, and some people say up to 80%, of our politicians on our powerful class are involved in this, are you saying more for the sexual purpose, or also the satanic underpinnings?

Det. R: It goes across the whole board. It's hard to separate them, because they lap over. Many of them, if they're in at one point, they end up going all the way. A lot of them, for some reason, we always figured it was this: When they got to the point where they thought they were so big nobody could touch them, that was what they could do, is use kids, and it gets very gruesome when you describe what the actual things are that supposedly they tried to gain, or what the ultimate sexual desires, how they're satisfied. It gets very gruesome.

SW: I've heard of the hormone adrenochrome. Is that something that they're trying to get to?

Det. R: I don't believe so. I believe it's just being people who think they can act and do anything they want to do, because of their power. The reason why much of this happens, and then they try to blame the gay community. There's many pedophile heterosexuals as there are gay. This is where, again, it's a misnomer. It is something that our society right now, what they believe this is about, it's been so misled, it's unbelievable. We not only work the criminal aspect. We had people from the policy science corporations, some of the most brilliant scientists on this working with us, but again, we also were able to interview and get the real story from the people involved.

SW: What is it about?

Det. R: Power and sex. That ever overpowering, that they can do anything they want, and get away with it.

SW: They're sick.

Det. R: Yeah. Yeah. They're sick. Baloney. They should get their heads handed to them, but it's. Again, like I said, you have to be politically correct nowadays. You can't tell the truth.

SW: What about the Franklin scandal?

Det. R: Yes. I had that. I was given that in a bar on West 57th Street, owned by an Irishman who I knew from my days, and yes, I know all about the Franklin cover-up. I know before John de Camp ever got it. I had it already. It was tied to the Omaha, Nebraska. The whole thing, which again, comes out of the Son of Sam stuff, and I had contacts in the intelligence world who had helped me with that.

SW: When they covered it up, who is ultimately behind the Franklin scandal?

Det. R: The whole Franklin scandal, John de Camp tried to do the best he could, but John de Camp also knew where it was leading to, because when you had King and them all tied in with the money movement, and again, it was human intelligence, human compromise, where they use this to compromise certain people. I know all the players in there.

SW: Was it all the way to the White House?

Det. R: When you say the White House, do you mean Washington? It was all the way to Washington, yes. It was part of that national, the whole national thing that was going on. It was just part of it. There was a small part of it. The Franklin cover-up was a small part of it, with the connections, and that's why Colby ended up getting killed, because Colby, and I know because of other involvements, had finally decided that he was going to help. The next thing, he went for a canoe ride, and was dead.

All Across the Country

SW: When you say this is just a small part of it, are you saying that there's stories like this all across the country?

Det. R: Yes, there are.

SW: They just don't become public?

Det. R: No, they don't become public because any media people who try to go with it, their careers are over. I can name, I have a list of them. People who have been here, people who I work with, what happened to them once they tried to go public with this.

SW: Their families are smeared, and ...

Det. R: Yeah, yeah, and their careers are over. The list is quite long.

SW: I would like that list.

Det. R: Yeah.

SW: Why is the Wetterling case in Minnesota so important?

Det. R: Because it's connected to that thing on East 64th Street, when those little boys were killed. The next case after that was the Pats case in New York, because my informant, Ben Rose, was observed there, and the case that followed that was the Johnny Gosh case. Then it's the Martin case. Then it's the Allen case, and the last one was the Wetterling case. There was a common name that I won't, I believe the guy is still alive, but there was something that followed this. Also, I know personally of the certain agent, with 19 men who followed these cases around. They were on the Wetterling case. I personally interviewed the guy, talked to him, knew who he was. Yes.

SW: When you say 19 men, what were they part of?

Det. R: Intelligence operation.

SW: When the Wetterling case went down, did they all ...

Det. R: They all knew. They knew how it all tied from that case that we had on East 64th Street, where they didn't want to kick back and expose that.

SW: They were actively covering it up?

The United Nations is Involved

Det. R: Oh, yeah. The sheriff, the new one you had here, effectively said this was a cover-up, but there's so much more into the Wetterling case. It's like again, look at the Pats case. The guy that they got guilty on that one, cops called the investigators at the time, and made me promise I wouldn't give their name, because my informant Ben Rose had been observed, and he was hard to miss. My original information is—just to show you how this works—I get called into the office of one of the top five bosses in the police department. He closes the door, turns up the music, and we're talking. He takes a piece of paper, and on it is written, Dr. Rockefeller looks like Quasimodo, supplies little boys to the United Nations. I nod, he nods. He crumples the paper up, puts it in the ashtray, and burns it, and with that, we kept talking, and when we got done, I walked out. That guy ended up being Ben Rose, and he looked like Quasimodo. That's how we know, but he was supplying those kids to the United Nations. We proved all that.

Det. R: The apartment where the two little boys were killed that I told you about was his apartment. That's why I know what happened, and he was also at the kidnapping site of Eaton Pats. Two detectives called me, and told me, "Don't ever tell anybody my name," because he said, "You know, first of all, he says, we can't find that you ever arrested Ben Rose." We didn't, because when we arrested him, we arraigned him. We took him to a hotel room, and arraigned him in front of a judge. There was no record. That's the way we worked, because you couldn't let anybody know you had them.

SW: When they brought those kids to the United Nations, what were they doing? Were they using those kids for blackmail?

Det. R: Oh, sure. Sure, they were using it to bribe people, blackmail them, and everything else. It was part of the operation.

SW: Were they mostly boys, or were they also girls?

Det. R: They were girls, too, but this Ben Rhodes operation was boys. Yeah, girls was a different group. Yeah, I was involved in that with the Profomo scandal, too. They came over on that, because one of my informants was very knowledgeable, and why they came ... This was after it happened. It was about 1968 when they came to see me because this is ... I think Profomo happened in '63 or '64, but in the follow-up, Scotland Yard and MI6 came to see me, to make sure of the political connection and information that might have been moved, so they came to see me because my informant was capable of getting into there.

SW: When they were bringing boys to the United Nations, was Jacob Wetterling one of those boys that was brought?

Det. R: No, no, no, no, no, no, no. That was part of a whole ... That was part of the ring. How this stuff moved, and the last I have it, the actual last killing was in Minot, North Dakota, when one of the car boys was killed there, but they ended up settling in Kanab, Utah, and years ago, I had somebody that came right here, and gave me all the information on that, and it was under best friends of animals that it was set up in Kanab, Utah, although people now have been looking at it. There was somebody here who I told this to, who actually found the person, and they have been on it, but they got stopped.

SW: My understanding is that Jacob Wetterling was taken right before Halloween, so more than likely those kids were abused and killed on Halloween?

Det. R: No. It goes with ... I used to know all this. It has to do with the full moon, and Halloween, and all these different signs and stuff that fed into it. There's a whole, whole, and I guess it changes when somebody dreams up a new cult thing, but yes, at one time we had all the seasons for this, and how it would fit in, and about the sacrifices, just like when I was up in Maine. The two priests brought a mother to me, and she, because they knew I was a detective in New York, so they came to ask me if this could be true, that somebody had approached this mother to sacrifice her six-month-old baby. Which I knew all about, and yes, it was true, and we ... I made sure it didn't happen, but there's all this stuff. You have that going on around here forever.

Politically Correctness Suppresses the Truth

SW: You state that Minnesota is one of the worst places, if not the worst places in the country. Why is that?

Det. R: There's many reasons, but one of it is everything here is politically correct. You can't tell the truth. You got to go along with the system, and over the years, the time I spent here, and every time you had a cop who tried to do the right thing, he was crucified. Lieutenant Gary McGaughey. If you look at the report I did on him, the kids that we helped, and brought to New York to testify and everything, and he was destroyed, just like his partner Kenny Tidgewell. It's just the way it was, and we couldn't, at that time, things that we saw, and observed here, was just unbelievable, and then another very sad part of this is, what happens to the girls in the Native American area? Again, example, I had the girl we brought. She was a thalidomide baby, and had a flipper for an arm, which made her valuable, and she had been sold into...

SW: Why did that make her valuable?

Det. R: Because how many people do you know with flippers for a left arm? This is the way-

SW: A cult world is.

Det. R: Yeah. Yeah, and when she came to testify in New York, we had 11 or 13 kids come to testify. Lieutenant Gary McGaughey brought him there, and they told us what happened here in Minnesota, and when he came back, because he was crucified. He ended up just totally destroyed, his family gone and everything. The biggest scandal I've ever heard in the state of Minnesota, and two years ago, I was up in Little Falls, and I gave a speech about this, and I mentioned Kenny Tidgewell, and his uncle must... I think it was his uncle said to me, "You know, Kenny just died, and he lived in fear his whole life after that because he was always scared somebody was going to get him for what he had done, trying to stop this stuff."

How Pedophilia Rings Operate

SW: Pedophilia operates in rings. How does that work?

Det. R: Oh, yeah, but it's not-

SW: But how does it work? How does the trafficking work?

Det. R: Oh, easy. They buy, sell of them. We had one guy, Willie Dunn, he actually ended up perfecting it. He got a Winnebago, and he would drive the country, buying, selling, and kidnapping little boys. He was a major operator, but you had that, that was going to the extreme, but they've... It's like an underground. I got this kid, I'm tired of him. You want him, and the next guy takes him. They'll sell him for ... Even this guy I told you that was out here in the Wetterling case. I had people that paid as much as $25,000 for a kid, from 2,500 to 25,000, and they sell them. It's like a market. Then we had in New York what was known as juice joints. These were places run by the mafia, where at night, you could go there. There'd be two, 300 kids, from 13, 14, 15 on up. They were boys and girls, but mostly boys, and you'd see the limousines come by looking to pick up the kids. Nobody knew where they came from, where they went, and whenever we tried to work on it, it got shut down, because I know who was running it.

Det. R: There were two, three of them at any given time in New York. I went to Minneapolis. There were things like that, so these things are set up, and that's how they move. They move them from one place to the next.

SW: Where do they get these kids?

Det. R: Oh, schools. In one instance we had a case where 200 kids disappeared in an operation, and nobody ever knew what happened to them. That happened more than once, where whole groups of kids over periods of time, from children's homes and such, would disappear.

SW: Are they mostly from children's homes?

Det. R: Oh, no, no.

SW: Or are they from everywhere?

Det. R: Everywhere, schools, everything. You have ... I just had a kid here the other year, right here, and I had alerted the authorities. The superintendent was very good, but after that, and the next thing she was being trafficked in South Dakota. Why?

SW: What happens to these kids? I know you say you don't know, but do they stay in the country, or do they leave the country?

Det. R: They do ... We also got into international stuff. Yes, they are used all over the world. I'll give you an example of another case. There was a young lady, and her pimp was Red Dog, and I got to know her, and again, in the work I did, my job was to find out what was happening. I got to know the girl. She was from Rockville, Minnesota, which is right down the road here, and I told her I was from St. Martin, and well, how do I know you're telling the truth, and she said to me, "I was brought into this world by Dr. Herman Koop," and I said, "So was I." She said, "Well, then you're from St. Martin and I'm from Rockville." That girl got killed by her pimp about 1971 or so. When I notified the authorities out here, and to this day, nobody has ever admitted that their child disappeared, and she's buried in Potters Field, New York, New York City, in Potters Field. I never knew her real name, because in the work we did, that's not what you did.

SW: You didn't tell your real name.

Det. R: No, no. Didn't even know my real name, unless I had to take action, but otherwise I was Jimmy Boots. You're discreet.

SW: How do they cover up their activities?

Det. R: You don't have to cover it up. Nobody does nothing to stop them. Why would they cover it up?

SW: Is all this stuff out in the open, the juice bars, and the rest?

Det. R: Yeah. Yeah, it's out in the open. You can go anywhere and watch it. God. God, I remember going to the mall, and I'm sitting there waiting for the kids to get done shopping. Just look at that. What do you mean? Look, that guy there. That's a pedophile. How do you know? Whenever he was looking in the window, right, a young boy comes by, he start looking at him. People, it's here, but you got to know ... You got to be able to believe what you're watching. These kids don't disappear for nothing.

SW: I heard that there's actually places where there's menus where you can order kids. Is that a true thing?

Det. R: Yeah, yeah. There are things like that. Yes. There's all that, but again, you get the bars. There were, again, I cite New York because I was here in Minneapolis with Gary McGaughey and Tidgewell, and we actually watched it happen. Right here in Minneapolis. Where they would come in and pick up the girls and stuff, right on, what is that street in Minneapolis? But yes, I was in Oklahoma City. Columbus, Ohio. It was everywhere.

SW: Do they have kill rooms and underground tunnels?

Child Sacrifices and Costume Fetishes

Det. R: I don't know. That I've never, other than the stuff we saw, like in Untermyer Park, with the sacrifices and that. I've heard of it, but I've never seen actual kill rooms, as they call it. See, some of that is there, but not the way they describe it. They do sacrifice kids. Why certainly. Look at Matamoros, Mexico. I never forget. Remember the kid in Matamoros that died a number of years ago, and it was lucky there was a reporter there.

Det. R: The reporter said, "Wait a second. There's a cigar butt there." He says, "I heard Jimmy Rothstein talk about this. That's a Satanic ritualistic killing." Because in this particular cult killing, they would cleanse the body with Cuban cigar smoke. Which is the same thing that showed up in the Epstein West and that case that we had in New York, where I first found out about it when they killed Shelley Bloom. There was a cigar butt there, and it was a Cuban cigar.

Det. R: What they do is before and after killing, they blow smoke on the body of that. There's all these different things. Every cult has its own little symbol, and they change as the new guy gets involved. But yes.

SW: Are they Satanic worshipers? Like Satan?

Det. R: Yeah, but you can worship anything. And they do. It's nice to call everything Satanic, yeah, but that's just a good name. But in the real world, it's a sacrifice.

SW: To whatever god they...

Det. R: Whatever god, or tree, or wind, whatever they want. For everything, there is a god. If you don't believe in God, you can't believe in Satanic stuff. That's what they do. You won't believe the weird stuff. You got the whole thing where they have these kids, for instance, like the JonBenét Ramsey case. Where you have these, it's called costume sex. It's like you had here where they would dress these kids up in cassocks, and the molest them. And they have these cult followings that watch these kids, and then do what they got to do.

SW: Was JonBenét, was that a whole child thing that she was a part of? The beauty contest?

Det. R: Yeah, but that whole thing has followers that have nothing to do. And everybody wants to blame the parents here. I got people that have been calling me since it happened.

SW: It was the parents with that case?

Det. R: I don't know.

SW: Oh, my God.

Det. R: But there's so much there because within two days of that happening, I had a phone call from somebody in intelligence who told me it was the cult following of the costume stuff. This guy was a military guy that called me, and this guy I knew very well. He knew this stuff. But I know these people been calling me since it happened trying to blame the mother and father. Again, I did not actively pursue it, but I know the call I got.

Det. R: They didn't even know that there was a following for this stuff. And that's a lot of this stuff too. Again, citing an example. I get a call from a bar owner in New York to come in right away. There was a girl that was there that was going to be put into prostitution that didn't belong.

Det. R: I came in, and the hookers were there waiting. They had gone to him to tell because they all knew to get a hold of me, you didn't go to the police department. There were certain people you had to see. And I got there, and yes. And we saved her, and we sent her back to Michigan.

Det. R: A number of years later, she came back to New York, and she went to this bar again. And the guy called me. He said, "Jim, you got to come in. Somebody wants to see you." And there she was. She had graduated from college, opened a business, and she came to thank me for having saved her life. Because see, there were so many of these people that you could help if you got [there], and knew what you were doing.

Det. R: In New York, after a while, there were a lot of honest cops. They had to work within, to keep their careers, and they would call me and tell me. They'd say, "Jim, I got this." It's like the Son of Sam case. The first inkling of the Son of Sam, a very honest forensic detective who I knew met with me in a bar out at Long Island. He said, "Jim, we got a cult serial killings going on." This was two years before it was solved.

Det. R: He knew, but he came to me because he knew I knew this stuff. It was tied to the stuff that I had been taken to Untermyer Park with.

Everyone Gets Blackmailed, Everyone Extorted

SW: How does the blackmail work?

Det. R: Blackmail, easy. Skull Murphy was the best there ever was, and you can look at an article that was written by Bill McGowan who happens to be the son of a Captain I knew who was a good informant. But Skull Murphy was my informant. And they blackmailed everybody.

SW: When you say everybody?

Det. R: Everybody. Congressmen. Cops. Doctors. Lawyers. Right to the highest levels. They would take them, like in some cases, they go right into the District Attorney's office, and say they were detectives. And they'd have the guy. "Well, it'll cost you $25,000." And they go get the money, and then they let the guy go.

Det. R: But extortion at every level, not only for money, but for power, for favors, and stuff like that. That's how it works.

SW: How do they bring the little kids in there?

Det. R: They set that up ahead of time. It's a different part of the outfit. First they set them up with the kid, then once they got them compromised, then they'll get them in a position where they can confront them. Oh, yeah. It's very simple, how they do it. You won't believe what they're extorted for. Power, corporations. I had some corporations that paid dearly to cover all that stuff up.

SW: They would compromise the CEO, or something?

Det. R: Or somebody in a high position, yeah. Yeah. And I'm not going to name any companies, but oh yes. I had two, three cases, actually, like that, yeah.

SW: How many of those compromised people were actively involved, and were dirty, versus were innocent and they compromised?

Det. R: There was never anybody innocent. They had all messed around, and it seems like once they got in power, they felt they could do anything. I confronted guys, and I'll give you a case. Uncle Charlie's in New York was a notorious hangout for high-level rich pedophiles. And one particular night, there was a man who was going to run for president. And we got the call, he was there with two little boys. So we walked in on him, and my partner and I said, we were a little out of the ordinary. He picked a piece of shrimp off the guy's plate and he ate it.

Det. R: This guy was a Senator at the time. And the guy said, "Hey, who the hell do you think you are?" So he calls Roy Cohen, the big-shot lawyer. We knew Roy Cohen, and Roy Cohen knew me. This guy is describing how these detectives came in, and all of a sudden he starts going, "Yes, sir. Yes, sir. Yes." And he hangs up the phone. He says, "I'd like to apologize if I insulted you detectives. Would you like to join me for dinner?" He never ran for president.

Det. R: But this is how it worked. And there were others. There were people who would use that. "Who called us?" We don't know. 90% of the things I got, I didn't know where the information came from. It's just the way it is.

SW: Is New York cleaner than Minnesota, for example?

Det. R: Population wise, definitely? When you go with the amount of people, because after, it took a lot of years after we got done, for a lot of things to start happening in New York. But it did. I haven't been there. The only time I go there is to do a TV show, or something like that, and then I leave. But yes.

SW: What other states are like Minnesota? That are bad.

Det. R: Ohio. Go down. Go to almost every one of them. Ohio is very bad. Pennsylvania. I worked in all of them places.

SW: But you were saying that the makeup of Minnesota makes it worse than other places.

Det. R: Yes it does.

SW: What other states have that makeup? And what specifically is it?

Det. R: Ohio.

SW: Ohio. How about Utah?

Det. R: That one's different. That's a whole different group out there. That's a different operation, but they have a problem too. That's not part of this group.

SW: What do you mean, part of this group?

Det. R: That's a different— religious beliefs, and stuff like that. But this one here, like I say, ended up in Kanab, Utah. That's what we know where they ended up, but these things all dove tail. You got that whole thing through Colorado, and the different part the Rocking X. Then you got the JonBenét Ramsey, and there was another ranch. I forget the name of it now, that was tied in with all of this stuff too.

SW: I heard California's pretty bad.

Det. R: Oh. Unbelievable. I spent a lot of time out there. Northern California had a whole segment. Then you had the central part, and then the southern part, Los Angeles and that was just unreal.

SW: Is there any state that's better?

Det. R: I don't know. A lot of states, naturally. I didn't get to spend enough time. We couldn't find anybody to work with, so I don't know. But the southern part, it was a whole thing that tied in with what we know as the Bible Belt that never, it had to do with the Jimmy Swaggart, when he went after that stuff. They had killed a couple preachers who tried to expose it, and that's another story that's never been told. It just goes on and on.

SW: Now the NYPD has expanded its reach and changed. Are the influential not only locally, but nationally and internationally?

Det. R: If they want to be.

SW: And why is that?

Det. R: Because there was a story a couple years ago. Associated Press did it, on how the New York Police Department works outside of the government. And I've got a copy of it. About halfway through, it says that it started in the late 60's and 70's. And right after that article came out, I had a couple of phone calls. They said, "Jim, they still don't know what you were doing."

Det. R: The New York Police Department is very effective. They reach all over.

SW: So they're good. Could they be a model for other?

Det. R: Well, yeah. They have a lot to protect in New York. You saw what happens when they got lax. You had 9/11 and a few things like that, but when they decide they're going to stop it, they stop it.

SW: And that's something I wanted to discuss.

Det. R: And I'm not going to go into that publicly.

Pedophile Rings Posing as Charities

SW: Well, maybe you can privately. What are the roles of charities in law enforcement?

Det. R: Oh, my God. Some of them are nothing but fronts. It's like that poster I showed you, of what it's known as. It tells you that you got these chicken hawks, which are the people use kids. You got to know the language to converse with these people. If you don't know the language, the minute you talk, you might as well forget it. They won't trust you. They won't tell you nothing.

Det. R: A lot of these are nothing more than candy stores. Where you can go and pick up kids. In the underground, they're called candy stores. Where you can go there and play goody two shoes, and take off with the kids. Which is everything you can imagine. School are, and everywhere I've gone and spoke on this, people have spotted it and done something.

SW: They become aware?

Det. R: Yes, yes. But the stuff that a lot of these people are going out and talking about, they have no idea what they're telling these people. It's only politically correct feel good do good. It doesn't tell the people the truth.

SW: There's a couple cases recently. The Laura Silsby case, where she was trafficking kids out of Haiti, and the Clintons actually came to her rescue.

Det. R: Well, I don't know about that.

SW: You don't know that one?

Det. R: Because those are, yeah you read about them, but I don't believe that. I don't believe that. If I didn't work at that, and physically went there, because I saw a lot of the things we worked on that were made public one way, that had no factual basis to it whatsoever. A number of things. I can go into them, but one of the saddest was Father Bruce Ritter, with the Covenant House. When he started doing something, they accused him of being a pedophile. And when I got word of it, and I came back to New York, that was the end of that because I worked with him. I knew what he had done, and we had investigated it personally.

Det. R: We never found any evidence to say that he was.

SW: There's another case. The Wetterling. Patty Wetterling was the chair of NCMEC, National Center for Missing and Exploited Children, which is the big one that works with the FBI. She was right, am I wrong?

Det. R: I guess that's what they're doing.

SW: Yeah.

Det. R: I haven't seen it, but...

SW: Supposedly.

Det. R: I met with them people personally at the last meeting in Iowa when the man came up and told me that they knew, because I had dealt with them, and he says, "I'm retiring." And he told me. He says, "You were the only guy that we could do."

SW: Well, Patty Wetterling was a chair.

Det. R: Yeah.

SW: Is she a good character from your experience and research?

Det. R: I don't know nothing about that, but first of all, just because you're a victim don't make you an expert. Why was she the head of it? I have no idea. I feel sorry for any mother, but I will not. Look at Noreen Gosch. You know what Noreen Gosch did? And in my papers, you will see a thing where me and Noreen made up a pamphlet on what victims should do when they become a victim. It has a picture of a mug of coffee with wings on it.

Det. R: Well, when she was told that, because she was really nobody. Her kid disappeared. She threw the mug of coffee, mug and all, right in the agents face. That's what she did.

SW: She's a good person. I've got some things on her.

Det. R: Yes. I've met her many times. I know the Johnny Gosch case inside and out, and everything that goes with it. She did not get rich by her son disappearing.

SW: Now, what do you know about that case? Was it tied into the network?

Det. R: Yeah. I told you. It's part of that, coming out of New York. It was part of that. It had to do with the whole Franklin cover up. The Omaha, Nebraska stuff, and what's interesting is the FBI agent who ends up up here. There's no connection. Why did they send Nick O'Hara up here from Omaha? And ask Nick O'Hara what he told the police chief in West Des Moines, Iowa.

SW: What did he tell them?

Det. R: To stand down. That's right from his mouth to me.

SW: So who was involved at a higher level that, were they protecting the ring?

Det. R: Yeah. It had to do, if they didn't want to expose what we had on East 64th Street. Can you imagine if they invoke National Security to protect a murdered 14- and 15-year-old boy? Huh? You tell me what part of the National Security Act allows that?

SW: That should be the one it's for.

Det. R: That's right.

SW: If you can't protect children, then what can we do?

Det. R: Yeah. Hey, they can go get the subpoena. There's still somebody alive that knows when I called that day.

What about Donald Trump?

SW: Let's get started on the Trump stuff. I'm already on camera right now. You know Trump personally.

Det. R: The only time I ever was with him personally was when one night he was having dinner with a bunch of other developers.

SW: What do you know about how, what Trump has to be like in order to be successful in New York?

Det. R: You got to be one of sharpest business men in the world to do what he did in New York, and how he did it. You have to know the system. You have to have the right connections. Then there's this thing that most people don't even know. It's known as the cash underground, where cash talks. Big cash. I personally was present when there were ten suitcases, each one with a million dollars on a business deal. This is the real world in New York, and how many people even know what that is. They never heard of the cash underground.

SW: And Trump would know this?

Det. R: Yeah, well, any business man in New York that's of that caliber. You had the Millsteins, the Zeckendorfs, and the list goes on and on. And there was one man in particular you, or a couple of them that, when they were found out, nobody even knew who they were, and yet they owned more buildings and stuff than anybody ever could imagine. These were the people I knew because again, like I told you, I had these hookers and pedophiles working for me, and they knew all these people. That underground in New York, once you infiltrate that and become a trusted part of it.

Det. R: I never took a payoff. That was the big thing. They knew they couldn't buy me. And many times, it was brought out, even after I retired. An old boss of mine was sent to talk to me. And he asked me, "Were you approached by this certain organized crime figure after you retired to come to work for him in a business he had?" I said, "Absolutely." "Did you take the job?" I said, "No. I told them." I said, "That would go against my principles because even if I'm retired, this was part of it." And the guy respected me. He says, "Yeah. That was on an FBI wire tap. That you wouldn't take it." But he says, "We just had to check."

Det. R: That's why there were instances in a lot of these things where people came to see me after I retired. Either to thank me, or to ask me.

And they came from all over the world, so yes. The Donald Trump, the part of business in that. At that time, you had the Grand Central Station, when that real estate all went up, I was in the middle of all that stuff with these people. That's big business. The Waldorf Astoria, you had the Biltmore Hotel. When that got sold off and Bank of America bought it, I was in the middle of all of that. They made sure that I was happy.

SW: Why was it important to make you happy?

Det. R: Well, they didn't want me mad at them, that's for sure. They didn't. I knew a lot of things. It's just the way it was. You don't go causing problems. There's respect. And it's like my rules of 8th Avenue. That's what that was.

SW: Is Donald Trump honest, and has integrity?

Det. R: Well.

SW: Is he going to tell the truth and do what he says?

Det. R: I would say if anybody is, he's going to do it. That gets interesting about, he's doing a business deal. He's going to say what he has to say, but I'll guarantee you one thing, he's going to get done what he wants to do. If you know the right people and the right thing, just look at what has happened. All of a sudden, people who've never talked to us, all of a sudden are talking to us. Why?

Det. R: You got to remember, New York is where the money is. They still got to have money. He was definitely one of the big players when it came to the big money. Oh, yeah. And people don't understand that.

SW: Would he have been compromised?

Det. R: No. How can you be compromised if they're talking about infidelities, what do, in mother nature, what do young boys and young girls do? When he was out there chasing women, or women chasing him, have you ever heard him say, "That's bullshit?" Well, what is he going to say? No? I didn't. He don't do that.

SW: They tried to tie him to pedophilia and all that stuff.

Det. R: I never, in all the years that I worked, ever, ever had any information like that on Donald Trump. And I knew the big boys. It's like I say. Cohen and them guys. There never was any mention of that with Trump. That's why, when I hear that stuff, and some of these people that are going out saying this, where do they come from? They read it on the computer somewhere?

Det. R: I ought to give you an example. A while back, a lady called me and she said, "Did you ever hear that this guy was a pedophile?" I said, "Yeah, I heard it, but I didn't work it. I have no idea." The next thing, Jimmy Rothstein says this guy's a pedophile. I never said that. You hear it, yes. But I don't believe it. It's like I said, unless I know, then it wasn't true.

SW: In Trump's case, you never even heard it.

Det. R: No, no. And in those days, listen, if he would have been, we'd have had it. There's no doubt about it, let me tell you.

Media's Involvement

SW: When you see all the media attacking Trump, what are your thoughts on that?

Det. R: I laugh. I said, "These people, the people that are attacking him are doing it to cover their own what-you-call-its." Because they should look in their closet. There's some stuff in the works right now, that some of this stuff that's been exposed, especially on this human trafficking, pedophilia, and the stuff with the church is not happening on its own.

SW: Do you think Trump is actively trying to bring it down?

Det. R: Yes. And I can't tell you why I know that. That certain things aren't coming out. And there was something supposed to come out. That's why, every Friday at 2:00, I watch the news, because normally, if there's a secret grand jury and the information comes out, it's on Friday afternoon. Now I understand it'll be not until after the election. In fact, something was on the computer this morning about, there's some big secret grand jury or something that they're worried about.

SW: What about the sealed indictments?

Det. R: That's what.

SW: This is it. When they say there's over 55,000 sealed indictments, do you think that's possible?

Det. R: No. I don't believe that.

SW: What do you think is really happening? There's something happening, but not that.

Det. R: No. There is. What it is going to do is show the vulnerabilities that we have, and the people who used it that were, again, I've been at these meetings where the stuff comes out on people. They're exposed. Things don't happen right. I was there.

SW: Do you think this is a National Security threat?

Det. R: Oh. More than that, you should hear all the military victims that call me. The people, the women who were in the military. Remember, if a General rapes or has sex with a Private, is he compromised? Yes, he is. I had that, and like I said, when you read the Ed Skull Murphy stuff, the stuff with Church and those people, I knew about that. It happened before I was there, but those were the things we knew. And over the years, the different things on people that fell into the same category. Look at the stuff you just had in the Far East with Fat Albert.

Det. R: This is what they do. In the Kennedy assassination, one of things when I arrested Sturgess, when I asked him, he said he was messing with Ellen Romitch. She was a Soviet spy. I knew these people. Why do you think they came from England on the Profumo case? That's what spies, women do. We got women spies. You look in that book right there by Marita [Lorenz]. One of the best I ever met in my life, and I had saved her life. So I learned a few things from her.

SW: The grandma might be the spy. Not the one that looks like James Bond.

Det. R: Yeah. Oh, yeah. She was the best. But again, these are the people I knew. The Piggy Peggy's, and the June's, and all of them. I had a whole. One night, again, I like to cite actual things. A Lieutenant needed some information on some very high level criminal activity. He came to me, and he says, "Jim, what can you do?" He says, "Come on."

Det. R: We went down to 36th and Lexington to an apartment building to see a lady that I knew. We got there, there were 13 women in various states of getting dressed to go out working for the night. They were hookers. We sat there, and we both had a can of beer. The girls, like I say, were in various stages, and when we got done, we told the girls what we needed, and we left. We're walking up the street, and the Lieutenant says to me, "Jim, would anybody believe we didn't have sex with those girls?" I says, "Boss, you don't shit where you eat because if you do, you lose all credibility."

Det. R: This informant had her bed posts hollowed out for microphones in case we needed it. Within two days, we had the information we needed. That's just an example of how that worked. The same in the pedophile world. You put the word out there. When I got the thing for Doctor Rockefeller, looks like Quasimodo, that's the only description I had. Do you know, it only took me a couple of days to find out who it really was.

A Message to Trump

SW: If there was one thing you wanted Donald Trump to know, what would that be?

Det. R: Keep doing a good job. Oh, yeah. Yeah. He knows what he's doing. You don't live at that level in New York without knowing what the real world is. 99 and 9 tenths percent of the people you hear talking about it, have no clue how New York works. None. And if you go in the Police Department, you'd be amazed at how few of them ever get to know. But then there are those who do know. And let me tell you, they know what they're doing.

Solutions: Ending Human Compromise

This show we focus on solutions. You will hear important information about what a family should do if ever your daughter or son is abducted. Detective Rothstein also lays out a set of laws that should be passed in every city to significantly reduce human trafficking. He also lays out a program for mothers to take back their power and force society to care about our children. He predicts that these activities would reduce human trafficking and human compromise by 85%. This would also significantly decrease most problems occurring in our society, including war, poverty, drugs, and the vast amount of decisions that only serve a small fraction of our society for the wrong reason.

If there is anything you should learn from this episode is that together we can make a difference and solve these problems.

SW: Welcome to Business Game Changers. I'm Sarah Westall. This video is the last in the series I've recorded with Detective Jimmy Boots Rothstein during over 20 hours of time I spent at his home in November and December 2018. This show, however, will focus on solutions to the epidemic of human trafficking. You will hear important details about what a family should do if ever your daughter or son is abducted.

SW: Detective Rothstein also lays out a set of laws that should be passed in every city to significantly reduce human trafficking. He also lays out a program for mothers to take back their power, and force society to care about our children. He predicts that these activities would reduce human trafficking, and human compromise by 85%. As a consequence, this would also significantly decrease most major problems occurring in our society, including war, poverty, drugs, and the vast amount of decisions that only serve a small fraction of our society for the wrong reasons.

SW: Because human compromise is keeping our politicians and our leaders from doing what's right, and it's time for us to solve this. If there's anything you should learn from this episode is that, together, we can make a difference, and finally solve these problems in our society.

SW: Okay, let's talk about some solutions. You did a booklet with Johnny Gosch's mother, Noreen.

Det. R: Yes, that's number one.

SW: Let's talk about that because this is about what victims can do and people who are associated with victims. Can you discuss what you've put in this booklet that are highlights?

Det. R: Yes. Again, like I have it. I got it put together here. In this thing, it goes right in that the minute your kid is gone, you start a diary, number one. Every minute detail has to be put into it because as time goes on if it is one of these cover-ups, they're going to change stuff. Don't blame the cops because many of the things, if these cops go after, their careers are over. In this booklet here, you got to work with the press right away. Make sure the press gets it so they know, but here is the cover sheet for what we did. It's basically four or five pages that outlined all the things you have to do to go with it and how to follow up to get an organization going.

Det. R: These things are very important because nobody knows, and you're going to be... Again, if it was like the Wetterling or the Johnny Gosch case in particular. That was the first big one. They tried to discredit the mother and everybody instead of going after the facts. I interviewed the lead guy down there when that kid disappeared. He got a phone call to, how did they say the words was to stand down on the investigation. This is how this goes, so you need something that has everything recorded. In the Josh Guimond's case here at St. John's, I had the family do that, document everything.

What to Do If Your Child is Missing

SW: Now, how quickly do they have to act on this?

Det. R: Immediately. The first thing is when you find out your son is missing, or daughter, or whatever it is, you write down, "I heard from so-and-so that my kids was gone, this time," and everything else. Then every communication, everything you have, you write down.

SW: Now, the media doesn't get involved until it's of interest.

Det. R: Yup, and you got to-

SW: How do you get them involved?

Det. R: First of all, you call them right away and tell them, "Hey, my son is missing and this and that," and get the reporters on it. Make sure you have a good working relationship. You also have to remember, they're kept very tight on what they can report and can't report. I can cite cases of that at the highest levels with stories that were never made public with the biggest papers in the country.

SW: Well, in the case of Wetterling, they're still covering up for it.

Det. R: Yes. Yes. For instance, there was another kid they tried to kidnap just before Wetterling. You've never heard his name. You've never heard him, and I'm not going to give it now, but yes, I interviewed this kid. I interviewed his mother. He was riding his bike, delivering the newspaper. Now, what was Johnny Gosch doing? He was a newspaper boy. Before the Martin kid was kidnapped, a man told authorities the kid was going to be kidnapped, and still, nobody did nothing, even the newspaper boy.

Det. R: These are the things, when you look at these pedophiles, they have fetishes. In those books, they describe what they pay, what their fetish is, and all that stuff. This is the things you have to know, and that's why, like I said, this book, there isn't a family in this country that shouldn't have a book, that little notebook that we made to help.

SW: Now, where can they get a copy of that? Can I get a copy of it and put it on the website?

Det. R: Why, certainly, right here is a copy.[1]

SW: Well, what I'd like to do is get the ... I'll have this, but if I could get the digital copy, and then I'll put that up on the website so people can have that.

Det. R: Yeah. I mean, it should be out there.

SW: Yes, it should be.

Det. R: That is just the basic things that you should do.

Generate Government Solutions

SW: Okay. Now, there are a couple other things that you have as solutions. Let's talk about your government solution.

Det. R: Well, yes. We had here in this town of St. Martin, right up on the street up here, there were two young girls that ... We have had a couple of pimps that moved into this town, and I knew what was going to happen, plus, I had an informant. When they were ready to grab the girls, I stepped in and stopped it because I couldn't get nobody else to do anything. As a result of that, my city council, and I've passed resolution, and you can find it on the Internet. You put in resolution number 2014-08. This resolution outlines, and there are three ... Let's see. Five basic things that are addressed, and if these laws were passed, I would guarantee you, it would cut down 85% of this activity.

SW: They can do it at the local city level.

Det. R: You write a resolution. [For example —>[2]] This resolution is addressed to the governor of the state of Minnesota to pass this law. This resolution was sent to every government official starting at the county level, and it was sent into all the people in the state and to the Cornyn investigation where they were working on human trafficking out of Texas, and that was done through Doug Caddy, the lawyer from the Watergate burglars who knew what I was talking about.

Det. R: Only one congressman ever, ever did anything about it, and that was Michele Bachmann here from Minnesota. She actually called a meeting at the Historical Society of St. Cloud. You know what? She never ran for office, just like the people in Congress that I went with through with the confidential report back in the '90s. Out of the five people on the committee, only one person ever ran for office again.

SW: After she did that, was it immediately that same year was it that she stopped running for Congress.

Det. R: No, I think it was the next year or something.

SW: Well, but it was that next cycle.

Det. R: Yeah, it was right the next term, she never ran. Michele was the only one that ever actively had her people contact me, sit down with me, go over this and work on it.

SW: Okay. Now, what are the five things that are specifically illustrated in this?

Det. R: Well, the first one is the most important. Any person or entity that uses human trafficking, children, child porn, pedophilia to compromise, extort, or cause another person to do an unwilling act will be guilty of a felony with a mandatory 25 to life prison sentence. It was the death penalty, but we had a couple of nuns that called the mothers of the church in our committee, and they didn't believe in the death penalty, so we made it 25 for life, but I called for a death penalty on it. That is the big one.

Det. R: Then the next one, any person or entity that buys, sells, trades, or in any way promotes, enables, or profits from human trafficking, pedophilia, human compromise, extortion, or use of children in a criminal manner, same thing, felony, 25 to life. The use of electronics by these people and other forms of communications to facilitate, promote, or further human trafficking and all those stuff, the same things, a million-dollar fine for each occurrence and a 10- year prison sentence. In other words, if you used a computer or if you signal by waving across the street at somebody, you're guilty. You're facilitating this. It's so easy to catch them on the computer because it's on there. Anybody could find it.

Det. R: Now, here's the one. Any person, agency, other entity that interferes, threatens, harasses, impedes, or in any way compromises an investigator, an investigation prosecution, or witness in human trafficking and all of that is guilty of a felony with a mandatory five-year penalty. That's what is the most important one. Let these cops do their job. I can name cops, FBI agents and stuff that did these investigations into the highest levels, everyone was stopped. It's been going on for 50 years.

Det. R: Then the final one, any enforcement agency, agent, prosecutor, elected government official or any other authority that fails to act with due haste on all of these things is guilty of a felony. Now, that would mean if you vote in a dog catcher and he's elected, and he don't do anything he's guilty of a felony. Can you imagine if all these people were responsible, the elected officials, what that would do?

SW: Well, if they know about it, they need to do something about it.

Det. R: Yes, if they're aware.

SW: At least report it.

Det. R: Immediately, not to stall it, and they have to make sure something is done.

SW: I don't understand why this is so complicated.

Det. R: It's not.

SW: I think we know why it's complicated because they're protecting themselves, but this is a pretty straightforward ...

Det. R: Very simple, and it's done in layman's language, so if you were to legalize it, then you'd have to rewrite it, but this is for the public to understand. As part of this, I even go into different definitions, how it works and that, and then we have finally were purpose and need, which describes why we need this.

SW: Okay, talk about why we need this?

Det. R: Well, number one, you got to let the people know what's really going on. You got to let the people know how this works and define it, and define what has to be done. Again, we did have here a little task force for a while until they asked me not to attend anymore because I didn't fit the Minnesota model, but if you got these mothers together and it is structured where you have organized effort. If somebody, like when I sent this to the governor, I didn't get nothing back on it until I had a couple of mothers call.

SW: I want to talk about your "mother structure" that you came up with because you defined the whole organization. Do you have any more elements that we need to discuss? Why else do we need this?

Det. R: First of all, we have to let people know what prostitution really is, and what pimping is. Right in here, you cannot talk about human trafficking without talking about pimps, and you don't hear pimps mentioned. Number one, most of them don't even know what a pimp is and the different grades and level of it, procurers, that's a different thing. You have to understand all this, and that's why I explained that in here.

Det. R: Oh, they got all these programs were to help in this—if you cannot eliminate the pimp—and I have documented cases right here in this area in the last three years and I have them from 50 years ago. A girl was up at a house in Brainerd, Minnesota. She was a victim. She had been put in when she was 15 years old. All of a sudden. She's a runaway. She ran away from there at 2:00 in the morning. At 6:00, she was turning tricks in Minneapolis. She ran all the way from Brainerd to Minneapolis. Can you imagine that in that period of time?

Det. R: The pimp calls and tell them, you better do this, and if you don't, the consequences. They do not factor in the pimps. All they do was, "Oh, they're runaways, then it's not a crime statistic." They don't say, "The pimp called and said, 'Here,...'" and they don't know what the pimps do to these girls. I do. I've seen it. I had it right here, and there was nothing we could do.

SW: Prostitutes, and these young prostitutes, 15-year-old, they're not what the media and all this, it's not this glorified deal. These people are victims. They're trafficked.

Det. R: I took a 15-year-old, and to me, from the day you were put into this, this girl, same girl that ran. We had her in front of the mayor of St. Cloud. She starts telling him what happen. He says, "Oh, you're a runaway." The girl goes, "What do you mean I'm a runaway? The man told me, if I didn't do this, they were going to hurt my mother and my little brother." Right? Is that a runaway? No, but as long you call them runaways and homeless, they're not crime statistics. That's the big thing.

Det. R: This is why you have to do something. When these kids, first of all, you got understand what they're talking about and if you want to get out to this. I've seen what they do to girls. It's called "running the train in them" is one thing. I've seen right here, and I had two witnesses that actually saw the physical assault that was committed on this girl, but there was no place to go with it.

SW: Now, some people say that the foundation of society will be rocked, but in your opinion, and this is my opinion, that the foundational society needs to be rocked so that we can start taking care of this.

Det. R: Oh, yeah, but like I said, you can take care, find out what the pimps are, how did they get there? That's another thing I had. Up here in the little town called Pillager, a group was going to open up a house for these victims and such. The lady brought up the fact, she says, "What are we doing to get to the pimps so they don't pimp?" I put pimps in jail for 65 years. What do you accomplish by putting man in jail for 65 years when you don't know any better? People say, "Oh, they know they shouldn't put ..." Baloney. They're part of the society.

SW: They start, they're groomed when they're young kids.

Det. R: When they're young, yes, yes. I had these pimps ... I talk to them. They trusted me. Pimps told me. Girls told me. They told me 50 years ago, and they told me three years ago. The proof is there right after we had that task force meeting and I got up and said about what was going on. I identified 31 pimps and 42 victims right here. That's after the police chief of St. Cloud got up at the meeting and said they had no information that any such activity was going on here. 50 years ago, I had that already.

SW: They're lying.

Det. R: No. No, they don't know.

SW: Okay.

Det. R: They've been told, "Oh, no," but if you don't know what you're looking at, and now, the greatest thing of all is you go on the computer and put on your 15- year-old girl, and you get the John to call in, and you lock up the John and fine them $2,500, where does the money go? It's just like in 1972 when Assistant District Attorney John Patton and myself went in front of a judge in New York. We would arrest the prostitutes. They get fined $300 and given 30 days to pay. We went in front of the judge and told him he was a pimp. Well, think about it. What were we doing?

SW: You were extorting money from Johns.

Det. R: Now, that wasn't the Johns. That's what's going on. This was the girls and the other day, one of the media had it on television, there's money missing. Where is it? I agree Johns should be arrested, but lock them up legally. What good does it do fining them? Give me a break. First, you got to understand what this is all about.

SW: The cities like to fine them, and then put them back out there so they can fine them again.

Det. R: No kidding. Give me a break. Mother Nature has never quit in the world. It is a real thing out there.

SW: Okay. Let's talk about your structure that you put together with ... Did you do this with Johnny Gosch's mother, to Noreen Gosch, the structure, the mother's group?

Det. R: Yeah. Yeah.

SW: Okay, will you talk about that, what we need to get something like that going? Leaders in different areas of the country, and how would this whole thing.

Mothers Together to Pressure Officials

Det. R: First of all, each community should have what we call the Mothers Against Trafficking, for a group, but then there should be five leaders. They should be structured in such a way that when you, as a group, go and you get no response, these five mothers go in there. You set up a thing like a phone bank. Now, the cellphones, it'd be easy.

You'll hit a button, and everybody calls. I've been there when it was used, and it works.

Det. R: I was in Washington one time, and they were the five ladies. They wore blue blazers, white ruffle blouses, white slacks, and the white high heels shoes. When those days, she got on the phone and called. Within 20 minutes, we had 26,000 people calling. We were in there 20 minutes later.

SW: Now, let me ask you, why did that group disband, or are they still running?

Det. R: Well, this was not for trafficking. This was on another situation, but here, I had them call on the resolution to the governor.

SW: Okay.

Det. R: I had, I think it was five mothers at that time called. It didn't take long. All of a sudden, they were calling me. I've got a letter that's back up that I was contacted, but lately, nobody is responding again. It works, and you set it up in these different groups, and then you'd have it at a state level, and then the national level where you'd have these, and then-

SW: The five would be at each state level, or the five be at ...

Det. R: Every level.

SW: Every level, you had to have five leaders.

Det. R: Yeah.

SW: At the city level, you have five leaders.

Det. R: Oh, yeah. Yeah.

SW: State level, you'd have five leaders, and then at the national level, you had five.

Det. R: Yeah.

SW: Then they'd all worked on the tree.

Det. R: You can make it seven if you wanted to, but yeah. Here, this is the task force set up.[3]

SW: This, I would like the other ... Just like the government resolution, I would like to get this document too, and I can put this up on my website.

Det. R: Yeah, and here is the other part of this, is how the Mothers Against Trafficking, as you will notice, there is a little hatchet with T. I call them the hatchet team. When they go there, no is not an option.

SW: Absolutely.

Det. R: you how the whole thing is set up with the different things. This was done based on past things in that. You've got all that, but the resolution here, any legislator or colony commissioner or anybody, and I took this in front of my country commissioners. What was very interesting today, and you've interviewed her, Diane Muehlbauer was there with her people sitting behind me. In the front row was a young lady, all by herself, sitting there in front of the county commissioners. I presentedthat resolution.

Det. R: When we got done, the county commission said, "Who is that lady?" I always said, "She was there in case somebody challenged my credibility. She was the victim where the pimps ran the train on her here in St. Cloud, and she tried to get out of prostitution. She was dressed in such a fashion so she could've shown you very easily how she was mutilated.

SW: That would've been a pretty shocking experience for them.

Det. R: There happened to be a camera there for some reason but ask Diane. She was there. That was the end of it. I never heard from her, other the fact that all you should do a formal ... No. No, I made my presentation, but that girl was sitting right there. This girl, if you want to see all of the things, and we couldn't find anybody to work with us.

SW: Let me tell you, so people understand how important an organization like this could be. You have Mothers Against Drunk Driving, mothers against all these things, but this is at a whole another level of how we can change society. Can you talk about if we actually made an 85% dent in this activity, how much would it change our country for the better?

Det. R: Oh, it would be tremendous. You would eliminate this human compromise, human intelligence. First of all, how come our scholastic people, education people have not been talking about human compromise and human intelligence. Why haven't we heard about this other than from the street level? First, we got to educate, but for the victims, right now, there's a girl missing in Wisconsin. Right?

Det. R: If we had Mothers Against Trafficking, and they started marching in and demanding, what do you think would happen? And holding people accountable? There's a whole structure out there that's been going since 1966 that I know of. It involves the people that were involved here, and with the Son of Sam case. This is filters. There was a priest, Father Kunz killed out there. One of the .44s that was used in the Son of Sam case came from Eau Claire, Wisconsin. is there something I don't understand here?

SW: Well, to give a clearer picture for people, this could clean up a lot of our corruption, the money being stolen from our government. It could reduce wars that we have. I mean, all the negative activities around the world, we could see be cut down because of this. This is how serious it is.

Citizens Must Support the Police, Help the Victims

Det. R: Yeah, and the other part of this, you know who needs this the most? The mothers or the cops. They need this.

SW: To help them do their job.

Det. R: You got to have mothers that would go, "Why are you picking on this cop?" Right? I've been with cops that... sorry, I can't tell you that. There's the Etan Patz case. When it happened, a detective called me. By that time, I had been shut down already. He says, "Jim, don't tell anybody I called you, but your man, Quasimodo, (which was Ben Rose), was seen walking with the kids." In 2002, another detective called, said the same thing, "Don't tell anybody I called you," and he gave me that information.

Det. R: Why? Why do cops have to worry about doing their job? If they had the mothers, when we were doing this, when we got shut down, and if they'd had the mothers? When we were doing this, when we got shut down, if I would've had five mothers to lead the charge and 20,000 mothers in New York screaming, do you think I would've been [shut down]? My partners and such, all our careers were over? Do you think that would've happened? Do you think the police commissioner would've had the guts to do it? Who stopped the commissioner? Where did it come from?

SW: They're afraid of the people. Mothers don't feel like they have power, but—

Det. R: Oh, they're the most powerful thing in the world, but I can't tell you why that is because that's not politically correct. It gets down to the birds and bees. Let me tell you, this came from the horse's mouth.

SW: Mothers do feel their power has been mentally taken away from them, and they need to stand up and get their power back.

Det. R: Why does a mother sit there and tell me she's been told to put it behind her? Why weren't there 50 mothers there to help her? There were three mothers there to help her, but that wasn't enough.

Why? Just go around these towns here. Right here, I'm just speaking now and check with how many little boys have committed suicide because they're victims.

SW: Because they can't talk about it.

Det. R: That's right.

SW: Little boys who are raped and as they've grown to older men, it's still shunned in society and they're ashamed.

Det. R: Not only that. It's why isn't anybody helping these people like a 55-year-old man three years ago, four years ago calls me, "I got to meet you. I got to talk to you." I never knew who this guy was. I met him, and five minutes into the conversation, he says, "You know, if you wouldn't have understood what I'm talking about, I was going to commit suicide tonight." He was 55 years old. His brother had been a priest, and he'd bring his friends home, and they'd rape him. Right?

Det. R: Here, there's a guy right now, he just found out that his mother was a hooker, and he don't know how to cope with that, so he's coming to see me. This goes on and on. What about all of the older victims? How many of them are out there? There's a lot of them, and they got nobody to talk to. What about that priest over there? My journey alone. You want to sue the priest that have been here and in New York who came to see me to talk to me. They were victims. This is what's so sad about this.

Det. R: What about the innocent people? What about the victims? Some of these victims may be 15, 16, 17. What about the ones that are 50, 60 years old? It's like the guy that calls me two years ago, 6:30 in the morning to thank me for saving his life. He had been a hustler in New York. For 40 years, he was looking to find me to thank me. You can help people. I got him out of the business. He ended up in Philadelphia, and that's what he does for a living now is work this stuff.

Det. R: You can help people. All you got to know is understand them and talk to them, and don't go trying to tell them what happened. They got to tell you, every victim, right, I'll stick with what happened around here in one particular family. You sit there, and you start talking to these people. Their eyes are empty, and all of a sudden, when they know that you understand what they're talking about, they'll tell you everything. It is heart-wrenching how they describe these things from the minutest details of what happened to them.

Det. R: Then they have this thing now, oh, the greatest: Recovered repressed memory. Yeah, but you can alter that by how you question them. You got to know how to talk to these people, or they use dolls to say to these young kids, "Oh, he touched you there." If you say yes, you get a lollipop. I mean, give me a break. You got to find out the truth. Do you know there's been an investigation out in Oregon?

Det. R: There was the one here in Jordan, Minnesota. When people who don't know what they're talking about go into this, they can destroy whole communities. That's why, like I said, we did all this work. The last investigation, we had the Policy Science Corporation. We spent millions, and everything was covered up, all the background, and anybody who wants to check, look up Harold Lasswell. Those were the kind of people that were on that committee.

SW: See, I think we got to start having more pride and say, "This isn't good enough for us."

Det. R: Yeah, that's right. In fact, the cops, get the ones that want to do their job, and if they don't do their job, lock them up.

SW: Support the ones that do, and we have more power than we thought.

Det. R: Yeah, and I've had law enforcement here, both federal and local. Well, not here, not from here. There was two cops in Minneapolis, Lieutenant Gary McGaughey and Kenny Tidgwell. Look up their history. I mentioned them to you once before. Go to the police chief of Minneapolis and ask them what happened to Lieutenant Gary McGaughey. That man, they had this thing going, and they were shut down, totally destroyed.

SW: The people who destroyed them should be thrown in jail for life.

Det. R: Yeah. We were here with them. I watched it. We sat there with them.

SW: If society would support them, the mothers would support them, the people would support them, their careers would not be destroyed.

Det. R: That's right. That's right. Here's another thing. Here in Minnesota, at that time, remember, I said, we were at the meeting, nothing like this was going on. They brought 11 victims from here to New York to test the five in front of the State Select Committee on Crime. How come we've never heard of that here? You want to hear what these kids had to say.

SW: Yeah. We keep it away from people. We can't protect people from the truth. The truth will help. They say it sets us free. We need people to learn the truth. It'll be traumatic, but it'll be a lot less traumatic than what the victims are dealing with.

Det. R: Yeah. Yeah. Then like I just explained what happened to the church. I am Catholic. Somebody mentioned I should have a yarmulke, but I am a Catholic. I was born and raised one. If a Catholic stood up for what was right, this wouldn't happen. Right now, they're throwing the church to the wolves. Why aren't they talking about how that started? They know how it started because there were government documents that I looked at.

SW: The people who are going after them, the authorities, a lot of them are the ones at fault for the whole thing happening in the first place.

Det. R: But why aren't we hearing this, and why doesn't the church get up and say? Maybe when Pope John Paul I did it, it cost him his life. Oh, yeah. Again, people say, "Well, how do you ..." I was there. I got the info. Why did they have to drive, the informant, from Detroit, Michigan to New York? Huh?

SW: Why did they have to do that?

Det. R: So I wouldn't get their name. This is the way this work. Why did I have to get anonymous phone calls? Why I'd be walking the streets of New York, 3:00, 4:00 in the morning, and some guy would come up to me, no ... Jim, you got to look at ... I knew he was an agent from somewhere, some agency. Did I know his name? No. My job at that time was when they found out that we knew nothing about prostitution, trafficking and such, and I'll give you an example. When the pimps killed an undercover cop by the name of Campisi, our intelligence division gave me a list of pimps. Not one of them on that list was a pimp.

Det. R: This is what I'm saying. That's when the New York Police Department cut me loose, and my job was to find out what was happening. Let me tell you, in New York, when they send you out to find out what's happening and they give you all the money you need, and there were times, there were 100 cops working with me, detectives. You'd be amazed what you can find out, and you go anywhere you have to go.

Get Involved! Children's Lives are at Stake

SW: What do you want people to know as we close this up?

Det. R: As we close this up, organize the mothers, and get that resolution. Every town, every borough, whatever you want to call it, should take this to their town's board and have a passed. You know what I found, there were a bunch of towns here that passed the five of them, but what's interesting is the ones that didn't.

SW: What were their reasoning?

Det. R: Oh, they didn't want to get involved and such, but check into it deeper. There was one town I went to, there was one council member that didn't show up, the only meeting he ever missed. What would that tell you?

SW: He's involved.

Det. R: Oh, God. You know what I'm saying, but that's the most important thing, and get the mothers organized. Get them and have the meetings, and do it. I will tell you one thing. Make sure you're not infiltrated, and you will be, just like when we had our task force here, one of the first things I said, "There's going to be somebody here to infiltrate," and there were.

SW: What did you do to get rid of them, and how did you identify them?

Det. R: They asked me to quit because I was not following the Minnesota model.

SW: They were the infiltrator.

Det. R: Yeah. Yeah.

SW: The goofball who messes stuff up is usually the infiltrator.

Det. R: Yeah, and we were getting things done, but again, get the mothers organized. When you go on this stuff, no is not an option.

SW: 100%, no is not an option.

Det. R: No, you go down here. We got a new governor coming in. Now, this reaches outside of this, but a lot of states have new governors and stuff. Go to your governor and demand. Go to your federal government. Demand them to act on this.

SW: Thank you so much for everything you've done, your life's work, and for talking with me today.

Det. R: Well, thank you for what you're doing. I want to thank all the cop, and FBI, customs, IRS agents who have worked with me over the years. You'd be amazed how many people are trying to do the right job.

About the Authors

Sarah Westall

Sarah is a successful entrepreneur and business executive. In the past 25 years, she has created and developed multiple companies including a successful management and consulting firm and a multi-million-dollar international import and manufacturing company. She has a dynamic leadership career spent building high-performance teams in highly competitive industries. She has an entrepreneurial attitude, energy, and style. Sarah is a partner at Galex Consulting, and has been an adjunct at the University of Minnesota's top rated Carlson business school teaching classes in leadership, ethics, management, and entrepreneurship, and the host of the national radio show, "Business Game Changers." Her national radio show features leaders in Business, Government, Society, and Science. Her significant experience and knowledge in technology, systems engineering, business, and entrepreneurship provides insight and depth unparalleled in the media.

Retired Detective Jim Rothstein,

As a member of the New York City Police Department and his retirement from the New York City Police Depart in 1980 to the present, Detective Rothstein has continued his work as a researcher and consultant on human trafficking. Det. Rothstein worked with various out of state agencies, officers, departments, professional groups, and numerous federal agencies to develop the expertise so vital to be effective. Det. Rothstein's assignment to the New York State Select Committee Crime was also the end of his career. These hearings were ordered by Governor Carey of the State of New York and a Bi-partisan Legislative Committee. The mandate was to find what the effects these crimes were having on society. The Dark Side of human trafficking, prostitution, pedophilia, and corruption go far beyond human comprehension. It is a world of "Smoke and Mirrors," where "Deceit and Deception" are the norm. The degradation, torture, and mental manipulation of the victims that were uncovered in the investigations, conducted by Rothstein (Boots), were never made public. They were not politically correct, or feel-good do-good. You cannot disguise decadence with the smell of clover or the pureness of a white lily. It is what it is, vulgar and despicable.

The documents mentioned can be downloaded for free at the following links: Link[4], Link[5], Link[6]

You can see all of the interviews with Detective "Jimmy Boots" Rothstein on my YouTube channel under the name Sarah Westall or here: Link[7]

The transcripts from all of my interviews with Detective Rothstein will be made available for free for my Patreons. You can join at: Link[8]

Transcripts will also be available for a small fee on my website. Link[9]

---

[1] https://sarahwestall.com/wp-content/uploads/2019/01/GUIDELINES-FOR-FAMILIES.pdf

[2] https://sarahwestall.com/wp-content/uploads/2019/01/Resolution-on-Human-Trafficking.pdf

[3] https://docs.google.com/viewer?url=https%3A%2F%2Fsarahwestall.com%2Fwp-content%2Fuploads%2F2019%2F01%2FPROPOSED-INVESTIGATIONS-AND-LEGISLATION-M.A.T..pdf&pdf=true

[4] https://docs.google.com/viewer?url=https%3A%2F%2Fsarahwestall.com%2Fwp-content%2Fuploads%2F2019%2F01%2FPROPOSED-INVESTIGATIONS-AND-LEGISLATION-M.A.T..pdf&pdf=true

[5] https://sarahwestall.com/wp-content/uploads/2019/01/GUIDELINES-FOR-FAMILIES.pdf

[6] https://sarahwestall.com/wp-content/uploads/2019/01/Resolution-on-Human-Trafficking.pdf

[7] http://SarahWestall.com

[8] http://Patreon.com/SarahWestall

[9] http://SarahWestall.com

One of the ways that Q followers are dismissed is by mistaken association with people and organizations that we, in fact, are not actually associated with. While nearly all are "MAGA" and Trump supporters, many of us approach this as Independents, rather than as traditional Republicans or Democrats. Like Trump himself, who was at one time a Democrat, and who still is undermined by "Rino Republicans" who are supposedly on his own team—for most of us there is far more at stake in the take down of the Deep State than a right/left political battle. We are on the Q Team, but if you think that automatically means we follow Alex Jones or watch Fox News, you may find this chapter enlightening. There are those who would usurp this movement to advance their own agendas or to ultimately destroy it. Our solution, as with everything else: to keep digging, keep researching and keep thinking even as our heros from the past fail us. We really, genuinely, are fighting a war that is more accurately characterized as "Good vs. Evil," and while we embody enough diversity that we simply can't agree on everything, we know to the core of our beings that this is a spiritual battle and WWG1WGA.

The Fake MAGA Problem &
The Day I Helped Q Make Alex Jones Cry

by Dustin Nemos

In an Era of Censorship, I Honored The Truth.
In an Age of Kneeling Slaves, I Struggled to Stand.

Hello friends, my name is Dustin Nemos and I am a truth speaker. I've been covering Q since Christmas Eve 2017, and following it closely from the start (I've been a 'Truther' since I was 16, and am always plugged in to the Internet, learning.)

I developed a bit of a reputation in the Q movement for logic, reason, and calling out the Fake MAGAs (I've a hobbyist background in debate which lends itself to this area.) And exposing deception in the Anti-Q movement in general has been something I considered paramount (primarily revealing the Fake News, at least at first.)

Q Spotted It First

Early on, Q warned us about the Fake MAGAs, telling us that a housecleaning was needed within the MAGA movement. I took this to heart and began earnestly to make content exposing trends I noticed among certain personalities on social media. This project eventually morphed into the Fake MAGA list on my website, which is incomplete but already extensive. Documenting trends of 'friendlies' in the pro Trump era who were using deceptive or sophistic tricks or emotional attacks against Q or even Trump from within the perspective of the MAGA. These deceptions came in the guise of concern trolling (for example, offering "helpful" feedback actually intended to alarm and undermine), spreading doubt within the movement, trying to turn people against Trump and trying to spread lies or insults and ridicule against those who supported Q.

Good morning

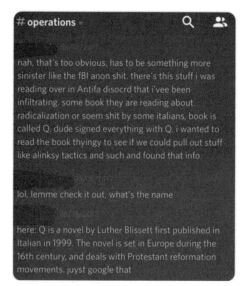

Jack enlightens us with his "research" on Q.

The occasional jab is bad enough, but when you notice the same personality doing it for 8+ hours a day, consistently over time, it becomes a bit more troubling. It certainly doesn't help when certain personalities (for example, Jack Posobiec) seem to line up in their 'attacks' within about the same period of time that the fake news went from full ignore to full attack on the Q movement. Perhaps you will recall that Posobiec went to the full extreme of building up weeks of suspense around chat logs that promised to reveal 'the truth' yet were themselves debunked as fake constructs within 5 minutes of finally being released.

Posobiec shifted his position about the identity and validity of Q numerous times and making among other claims: that Q was fake, that he was a psyop, that he was in fact John McCain, etc. I can't even remember all the positions he took. Then, of course, claiming that he actually knew who Q was and would reveal his identity in a big upcoming release! Such suspense! Then, we are told that not only will he reveal WHO Q IS, but first he has to make sure the equipment is configured properly for masking Q's voice so he can protect his identity. Huh? Exactly.

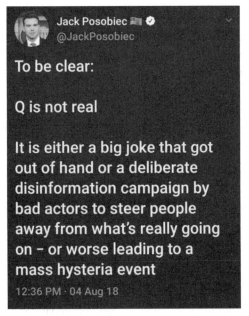

Jack Posobiec
@JackPosobiec

To be clear:

Q is not real

It is either a big joke that got out of hand or a deliberate disinformation campaign by bad actors to steer people away from what's really going on – or worse leading to a mass hysteria event

12:36 PM · 04 Aug 18

Scary about that non-existent mass hysteria.

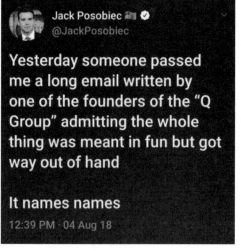

We're still waiting for those names, Jack.

Jack Posobiec 🇺🇸 ✅
@JackPosobiec   ⌄

Working on a new @OANN piece
debunking QAnon. I am in contact with
one of the people who started it of it
who is ready to go on record

They could have done their own Q posts yes	But Dems gonna use this Q s' in Midterms that's why media starting to talk about it now
I'd believe it	
Like i said more and more people started doing it	Up to you but I'm all for helpii kill Q it's toxic
I made 3-4 posts acting as Q	
These people seem to have been doing similar things	Some good friends of mine believe it and have gone craz because of it
I'll go on record saying I did these things	
I don't care if that helps squash this Q thing I'm all for it it's become an embarrassment	🖉 New Message

1:08 PM · Aug 4, 2018

Get ready! Get ready!

Sowing the Seeds of Confusion and Deception

There is more to this than randomly guessing wrong or innocently making stupid mistakes. It is as intentional, coordinated and as sophisticated (at least) as the Establishment Media itself (with its 4:00 a.m. talking points). I've documented and video-showcased numerous instances of this behavior and have even used Jack Posobiec's own videos/words to prove his deceptions. (I am referring to a situation where, within a few weeks, Posobiec both claimed he would never doxx anyone (intentionally revealing private information such as a home address), then doxxed me, then claimed he never doxxed anyone.)

Fortunately, it only took a few seconds to smash the videos together to illustrate his deception—all in his own words—and prove my point: that he lies. He later was involved in having me removed from the roster of those speaking at the American Priority conference in Washington, DC. But hey, it was worth it. I went anyway.

Perhaps the most troubling of all the apparent "Fake MAGA" that I have run across, is Alex Jones himself. Again, I need to preface this with a little context: I worshipped Alex Jones as the sole figure holding back the Darkness and speaking Truth in a darkening world. He was my hero for 16 + years straight.

Jack's reader seems to understand him.

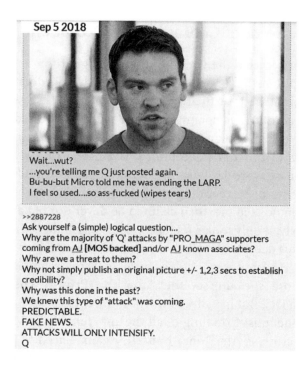

Sep 5 2018

Wait...wut?
...you're telling me Q just posted again.
Bu-bu-but Micro told me he was ending the LARP.
I feel so used....so ass-fucked (wipes tears)

>>2887228
Ask yourself a (simple) logical question...
Why are the majority of 'Q' attacks by "PRO_MAGA" supporters
coming from AJ [MOS backed] and/or AJ known associates?
Why are we a threat to them?
Why not simply publish an original picture +/- 1,2,3 secs to establish
credibility?
Why was this done in the past?
We knew this type of "attack" was coming.
PREDICTABLE.
FAKE NEWS.
ATTACKS WILL ONLY INTENSIFY.
Q

And I mean, I watched *everything* Alex Jones put out, and Owen, And David Knight, And Millie, and Paul Joseph Watson (The Great) and was pretty much an InfoWars superfan. In many ways, I still am. I forgave Alex his sensationalist tendencies because I was about the message, not the messenger. Looking back, however—I think he was always just trying to make us look stupid.

Let's get two things right. Alex Jones is a brilliant man: an autodidact polymath, an expert on human nature and condition and the geopolitical situation and many other topics, including history. Yet, he has a deeply disturbing tendency of always dropping the ball anytime we get a chance of making a touchdown. And his butterfingers are costing us needed victories. Let's consider:

Sandy Hook: He backed down and allowed himself to be demonized and he defended the wrong points.

Gun Control: (Consider the Piers Morgan Debate) Did he represent gun owners in a rational and reasonable manner? Or did he play into the stereotype of violent gun nut when he shouted that 1776 would commence again? At the time I lauded his passion.

What about Pizzagate? Was it not conveniently dismissed as 'debunked' after Alex Jones apologized on air to James Alefantis? At the time I told myself that Alex had to make a tactical decision to save InfoWars from lawsuit death spirals. But, still. At what cost?

You see the pattern. I'm not saying a man can't take losses. But then also consider what Q said:[1]

AJ is MOS? Mossad? A traitor? His 'network' certainly seems to be filled with the Fake MAGA types. Posobiec, Cernovich, etc. But let's address this in a bit more detail. First a little backstory.

You Have Your Q and I Have Mine

At first, Alex (like the mainstream media) seemed to ignore Q, only paying real attention when Jerome Corsi rushed headlong into the media void by trying to gain control of the Q narrative with his own decodes. Then Alex downplayed and ignored Q largely while playing up his own 'Q' insider, Zachari Klawonn, known as 'Zach.'

> *Alex Jones said, "...I don't follow QAnon. At first*
> *it's like "oh cute, you know we're gonna win,*
> *everyone's gonna get arrested. Oh it's cute and*
> *funny, some 4chan thing."*

If you watched InfoWars at the time you may remember Zach. Strangely, he was featured prominently largely by 'revealing' already released public information and playing the expert with insider knowledge. It even sounded like he was implying he was part of the Q team at one point. Eventually Alex Jones called Q a liar and fake and claimed to have spoken to him over the phone while golfing or some such nonsense.

I feel it's worth mentioning that, at first, I defended Alex Jones from Q himself. Q had, early on, brought up the 'performance artist' claim in reference to Alex. However, after such blatant lying about Q from Jones, and Q responding by connecting him to MOS and other researchers drawing potential ties between Jones and Stratfor and even the Bronfmans of NXIVM fame. I produced a video where I explained my reservations about Alex and why I believed him to be a fake MAGA and I asked the question: If he truly is Mossad, does that mean he would be headed to GITMO as well with a sealed indictment? After all, Q said no one who plays the game gets a pass and Alex is a major player in the game of influence.

I must have struck a nerve. It didn't take long before Alex Jones himself zeroed in on yours truly (without the courtesy of mentioning me by name, mind you, but it's unmistakable with the very clear references to statements from my video released online just hours before his own. He loosely quoted me about following him for 16 years and asking if he would go to prison over QAnon, etc. He spent nearly 30 minutes attacking me, insulting my mental capacity, my looks, my mannerisms, blatantly lying about things I said to make me look stupid, and overall using "Appeal to Ridicule" and "Ad Hominem" attacks. I'm surprised he didn't call me racist. He did call me "Satan's ankle." That's a new one.

> Alex Jones said, "... and then you see who've they got and it's like some bombed out weird guy going, 'Jones is the enemy. He's going to go to prison, the plan is in place, everything is good, Mueller will soon arrest Jones...'"

I damn sure never expected Alex Jones would attack me and on his show but he did.

> Alex Jones said, "I'm like 'Jesus they just put a QAnon post out that says 'kill me or arrest me' and it's got 50,000 views an hour.'"

This breaks my heart. Alex, why would you try to imply that I'm encouraging people to kill you? Please quote me in the video where I said that. You won't be able to so I'm not gonna hold my breath. I never wanted it to come to this. Who would have thought the Q would be re-message or re-share something that I posted and who would have thought that Alex Jones would be attacking me? I'm nobody. Wow. but hey, I have to expose liars right?

So it's clear that he's discussing the video that I made. Basically asking the question: Will what Q is saying ultimately lead Alex Jones to prison for treason? For cooperating with a foreign enemy? I mean that's basically what we just saw at the hearings with Kavanaugh right? They basically reaffirmed that if you're cooperating with the enemy your constitutional rights are gone and you are going be tried by military law.

It's also interesting that Alex Jones does a caricature of me. Because he actually complains about this when people do it to him. and I'm going be fair, you know I don't do that to people. So he does this thing that you know he's trying to imply that I'm some sort of a, what did he say? A bombed-out dead-eyed person. And then he caricatures my argument instead of addressing my points and then he needs to starts lying. I mean he's putting words in my mouth to try to "straw man" my arguments.

> *Alex Jones said, "I was watching this morning, I was cookin'*
> *eggs for my kids and watching it and I started crying and not*
> *in a wimpy way... I never saw satan's ankles like this.*
> *...Cause I was looking at this where I'm this enemy and I'm*
> *this agent and I'm watching this and there's these weird*
> *whacked out people believing it. ...I was watching this one*
> *guy. He looked like a dead zombie and he was like 'I used to*
> *believe in for Alex Jones for 15 years but he's the tree of*
> *poison, but now I believe in QAnon and Trump."*

Dustin Nemos or Dead Zombie?

I have learned that the fruit of Alex's tree IS poisonous. He screwed us over when it came to Sandy Hook. He let us down when it came to Pizzagate. He made us look like crazy gun nuts when it came to the Piers Morgan debate and it's a pattern, a trend. Q has called him out multiple times.

But please do not think Alex is alone. There are many. I've identified only a few. But it goes all the way to Fox News itself, the largest Fake MAGA in the room. Under Bill Sammon Fox just tried to hand the 2018 midterm elections to Dems by calling the election while the polls were still open and thousands of votes were uncounted.

Get Ready for the Unveiling

After ignoring QAnon for nearly a year, the MSM Mockingbird Media switched from "ignore Q" to "attack Q." All on the same day, hundreds of articles began pouring out ridiculing Q with the usual "conspiracy theory" labels. Alex Jones collaborator Jack Posobiec "activates" to begin his big "debunking Q" attempt. Building up weeks of hype for his faked chat logs attempt which were debunked literally within minutes (And Q even used my video to hammer this point home! Thanks Q!)

Owen Shroyer, another Alex Jones associate, fell right into line.

> *"As far as the Q thing is concerned, I believe that whatever was going on with Q in the beginning— legit, or not—co-opted everything. There was an article—it was after a Trump rally... big Trump rally, and there were a ton of Q signs at the rally— first time I had ever seen that. Well then the next day NBC writes an article pumping up Q, of course says it's fake, but ya know, covering it. So now it's in the mainstream right? So they covered it. It doesn't matter no one's gonna read the story anyway."*

Shroyer also pointed out that Trump was no longer allowing Q signs (or tee-shirts now) at his rallies. They have been banned as a security measure since threats, reportedly from Q followers, are called in before every Trump event.

The night of the 27th April Q posted:

Q #1295

Be careful who you are following.
Some are profiting off this movement.
Some are building a big following off this movement only then to retreat and go mainstream.
Patriots make sacrifices.
Some, the ultimate sacrifice.
Patriots are SELFLESS.
Do they ask for monthly payments to remain Patriots?
Think logically.

To some, it's only about the money.
Those who would seek personal gain at the expense of others in this
movement have an agenda.
You decide.
This is not a game
The only profit we should all be striving for is TRUE FREEDOM.
God bless you all.
Q

Author Jerome Corsi was an InfoWars frequent guest who, with a
group of his followers, had been decoding QAnon posts regularly on
YouTube. His approach to decoding according to the man himself: He
took his own "good" source information and was blending that
information into "the Q anon narrative." This is a CIA technique that
suggests that he had been intentionally MIS-decoding Q posts perhaps
prompting QAnon to post #1295 posted above. From the day following
#1295, Corsi claimed that QAnon had been subverted, therefore
hedging his bets on whether this post itself was "legit" or not.

"Some are building a big following off this movement only then to
retreat and go mainstream." When Q posted this, every Anon started
to have a damn good think!

At least one took it personally: Corsi immediately cast aspersions
on Q's credibility on his YouTube channel, calling Q a "communist."
One week after Q posted this warning, the questions that couldn't be
answered, increasing suspicion, and the loss of control, drove Corsi to
the limit. He blew up on Twitter, making wild claims against Q, and
Code Monkey, the admin of 8Chan where Q's posts appear. The
backlash against his clownish BS was so fierce, he went into full retreat,
and deleted his tweets within hours. Pointlessly. Too late.

And then Corsi and Jones echo back and forth between themselves
on InfoWars: that Q is "infiltrated," that Q is not reliable, should be
rejected, etc. But for all of these claims, and the echo-effect
amplification, there was ZERO sizzle on this sausage: Not a name. Not
an example. Not an ANYTHING. Jones and Corsi were talking hot air,
making utterly false claims.

Corsi then said that 6 months previously the WHITE HOUSE told
him Q was "good." Good information; sound source; White House
backing. But now they don't. Apparently.

How interesting, that Corsi was therefore also saying that from Q's
first appearance on October 28th 2017 to April 28th 2018 that Q was
legit and backed by the White House. Corsi then spoke about

"backchannels" that allowed him to know who Q is. Alex Jones pipes up and laughably claims to have personally spoken to Q on the phone. But no names, no details, not a thing except lies.

Q 513

8 Jan 2018 - 10:29:38 PM
IMPORTANT:
NO private comms past/present/future.
NO comms made outside of this platform.
Any claims that contradict the above should be considered FAKE NEWS and disregarded immediately.
WHERE WE GO ONE, WE GO ALL.
PATRIOTS.
Q

I don't mind being pro Israel. I mind selling out the country to Israel's version of the CIA.

Of course, the saga of what has happened subsequently to both Alex Jones and Jerome Corsi is worthy of a whole other book. But the point here is to simply understand that there is much more to the events around QAnon and the hidden agendas of both the mainstream media and its controlled opposition— fakery from both right and left. There is a dangerous game of corruption and intrigue going on, a high-stakes mostly invisible war where people are killed and careers are ruined.

A man can be killed, but an idea is bulletproof. Our Founding Fathers started as a group of anonymous Patriots handing citizen-produced pamphlets to their neighbors and friends, very much like the Q movement does today with citizen-journalist video broadcasts and online Anon groups working together to discuss and decode QAnon posts. Did you ever read Common Sense by Thomas Paine?[2] It is in the spirit of Thomas Paine that we are working together today as Patriots.

> *"Of more worth is one honest man to society and in the sight of God, than all the crowned ruffians that ever lived." —Thomas Paine*

---

[1] https://qmap.pub/read/2102
[2] https://www.pagebypagebooks.com/Thomas_Paine/Common_Sense/index.html

When Chrystal (Scorpio) says, "There is a forever fierce passion for God, Country and Our People in my heart that evil can never take away," you know that she means it. She plain-speaks the love and concern most Anons feel for God and country, and YOU dear reader. Indeed, we are Patriots, full of spirit and righteous passion, grateful for all this country has given us and eager to let you know about the danger that surrounds us, how duped we have been, how trusting. We are warriors in the battle of Good vs. Evil and this is not a game. If you are convinced that there is nothing to see here, we beg you to look again. They are hiding their hideous crimes. People have died attempting to show you, to save you. Chrystal, like so many of the authors featured here, has grown followings on Reddit boards only to be censored and banned multiple times. Nevertheless, do not underestimate this dynamo. She makes things happen. She is unstoppable. She has been working for years to protect us, our children and YOUR CHILDREN, from those who would harm or enslave them. This is a wakeup call and your invitation to the Great Awakening.

The Resistance is On

The Message to The Resistance

I know many people wouldn't give "shills" (paid antagonists) the time of day. I decided to tackle this everyday issue on the boards differently. In my mind, I think deep down there is something inside everyone that deserves to know the truth and who deserves a good life and wants that for themselves and others.

That being said, knowing that 95% of the time people who tend to bark up the wrong tree, tend to be misinformed and have a hard time believing the mindset they have been trapped in. So, here is my "Message to The Resistance."

Our movement comes off as being toxic to the left/liberals (and even some on the right) because it's exposing everything, they (or at least their leadership) have worked for the past 200 years to destroy. They have been trying to bring the world to its knees, in efforts to bring about the "New World Order." They have made it well known—what their plans are and would be, when they gathered from all corners of the world—to write them on the Georgia Guidestones.

There is an evil that our world is facing, starting with the original 13 wealthiest families, whose bloodlines date back 6000 years to

Babylonian times. These families are some of the most twisted Satanic people in existence.

They basically have every avenue of "kill order" working in their favor. That includes all platforms of Media/ TV/Movies for Mind Control, (with their Luciferian symbolism planted everywhere—think pyramids with an all-seeing eye in middle), Food Giants for GMO/slow kill, Vaccine Industry for Agenda 21 /depopulation, water fluoridation for/calcification of the pineal gland, H.A.A.R.P Weather Modification for creating natural disasters, etc. They reap the benefits for themselves in so many ways it's disgusting to think about.

This is not even getting into the MK-Ultra programs that they use with False Flags around our country and the world, just to push their agenda on and through the media, politicians, soldiers, actors, musicians and more.

This doesn't include, the operations they have used for so many years, that have the CDC/random disease outbreaks and creation of diseases (Aids, Polio, STDS, Lyme Disease), using countries/entire villages as their lab rats. Many of the results never see the light day.

This doesn't include owned, funded or contracted organizations involved that "legally' take, steal or lure children for the sake of using them as sex slaves, or in slave labor camps/mines, using them like toys in their pedophilia fantasies, and then to literally sacrifice them, in their cult ceremonies. And then they have the nerve to blast it in your face as they do in movies like "The Dark Crystal," "Indiana Jones and the Temple of Doom," "Monsters, Inc." (The Fear Meter), etc. showing how to gather adrenochrome that gives them some form of high and youthful looks. We can't forget about organ harvesting operations, which are big money (Planned Parenthood).

You seriously don't have to take my word for any of this. Just think long and hard about the side you align with. When you start seeing the news released from the grip of the enemy, and their narratives start changing as we shine the light on these Elites, join us instead of running with them like a pack of dogs.

Then, you will know that the world is about to get a whole lot more "interesting." That those who have done us all wrong for decades, will finally be answering for the crimes against humanity they have been involved in or committed. Best of luck in your search for Truth. It could be right in front of you.

Here are the facts. Over the years, from points of power, all the way to big-screen movies and every perch between, our history to the present day has tried to warn us about the "bad players" working to ruin our country and ultimately the world.

We just had to listen.

This is our Great Awakening.

A Fierce Patriotic Passion

When this "Q" movement began, and everyone was up in arms wondering the direction Qanon was trying to take them, or waiting around wondering when the next crumb would fall. I knew someone needed to speak up with a little direction.

So it began with this post I made.

I think more people should be focusing on the underlying cause/reason for "Q" to be doing what he or they are doing; the reason our country and the world is in a complete uproar. You don't learn that, by simply connecting puppets to puppets. You do that by starting at the base of it all, "the foundation," and work up. I can tell you doing it the way everyone is assuming should be done, is like a train wreck and when you stand back after just a few months and try and look at who you connected to who, that list is extremely small in comparison.

This web is like the size of the world, and each bad player has thousands of connections to someone else. Imagine an "agenda" that was written 200 years ago. Now imagine how many people are affiliated with that one main objective. You need to comprehend that main objective first, to understand what's going on.

This is way bigger than the U.S. This is way bigger than Q, Trump, or a memo. We need to do good by them by investigating the shit out the original players, the ones who made all this possible. They formed the real "Secret Societies" and through those societies, they formed the most twisted framework to kill off 80 percent or more of the world's population. All these puppets are either descendants of the members of these societies, or extremely well connected and trusted advocates.

Start at the Illuminati, New World Order, the 13 "original bloodlines" and the wealthiest families in the world, and branch out from there. Pay mind to where each family member is currently working and what they do, or what they are known for. At the base of each of these families is some form of cult worship, so at each core is most likely going to be some form of human trafficking, either openly involved or hidden behind companies that they are connected to. These companies will likely be ones seized in Trump's Executive Order about human rights abuse.

These families are scattered all over the world and each company they invest in, or possibly own, should be investigated to the fullest for bribery, laundering, trafficking of drugs and humans of all kinds and sizes.

This is how we stay focused and ahead of the Q phenomenon, instead of scatter brained and all over the place. This will be 10 times more productive than sitting around waiting on a crumb of info to drop. Q is mainly dropping these crumbs to connect to current events that connect to the bad actors they are trying to take down in due time. Our job is "red pill" the public within and around our country and the world.

I've got a game plan to get this rolling into something massive. That is by dividing people into work categories that can communicate efficiently and work around the clock on things such as Meme Productions, Social Media Teams, Investigative Researchers & Bloggers, and Semi Community Organizers for a Mobile Movement so we can help push the vetted info that we find and we become a Go To Source For Investigative Info when other news or once reliable sources become unable or unwilling to do the people's work. We are far too many and far too PRQ PATRIOTS IN AMERICA & WORLD WIDE to fail.

I would like to start talking about a plan of action with those who wish to be apart of it. I also wish we had one board to go to instead of like 4 or 5 main ones. I keep having to post the same stuff to all these boards but we can figure something out but. I have made a Discord and wouldn't mind discussing further plans via it if you message me. I just created it and put a few sections up in it for people to chat openly in. All shills looking to disrespect or disrupt will be banned. But please message for the link for Discord. It's called PRQ AMERICA.

But yeah, just keep an eye on future posts about the progress.

God Bless & As Always, Stay Informed Patriots

The Idea, Speech & Their Commitment

One of the biggest "Q proofs" in my eyes was the moment I posted an "at random" idea I had across the 3 Reddit boards I shared Red Pill material on. Now before jumping into this, there were multiple other "Q proofs" involving me, but I don't think I have the space here to break all those down for you. However, this one hits home directly. Here was my post:

The Idea

Nine months ago I made an "at random" post speaking about an idea/suggestion I had for businesses to start getting involved in small-town communities, plus ideas about what they could do and what impact it could have on these areas if they did.

I gave an example of the Ohio town I grew up in these post. I'm going to post what my original random post was, then the second post where I highlighted the Q proof, that stemmed from that original post. That should open everyone's eyes.

ACTIVATING SMALL TOWN COMMUNITIES

I'm suggesting we start an "Activate Small Town Communities Projects." I'm not sure if you are completely over seeing our kids tormented in some way, shape, or form at SCHOOL but I am after seeing this post I saw about 5 mins ago about 8 or 20 kids who got sick or were hospitalized after someone brought in some candy in some Perry township school in Ohio.

I wanna say it kinda forced me to reply with the message I wrote below, and then I got to thinking...maybe I should share the message because it might actually serve to some as a motivation, and I would very much love that. If it helps people and gets their gears moving on ideas to assist in their own communities or go to helping others in theirs.

Here is the message:

Is it just me or is it time for people to go back to staying home teaching their own kids? SCRATCH THAT...IT'S OVERTIME.

Time for HOMESCHOOLING THE KIDS, ALL COURSES TAUGHT ONLINE. THEN PROVIDE TRADE SCHOOLS FOR

FURTHER PURSUIT. No elite Common Core/Scrubbed History Indoctrination. No elites forced vaccinations. No elites pro bullying atmospheres even when they promote it being the opposite. I mean the incentives for homeschooling your kids are priceless. Just so you don't have to worry bout the above mentioned.

I mean seriously these schools are in worse shape than prisons, as far as decor /shape of their foundations. Its pretty sad, that the fast food restaurants in some of these communities look like a palace to these kids, in comparison to their houses & schools. How the hell will they get any motivation being forced to attend in these places? Some have been in use so long, you have to wonder if they still have rooms with LEAD paint on the walls.

I was born in '81 and lived in Ohio about an hour from Pittsburgh. So basically between Zanesville and the PA border. Everything between those areas has always been heavily run Democratic operation zones. They are gutted. It's soooo disgusting. If more businesses started branching out instead of staying localized around a big city scene.

These little towns could benefit so much from them doing so, maybe start modernizing the towns, they currently look like creepy towns with broken down old buildings.

There are soooo many hard working men and women out there and they have to drive over an hour to find a job. When they don't have a semi local job, it forces people into everything else, since they can't afford a dependable vehicle to travel to a good job. It forces people to supplement their money because what they are getting isn't enough to cover, these electric bills that are like $500 a month or more and that's being modest.

That's why these small communities are heavily into drugs and welfare, the towns are nasty, and the people feel and look like they been through the wringers and back.

Most people have not even been able to afford themselves a new outfit let alone anything else. So many ways people can band together across our country and make a difference in these little forgotten towns and depleted cities.

I mean, if jobs could start paying enough to where one parent can stay at home to raise the kids & do home school, it would be huge.

If more big businesses branched out to small communities, that could change the outcome of people's lives on so many levels.

All these things can turn our country around from the inside out. If people start getting together on certain days and making it a town wide cleanup day. People can plant flowers, clean up the streets, just do little things to help improve your communities.

I don't live like I did when I was growing up, but I did grow up working for everything I had, and I can tell you, it makes people appreciate everything they got and it brings families together. Jobs brought to these small towns across our county will do the trick.

Sorry, about the straying. I'm pretty passionate about this stuff, and I know there are millions of stories just like this around our country. We can't rely on our president and others to do all the hard work alone. It will take communities banding together.

Local businesses can create days where you sponsor a group that can run around the town cleaning up and provide lunch or a community picnic where everyone brings a dish. Whatever it takes. Get people out in the sun and active. No more doom n gloom.

We go forward as Q-N-E.

What Happened Next

This is an update. I excitedly posted this 7-months ago and 2 months after my original post above.

MY IDEA, HIS SPEECH, THEIR COMMITMENT

God Blessed Our Country in every way... THANK YOU #45 & TEAM.... This is without a doubt proof from start to finish of how they care, they listen, they respond. If this truly comes true, there is gonna be pockets of light sprouting up from all corners and all crevices of our Nation. Blooming with Happy Families & Happy Workers.

It will be Beautiful on so many levels. I'm from a tiny little town between Cadiz, Ohio & New Philadelphia, Ohio and I can tell you these people over there are HARDCORE WORKERS—yet have Zero work.

Hell, zero money to buy anything. It's been a run down Democratic zone since I can remember. I don't think its ever been anything else actually. Seriously it's like an hour drive to the nearest major city and almost an hour out to just get a job if you're lucky.

These families, like others in these small-town areas, are trying everything to stay afloat and there is nothing. Not even assistance, (that's been in place for decades), even comes close to keeping up with the bills and food.

I no longer live there, I live in Camby, Indiana, but all my family still do. So, I decided to post an Idea I had to try and perk these small towns up, and you can find it [above]

Someone else got wind of it, and then today I jump on wh.gov [the White House website] and find something I'll link at the bottom for you. After reading and watching everything, you tell me if they are not listening to our concerns & things we throw out here. All I know is, at least this PATRIOT is Thankful BEYOND WORDS.

Hope y'all have Smiles on each of your faces. Q Team/Trump Team, I'm gonna come up with a new nickname for the whole bunch of ya. Maybe "MAGA ADMIN" even if nobody else adopts it. it will be my thing for you all.

Their Commitment

Trump Administration's Approval of Opportunity Zones[1]

"During his inaugural address, President Trump declared that "the forgotten men and women of our country will be forgotten no longer." It is critical that every American shares in the gains of the past two years.

Today, the President is establishing the White House Opportunity and Revitalization Council through an executive order. I'm pleased to chair this council, consisting of members across 13 agencies whose mission is to jumpstart the development in urban and rural communities through the creation of Opportunity Zones.

Located in economically distressed communities across this country, Opportunity Zones are home to approximately 35 million Americans. The Department of Treasury estimates that the Opportunity Zone legislation could attract over $100 billion in private investment, which will go a long way to spur on jobs and economic development.

This kind of medicine is precisely what a doctor would prescribe to heal communities where nearly 1 in 3 people live in poverty, and unemployment is nearly twice the national average.

Too often, new investments into distressed communities are here today and gone tomorrow. By offering incentives that encourage investors to think in terms of decades instead of days, Opportunity Zones ensure that development is here today and here to stay."

Listen to every inch of this speech about the plan for OHIO and read EXACTLY what I wrote about above, again if need be. Link[2]

Everything Happens for A Reason PATRIQTS.
GOD BLESS.

UHRICHSVILLE, SCIO, BOWERSTON, NEW
PHILADELPHIA, OHIO & HARRISBURG, P.A.
HELP IS ON THE WAY!

GET TO WORK.

Much love from
A HARDCORE DEVOTED PATRIQT ANON

GOD BLESS PATRIQTS WORLD WIDE

Stay Safe, Stay Vigilant, Stay Bad Ass & Most
Importantly, Stay Informed.

WWG1WGA

After the Storm

Evil had infiltrated most of the original Q-following boards with paid shills posing as Mods. They were deleting the good finds of hard working Anons. Coincidentally, right after that, these seeds of FAKE ANONS started popping up across the Reddit boards with racist rhetoric that these so called "new Mods" were not removing and when they didn't remove it, and that allowed the shills to setup camp and dump post after post of fake news and more on our boards.

Once they had more help from other planted operatives, they then could create a case against a Q board for HATE speech and ultimately have it brought to its knees. I tried to WARN everyone this was going on the moment I realized it. That's why the CBTS (Calm Before the Storm) board was banned then onto the Great Awakening.[3]

The FIGHT FIGHT FIGHT was very real. Let's just say, this Scorpio went on a RAMPAGE spreading this Warning Message far and wide.

TIME'S UP

I've seen your crazy rhetoric posts on all your sub-Reddits. You people have nothing on us. You are paid plants devising how to bring us down by planting racist posts, hate memes and fake freaking news.

I wasn't born yesterday. I also know the Daily Beast and the Washington Post get their talking points from you, "their sources."

(Man, if they'd seen your discussions. The ONLY hate being spoken was from you people—to the point that people should be looking into it.)

Wait till the world finds out about your little operations to bring down websites by attacking their advertisers on their sites across the net, claiming the websites are spreading racism (when I know it's y'all or the bots you deploy.)

I'm onto your shit.

You people have nothing on good hearted Americans who are in here minding their own business, sharing info among the people. Not one single racist comment has been spewed, other than from a paid planted shill.

From here on out, we will be all over your posts on our boards. We will be hunting them down.

ACTIVATING OPERATION DOWN VOTE NEGATIVITY

From here on out, down vote negativity. The mods will know to remove fake news. We will not allow shills to setup shop and lay their seeds of hate here. Not happening on our watch and it will be around the clock patrol. Patriots don't sleep.

We are not gonna take it anymore.

This is our country and we are gonna fight evil ludacris hate, with the LIGHT.

GOD BLESS PATRIOTS AROUND THE WORLD

AND TO THE SHILLS
MAY GOD HAVE MERCY ON YOUR SOULS

THE CLOCK IS TICKING

In closing, this is my tribute to my red pill board AFTERTHESTQRM, that acted as a go to place for shareable red pill material, that other Q-following Anons could use as they wish, and share with friends and family to help them inform and awake the masses across all social media platforms and their other subscribed Reddit boards.

The board was just shy of 1200 strong, and acted as a guiding light and a safe haven for Anons worldwide, all the way up until it was the last board to be brought down due to a Reddit-wide Q Board Ban that took everyone by surprise and swept across not just their platform, but other platforms on the net that joined in. The Internet was on fire banning Q-related material. We obviously hit a nerve.

However, my story didn't end there. I came back swinging not 1 time or 2 times but 3 times creating a New Board each time until THEY finally gave up trying to stop me with the creation of WEREALLPATRIQTS.

My message to all Anons would be: The military is on the front lines and "WE, THE AWAKE" are the backbone with the Administration and QTEAM as the driving force. If any part of that fails, so will our country.

OUR ONLY JOB was and still is to guide the asleep out of the dark, and expose every aspect of what's been killing our people, country and world from the inside out for years. Have Faith, Strength & Determination.

AFTER THE STQRM, JUSTICE, WILL BE SERVED
FREEDOM FOR ALL WILL PREVAIL.
WE DON'T GIVE IN, WE DON'T GIVE UP
AND WE NEVER BACK DOWN
THE "NEW EMPIRE" AWOKE IN 2016
& WE'RE TAKING OUR COUNTRY BACK
GOD BLESS, PATRIQTS WORLD WIDE

Stay Safe, Stay Vigilant, Stay Bad Ass & Most
Importantly, Stay Informed.
WWG1WGA

YOU'RE ALL LOVED

Signing out /ScorpioPatriot

About the Author

Chrystal/ScorpioPatriot

A little about me: My name is Chrystal. I'm 37.

I was born in Ohio. My mom and real dad never married but her 1st husband was a high ranking Sargent in the military and retired from it. His name was Larry Bair and he just passed away from cancer last year. Her 2nd husband was in the Army and was involved in the Vietnam War. She had 2 boys with him.

I grew up in a town so small you could sneeze and be through it. At the age of 17 I attended a trade school and completed a 2-year Law Enforcement Program at Buckeye Career Center in New Philadelphia, Ohio. Six months after graduating, my real dad was killed at his work. His was the 2nd death within 6 months at that company, resulting in them closing their doors that day. It threw his 4 kids into a wrongful death lawsuit that dragged out for 6 years and went all the way to the Supreme Court where it was thrown out.

Moving past that, I moved to Indiana in 2003 and became a pretty hardcore online gamer at the age of 21. I played old-school games like Counter Strike 1.6 and Source. I realized playing that game that I had a very big passion and love for leading people. I started an in-game clan, then competed from there. I started running my own clan servers and taught myself how to build and run my own website and the ventrilos (Voice Communication Servers) for my clan.

I was confronted one day by one of the kids in my clan who suggested I try this game that he and a buddy had been playing called "World of Warcraft."

I'm like, "There is no way, I'm paying a monthly fee to play a game."
Well, it took them hounding me for 6 months to say the only thing
that could sway my decision, which was, well, "You can COMPETE in
the game."

I'm like, "How?"

They said they have servers called pvp servers and they have a
trial—up to level 20 for free. "You should try it and see if you like it."

I was like, "Maybe I will." cough

So I did, and HELLLLLO AMERICA did things start getting real.

I went from being miss nobody at level 20 in the game to paying to
play a game and then running what would be the oldest active pvp
ONLY guild in the world for 7 years! (It was called Miller Time and the
server was Bleeding Hollow.) Let's just say, everybody knew my
character which was Chrystal :). ENEMIES KNEW MY NAME.

Let me put it into context, there was people talking about my guild
in places around the net you never would have thought. I had people
transferring servers just to be in my guild.

I was the most hated person in that game, all because I did what
should be done on a pvp server—which was to PROTECT OUR
CITIES AND MY GUILDIES.

I've commanded 200+ person raids for years on that server, with
videos scattered all over YouTube showing the action. This might
come as a shock, but I worked (top notch at my job), had a spotless
"owned" house, cooked full-course meals (not in a basement) and at
age 26 had my first child. I tell you this to lay all Gamer Myths to rest.

As time went on, I met my Soulmate—rawr—another Scorpio (and
married him I might add. lol). I KNOW THOSE MYTHS TOO. Aside
from that, we began our journey introducing his 2 girls to my 1 girl and
then, bam—here comes our shared little boy 1 year later. :P

It was then, us meeting, that led me to start doing massive research
into the powers that "was," and their plans to ultimately take down the
world, and I have worked every day since 2011 to personally investigate
and wake up others.

Every hardship and experience in life lead me to this point, this
movement, and it wasn't until this point that I finally realized—

THIS IS WHAT I WAS BORN TO DO

THERE IS A FOREVER FIERCE PASSION FOR GOD, COUNTRY
AND OUR PEOPLE IN MY HEART THAT EVIL CAN NEVER
TAKE AWAY.

WE ARE THE CHOSEN "Q-N-E-S"

WWG1WGA

---

[1] https://www.whitehouse.gov/briefings-statements/remarks-president-trump-signing-executive-order-establishing-white-house-opportunity-revitalization-council/
[2] https://www.whitehouse.gov/briefings-statements/wtas-support-trump-administrations-approval-opportunity-zones/
[3] https://www.dailydot.com/layer8/reddit-bans-r-cbts_stream/

It's Time to Wake Up

If you are ready to give up the senseless rage you are surrounded by, wake up and join the forces of Light. We welcome you.

We are not a political party. There is corruption on both sides of the aisle. Most of us are Independents in some sense. We think for ourselves.

Instead, we are a movement of awakened individuals working together to discover and reveal the truth that has been hidden from us and to eliminate evil and corruption. Our goal is to protect others, to share the truth and to restore sanity. We have friends and supporters all over the world.

Here are ten things you can do to awaken others and help in the war we are fighting against the Deep State.

1. Love and support our Nation, our Constitution and yes, our President. Donald Trump has given up the life he could have had in order to play an essential role in freeing us from darkness. But he can't do it alone. Supporting him is the least we can do.

2. Get an education. Nearly every major national event involving the Deep State—both the good and the bad things that have happened—have been suppressed over the last two years or more. You can catch up. The Russian collaboration story that the media has fixated on is both untrue and a distraction from many important stories the mainstream media will never tell you. Follow independent journalists. Subscribe to their channels.

3. Share what you're learning. Tell your friends and family. Send posts, email, Tweets, etc. sharing news, videos, memes. Have conversations. Give this book to someone you care about. Ask them to share it when they are done reading. If you can, buy more copies and give them away.

4. Pray for our leaders, our families, our communities, our children and our movement. Please pray for protection from those who would harm us and for the power to overcome evil. One of the things we've learned is that evil is real. Many of us are Christian and we seek God's help daily.

5. Be there for friends and family as they awaken. They will be in various stages of disbelieve, denial, fear, depression, anger and misunderstanding as they process the new realities they are learning. Be patient, tolerant.

6. The Deep State will do and say ANYTHING to retain power. False flag events, potential biological threats, violent mob actions, etc. are real possibilities. If you see anything suspicious, please report it. Avoid violent confrontations. Stay informed.

7. Be prepared. Things could get rough at times. Maintain a stock of food and water, enough for a couple of weeks at least. Communications could break down. The banking system may be offline. This isn't intended to frighten you. It is simply to say it is wise to prepare for breakdowns and delays in times like these.

8. Give peace a chance. The Deep State has been the hidden hand in conflicts and wars all over the world. They benefit from war and chaos in many ways. While it is important for nations to be ready to protect themselves, as we eliminate the bad players we pave the way for peace and prosperity.

9. Join us in creating a positive future. Whether we realized it or not, we have been working indirectly for the Deep State as they have stolen from us in many ways. As their grip weakens, some of the stolen resources will be returned to us and we will have access to advanced technologies they've hidden from us and kept for themselves. Better days are ahead.

10. Get involved. This is a movement that is entirely voluntary. We contribute what we are good at, what we are moved to do. We take action where we see we can make a difference. There is a place for you too. Welcome aboard, Patriot. WWG1WGA

The Great Awakening email signup: http://eepurl.com/ghR_5f

QAnon's messages are often conveyed using code, abbreviations and with both political and military jargon as well. In turn, the subcultures of Reddit, 8Chan and even YouTube have their own jargon. Thus to fully understand some of these chapters you'll have to do a little decoding of your own. We've created this glossary to help get you started.

Glossary

187	To murder, assassinate. Q's reference likely comes from California Penal Code 187.
4:00AM talking points	This refers to the fact that for many years, the Main-Stream Media (MSM) receives the daily agenda to be broadcast that day at 4:00 AM. Note that this information tells them word-for-word what to report so you often hear the exact same information being sent out to the world, often with the EXACT same words. Visit link for an example: Link[1]
5:5 or 5x5	Loud and clear. We hear you.
8chan	Refers to the discussion boards at http://8ch.net[2] which Q uses to post drops and Anons use to post research information related to Q posts. You can read the Q-related research posts here: Link3 Warning: Do not post until you have lurked for some time and understand how it works.
A1Z26 cipher	A simple direct substitution cipher. It goes by other names (Letter to Numbers or Numbers to Letters). It is also known as letter-number code. You can learn more here: Link4 Here is a calculator you can use to encode or decode: Link[5]
Admin	In IT, the person responsible for running a network or website. Short for Administrator.
adrenochrome	Adrenochrome is an adrenaline metabolite that was investigated in several very small studies in the 1950s and 60s. It is supposed to cause mental disorders, derealisation, and euphoria. Some reports tell us that blood of sacrificed children is used by Satanic worshippers after the sacrifice and can allegedly extend life.
alt media	alt = alternative. News sources outside of the mainstream media that have sprung up on both sides of the controversy. Often they are citizen journalists trying to get the truth out. But, be careful who you follow. Not all are telling the truth.

Anon	Anonymous.
AS	Antonin Scalia
autists	Autistic decoders often found on 8chan.
Bakers	The people on the chans who do the Baking (*see below*).
Baking	On the Chan boards, as a thread comes to its limited end, someone needs to create a new thread and carry over relevant links and subject matter from the old thread. The act of doing this is called Baking.
boards	Before the World Wide Web, we had bulletin boards. They are a place you can go (now on the Web) to have discussions with others on a common topic.
BOOM	An expression Q frequently uses to let us know something big is coming or just happened.
bread crumbs	Clues.
Bronfmans	The Seagrams family who have a very shady history. Clare Bronfman, the Seagram's heiress was recently arrested in connection with NXIVM, an alleged sex cult.
cipher	A coded message needs a cipher to decode it. See A1Z26 above for an example.
controlled opposition	People who appear to be supporting the white hats but are actually controlled by the black hats.
comped	Compromised
crumbs	Same thing as 'bread crumbs' above. Clues.
D5	A reference Q gave us in Post 2494 that referred to Dec. 5. (Also a chess move and avalanche classification.)
DECLAS	Declassification, specifically of the FISA applications.
de-platforming	Censorship by banning.
Decodes	Code breaking or understanding hidden communications through decoding them. Gematria is an example of a code.
Deep State	Corrupt people who have infiltrated and work within or for governments around the world including working in businesses, charities, pharmaceutical companies, manufacturing, military

	and others that often control government outcomes through blackmail, kickbacks, protection rackets and bribes.
DoD	Department of Defense.
doxx	Practice of researching and broadcasting private or identifiable information about an individual or organization who wishes to remain anonymous.
Drain The Swamp	Indicting and arresting corrupt deep state workers and leaders.
fake MAGA	Someone who is using the MAGA or QAnon movements to build an audience for a hidden agenda, disloyalty. This is an example of "controlled opposition" above.
Fake News	The mainstream media outlets that control the primary broadcast stations on Cable TV endlessly release lies and propaganda that President Trump refers to as Fake News. Fox is the only one that is not considered Fake News, however, beware as even Fox is owned by a liberal globalist. Rupert Murdoch is a member of the Council on Foreign Relations, a known globalist think tank.
false flag	An event, usually a terror event, that is planned in advance and carried out for nefarious reasons. Example: For many years the black hats have carried out false flag mass gun shootings around the world. This was an effort to force gun control and eventually ban guns worldwide.
fetish	An obsessive sexual attraction to objects, body parts, clothing, children, etc.
Gematria	Cryptograph in the form of a word whose letters have the numerical values of a different word taken as the hidden meaning.
GITMO	Guantanamo Bay Naval Base military prison and detention camp.
human trafficking	Trading in human beings, including babies and children, for the purpose of sexual abuse, prostitution, slavery, ritual sacrifice, cannibalism or organ harvesting.
Hussein	Barack Hussein Obama.
John	A prostitute's customer.
larp	Live action role play(er). (Civil War reenactments for example.)

261

lurking	Reading online posts without revealing your presence.
MAGA	Make America Great Again.
Mockingbird media	The mainstream media outlets that control the primary broadcast stations on Cable TV and receive their 4:00AM Talking Points.
Mods	Moderators.
MSM	Mainstream media.
narrative	The media talking points of the day. There is a constant struggle for each side to "control the narrative" on a daily basis. Whoever controls the narrative is then in control.
No Name	John McCain
normie	A normal person.
NXIVM	The sex/slave cult that Keith Raniere created. He, Clare Bronfman and Alison Mack have been arrested in this case.
Patriot	Someone that supports freedom and truth.
pedophilia	Having a fondness or affinity for sex with children and babies.
pimp, pimping	Someone who forces women to work in prostitution.
Pizzagate	A pedophilia sex cult allegedly involving Comet Ping Pong pizzeria in Washington DC. Despite the fact that Wikipedia (controlled opposition) claims it has been debunked, stay tuned. More to come.
POTUS	President of the United States.
psyop	Psychological operation. Any operation (possibly false flag) intended to affect people psychologically.
Q-drop	Posts created by Q are often called Q-drops.
red pill	A reference to the movie "The Matrix" used to indicate someone has opened their eyes and seen the truth.
Reddit	A website used by many Q followers in the early days. Reddit has many boards that people can converse on many subjects anonymously. Link[6]
Rino Republicans	Republican in name only.

ritual abuse	A child or adult tortured, sexually abused or sacrificed in Satanic ritual worship.
run the train	Gang rape.
SCIF	Sensitive Compartmented Information Facility. A place where confidential or secret information can be verbally shared without being overheard.
shadow banning	Defacto banning by making a channel difficult to find or otherwise using censorship to limit its audience.
shill	A paid antagonist
Socratic method	A teaching method that emphasizes questions and deep inquiry.
Stratfor	A self-described "geopolitical intelligence platform."
straw man	A common form of fallacy based on giving the impression of refuting an opponent's argument, while actually refuting (or attempting to refute) an argument that was not presented by that opponent. One who engages in this type of fallacy is said to be "attacking a straw man."
Subreddit	Each primary created discussion topic on Reddit is referred to as a Subreddit.
the chans	Reference to 4ch.org (4chan) and 8ch.net (8chan). Q began by posting on 4chan but moved to 8chan when 4chan became compromised.
The Great Awakening	Refers to the event currently taking place that involves waking up the public to see the truth of the world they live in; the world that has been previously and deliberately hidden from them.
trip code	A code that Q uses when logging in to 8chan that is also displayed in each of the Q posts.
Truther	One who believes in seeking and telling the truth.
WWG1WGA	Where we go one we go all.

---

[1] https://www.youtube.com/watch?v=xefMM7m2YfE
[2] http://8ch.net
[3] https://8ch.net/qresearch/catalog.html
[4] https://kifanga.com/what-is-a1z26-cipher/
[5] https://planetcalc.com/4881/
[6] http://reddit.com